W9-ALJ-549

PRAISE FOR

A Haunted History of Invisible Women

"Thought-provoking and deliciously eerie, this intriguing study of phantom females not only delves into the history behind the legendary hauntings that chill our blood but also gives detailed descriptions of real-life ghost encounters."

—Leslie Rule, bestselling author

"This book accomplishes the impossible—to tell true stories of abuse, murder, horror, and the plight of women, and somehow make that an elegant and compelling piece of writing. This should not only be read . . . but taught. Brava!"

—Jonathan Maberry, *New York Times* bestselling author of *Relentless* and *Ink*

"*A Haunted History of Invisible Women* is an absolute must-buy for the spooky people of the world. Hieber and Janes lead the reader on a guided tour of America's most fascinating and noteworthy female ghosts that is utterly brilliant and deeply compelling. The authors examine these stories with a keen feminist lens and resurrect the real women behind them with respect they were seldom afforded in life. It's extraordinary to find a book that is so chilling, yet so full of heart. You'll find yourself haunted by these stories."

—Mallory O'Meara, bestselling author of *The Lady from the Black Lagoon* and *Girly Drinks*

"Deeply researched and lovingly written, *A Haunted History of Invisible Women* is the ultimate paranormal compendium on female ghosts of America. Not only is this a compulsively readable book, it'll send a chill down your spine while illuminating the dark shadows of a nation."

—Kris Waldherr, author of *The Lost History of Dreams* and *Unnatural Women: A Novel of the Frankenstein Women*

"*A Haunted History of Invisible Women* looks beyond the legends of maligned female ghosts and gives us their real histories. It is both a meditation on the misogyny of a ghost-hunting culture that capitalizes on false narratives of sex and death, and a fascinating look at the flesh-and-blood women behind the ghost stories. This book is a long-overdue search for historic truth, yet it recognizes that 'When it comes to ghosts, truth is as elusive as the spirits themselves.'"

—Chris Woodyard, author of *The Victorian Book of the Dead*

"*A Haunted History of Invisible Women* is a beautifully researched and well-written observation of women's ghosts across time. From the famous to the not-so-famous, their stories and the history surrounding them both fascinate and mesmerize. If this book doesn't leave with you a sense of wonder and a healthy dose of goose bumps, check your pulse—you may already be among the spirits."

—Marc Hartzman, author of *Chasing Ghosts: A Tour of Our Fascination with Spirits and the Supernatural*

"This is the book I have always wanted to read. Expert storytellers Hieber and Janes take us on tour through the lives of real women who would become legendary ghosts, adding depth to stories I thought I knew and introducing me to characters I've never met before. With wit and empathy, *A Haunted History of Invisible Women* brings the spirit of these women to life. Their stories are touching, shocking, inspiring, and intimately relatable. They tell the ways women have learned to navigate their world, to thrive, and live authentically against the odds. They reveal the ways society objectifies and classifies women who defy norms and challenge the expectations of their time. These ghosts still have something to say and have much to teach."

—Leila Taylor, author of *Darkly: Black History and America's Gothic Soul*

"*A Haunted History of Invisible Women* is what ghostly nonfiction *needs* to be. The stories recounted are an assortment of delights—by turns wistful, romantic, and genuinely creepy—but illuminating the women who may or may not be at the heart of them gives a depth and luster that is often missing from ghost story collections. The authors care about doing their best by their ghostly subjects, including a nuanced look at how women's stories—even after death—are often molded into archetypal shapes that have very little to do with life or afterlife. It's a jewelry box of haunted heirlooms. Light the candles and sift through it."

—Jillian Venters, author of *Gothic Charm School: An Essential Guide for Goths and Those Who Love Them*

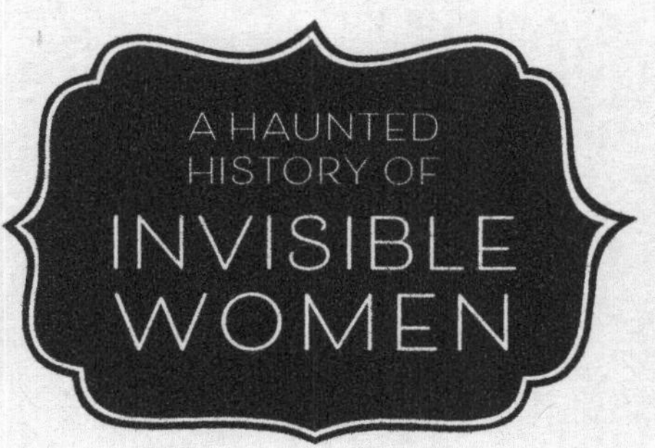
A HAUNTED
HISTORY OF
INVISIBLE
WOMEN

A HAUNTED HISTORY OF INVISIBLE WOMEN

TRUE STORIES OF AMERICA'S GHOSTS

LEANNA RENEE HIEBER
AND ANDREA JANES

CITADEL PRESS
Kensington Publishing Corp.
www.kensingtonbooks.com

CITADEL PRESS BOOKS ARE PUBLISHED BY

Kensington Publishing Corp.
119 West 40th Street
New York, NY 10018

All Kensington titles, imprints, and distributed lines are available at special quantity discounts for bulk purchases for sales promotions, premiums, fund-raising, educational, or institutional use.

Special book excerpts or customized printings can also be created to fit specific needs. For details, write or phone the office of the Kensington sales manager: Kensington Publishing Corp., 119 West 40th Street, New York, NY 10018, attn: Sales Department; phone 1-800-221-2647.

CITADEL PRESS and the Citadel logo are Reg. U.S. Pat. & TM Off.

ISBN: 978-0-8065-4158-7

First trade paperback printing: October 2022

10 9 8 7 6 5 4 3 2 1

Printed in the United States of America

ISBN: 978-0-8065-4159-4 (e-book)

First electronic edition: October 2022

CONTENTS

Introductions

Part 1: Death and the Maiden

Part 2: "Witches"

All Is Vanity by Charles Allan Gilbert circa 1900, courtesy of Alamy Stock Photo

INTRODUCTIONS

WOMEN, DEATH, AND GHOSTS

ANDREA JANES

I HAVE A FUN DAY JOB: I RUN A GHOST TOUR COMPANY IN NEW York City. After about three years in business, I began to notice something about my customers. It came to me one day as I was leading a "Ghosts of the Titanic" tour. As I stood in Astor Place on a warm spring afternoon, explaining the gender breakdown of the first-class lifeboats aboard that ill-starred vessel, I informed my tour group that those lifeboats carried almost exclusively women and children. "There were almost no men aboard the lifeboats," I said, staring at the group of about twelve or fifteen guests standing in front of me, all of whom were women. "Kind of like this group."

Everyone laughed, but I realized what I had said was very true: our customer base skews heavily female. That moment of revelation left me scratching my head, wondering where the male customers were. Oh sure, every once in a blue moon a man would come along, usually dragged there by a date or spouse, but as a general rule, female-identifying people made up 90 percent of my customers. Which was fine by me, and yet it made me wonder: Was I doing something to alienate half the human population?

It wasn't until a reporter approached me for a story on why women are obsessed with seeing ghosts that I realized: ghosts are gendered.

The more I thought about it, the more it made sense. Women are profoundly entwined with ghosts and ghost stories. There are several notions in Western culture that connect the intrinsically "female" with death. Of course, the very notion of gender is culturally constructed, just as ghosts are culturally constructed. Edith Wharton once asked, "What in the world constitutes a ghost except the fact of its being known for one?" Ghosts and gender both require naming and performing, and are not at all uncomplicated, innate, or inherent things. Part of this constructed identity has to do with the cultural roles of women in the United States in the last two centuries.

Historically, women have always lived cheek by jowl with death. Married women tend to outlive our spouses, becoming widows sooner, longer, and more frequently. We hover near the border of death for hours, sometimes days, during the delivery of children, and historically, we have very often died in the process. (As of this writing, the maternal mortality rate in the United States, where I live, is actually on the rise.) In the nineteenth century, when infant mortality rates ensured 1 in 5 children did not live to see their fifth birthday, women suffered heartbreak and arranged for funeral preparations with great frequency, and whenever a family member of any age died, it was often women who were in charge of arranging the funerals for their loved ones, as funerals one hundred and fifty years ago fell within the domestic, and hence female, sphere.

When it came to the spirit realm, women received special status there as well. The American Spiritualist movement of the 1800s was mainly led by women, and allowed women for the first time to assert themselves as vocal spiritual leaders. Its primary adherents were women, many seeking comfort after the death of their loved ones following the Civil War, or solace after the too-frequent deaths of infants and children. Women were thought to be perfect mediums, conduits for spirit communication, because they were open, receptive, passive, and less rationally minded than men.

Women figure prominently in ghostly folklore around the world, often as tragic or terrifying figures damned to become specters because of their very femininity. La Sayona in Venezuela, La Llorona in Mexico, Kuchisake-onna the Slit Mouth Woman in Japan, Mae Nak in Thailand, and any number of "women in white" or "women in brown" in various European traditions, demonstrate that the unleashed feminine, that awesome maelstrom of incredible sexual and physical power—multiple orgasm, gestation, birth, breastfeeding—so often feared, is dangerous and often leads to a terrible afterlife.

In the arena of supernatural fiction, women appear with great regularity both as gothic, ghostly tropes *and* as authors. In fact, women authors accounted for a large percentage of the short stories published during the golden age of ghost stories, from 1840 to 1920. Women triumphed in the critically marginalized world of genre fiction, and excelled in the format of the short story, the ideal format for someone squeezing out a living between her other labors. In fact, this era gave women the means to profit from their own labor and to earn a decent living from the sale of their short stories, which leads us to the most interesting line of thought when it comes to women and ghosts: that in their intersection lies a kind of power.

Though women are traditionally marginalized, and though many female ghosts are the spirits of women who died in awful, often misogynistic circumstances—i.e., murdered by a spouse—not every female ghost is a tragic victim. Many exact vengeance, assert power, and subvert gender roles in ways unavailable to living women. As cultural critic Andi Zeisler writes:

> *[Female ghosts] have every bit of anger that makes living women sources of fear, but none of the societal restriction. In*

> *this way, ghost stories are often protofeminist tales of women who, if only in death, subvert the assumptions and traditions of women as dutiful wives and mothers, worshipful girlfriends, or obedient children by unleashing a lifetime's worth of rage and retribution.*

Spectrality can potentially bestow agency on a woman who was denied it in life, forcing her haunted victims to reckon with her whether they want to or not. While it's easy to dismiss and belittle a living woman who dares to be vocally critical or angry, it is much harder to silence a ghost: She has remarkable staying power.

Engaging with the spirit realm could even (quite literally) grant living women a voice. Spiritualists were able to advocate for social change—from abolition to women's rights—in public arenas, speaking on stages in ways that would have been unthinkable before 1848, the year the Fox sisters first heard the spirit rappings that led to Spiritualism and, incidentally, the year of the Seneca Falls Convention on the rights of women. (1848 was also the year Catherine Crowe published her ghost-hunting manual, *The Night-Side of Nature*, in England, inextricably establishing women in the world of paranormal research and investigation. It was a big year for women and ghosts.)

It's the complicated intersection between the tragic/conservative side of ghost stories that represent women as victims and the unleashed, unsilenced, undaunted aspect of female ghosts we find compelling. Neither victims nor heroes, our female ghosts have, as Avery Gordon calls it, the right to "complex personhood," possessing "sometimes contradictory humanity and subjectivity that is never adequately glimpsed by viewing them as victims or, on the other hand, as superhuman agents."

They're also just really damn interesting tales.

In this book, we have collected some of our favorite female-centered ghost stories from around the country, what we consider to be the most thought-provoking and significant ghost stories. In a cheeky nod to the way gender is a societally constructed norm, we've decided to organize them by trope: surely you will recognize the categories of "Spinster," "Witch," and "Fallen Woman," just some of the types we have compiled here.

We want to examine how—and why—these stories are told in local legends, on ghost tours, and by generations of Americans, as much as the stories themselves, many of which do live up to the cliché "stranger than fiction." This book is an exploration of what ghosts and hauntings tell us about ourselves, and about the historical role of women in this country. By understanding our ghosts, we may better understand ourselves both past and present, and how female-identifying individuals are represented in the (margins of) historical record.

History, and ghost stories, function for us as a kind of mediumship. We humbly ask questions of the dead to see the deeper meaning in their stories. We seek out the facts of their stories to the absolute best of our ability, as much as historical research allows. We come to inquire, to reveal, to listen, and to share these women's often forgotten, sometimes misrepresented stories. We are glad you are here on this journey with us. And to you we say the same thing we say to the ghosts who allow us to share these stories: thank you.

EXISTENTIAL QUESTIONS

LEANNA RENEE HIEBER

I HAVE ALWAYS BEEN HAUNTED. NOT IN A SCARY-MOVIE WAY, BUT in a wistful, melancholiac kind of way. The way that made Poe's stories and poetry resonate with me at a too-early age. With that odd understanding of sadness and an inexplicable draw to the nineteenth century came an equal and enthusiastic desire to *discover*. To query. To contemplate the big, mystical questions that keep folks up at night. To play hide and seek across the veil. But I've done so trying not to take myself too seriously. A life in theater, playwriting, and fiction *must* be taken with a sense of humor. Still, I'm passionate about my work and consider it a calling.

Spirits have always been with me, asking me to tell their stories. That request has come in many forms: a sharp instinct, an odd synchronicity, something I know but don't know how I know it, a sudden inspiration, or a whisper on the wind. So, I do what has been asked. I tell spectral stories as a novelist, as a tour guide, a lecturer explaining the importance of ghost stories, and now sharing these tales. Widening history and experience.

This book isn't here to tell you what to believe, to convince you ghosts are real or they're not. But disbelief will not make the lived experiences described here untrue. I think one's relationship to the spirit world, like religion and identity, is fundamentally personal and contains multitudes.

Personally, I don't believe hauntings are, by their nature, inherently or always scary. I think they can be beautiful. Sometimes funny. Often endearing. A paranormal experience can say as much about the living as any entity in question. The thing that surprised me most about becoming a ghost tour guide was that I became a sort of "paranormal chaplain," guiding my audiences through their own questions about the beyond. In some cases, my reassuring them that they weren't out of their mind for sharing with me something inexplicable provided comfort.

I'll never forget a bright young man from the South who, between stops on the tour, just needed me to tell him it was okay that he sometimes saw his beloved, departed grandmother in their living room. I asked him if he was glad to see her, and he was. So, I said there was nothing to worry about, but to take heart that she was still looking out for him. He seemed relieved.

What I did caution him about was that there would be some places it wouldn't be safe or welcome for him to share that knowledge, and I trusted him to figure out where he could and couldn't be honest about his experiences. I was thanked heartily by his kind father, who seemed to need to hear all of that too.

Ghost stories have an intimacy to them. I believe the thrall of ghosts, compared to other paranormal "creatures," is that they are *of us*, and we all may someday *become them*. Our loved ones may at any point become a startling story. We too may become legend. Ghosts can't be discounted as easily as any other paranormal entity. It is the unknown, mysterious echo of something human that makes ghost stories eerie, the familiar instantly strange.

Telling a ghost story in combination with a precise historical location infuses a dynamic mysticism into what is otherwise taken as historical "fact." It gives us, as tour guides, other angles and perspectives by which to consider the past and present, merging time lines to make figures of history contemporaneous in haunting.

In this book, we focus on a personally curated selection of stories. By *no means* is this an exhaustive list, nor is it an encyclopedia or compendium. We hope to examine and unpack some of the inherent tropes of ghost stories, gothic fiction, haunted houses at various crossroads of women's history. We hope to expand this concept in future volumes to be able to include many more stories.

In my Spectral City series of novels, my spiritualist and psychic medium heroine, Eve Whitby, confronts her pressing and often debilitating sensitivities by devoting her career to them, by giving the ghosts voice and worth. The idea that a soul still has something to say. I gave this drive to Eve because I have it myself. This book is another way in which I can honor my lifelong quest to examine whispers across the veil and why the living are so keen to listen.

During the course of my career, I had the pleasure of meeting paranormal superstar Katrina Weidman, host of television's *Paranormal State, Paranormal Lockdown, Portals to Hell,* and more. I thought of her immediately when this book became a reality and wanted to ask about her experiences dealing with ghosts on such a large scale and for such a wide audience. She was gracious enough to answer:

"One of the aspects that is hardly talked about in paranormal media is the emotional toll this work can take on you. There seems to be a connection between tragic history causing places to have a high amount of activity. When I'm working (on camera or privately), I'm bombarded with traumatic stories from the past. Suicide, murder, neglect, and abuse are part of the daily conversations we have in the field. I'm often asked how I go into and, in some cases, live in these terrifying locations? The truth is: yes, unexplainable activity can be scary, but I find that the history leaves more of a stain on my heart than any supernatural occurrence I could encounter.

"Does the emotional ride change if the supposed spirit is believed to be female? What I will say is I often find myself being, again, more affected by the history we encounter involving women. For instance, one case I worked involved the murder of a young woman by her boyfriend. Other cases involved women who were unjustly placed in mental health facilities simply because the men in their lives could do it. Then there are the present-day cases where some of the women I've assisted are being called 'bad mothers' for exploring the paranormal realm even though they've exhausted all other options when it comes to finding natural explanations for the phenomena in their homes.

"All of that, for me, is hard not to take on. I feel that emotion on a deeper level because even though I may not have experienced their exact situation I can empathize due to the hurdles I have been through by simply being a woman."

When I asked if being a woman in the industry of ghost hunting affected or informed her experiences, she had this to say:

"It's no secret that when it comes to the media side of the paranormal field it's mostly been men who get to take center stage. I always find that interesting, considering the field and the audience who indulges in the media itself skews and identifies as female.

"So why do we have so many men running the show? I can only speak to what I've seen and experienced personally. I've noticed a lot of old rhetoric that refuses to die. 'Males lead and females follow. Males are protectors and females need protecting.' With the added element of television, we're also harshly critiqued, in comparison to our male colleagues, when it comes to our looks and body types.

"Now, is paranormal media unique for this? Certainly not,

there's a lot of industries where you can see the same challenges, but it has bled into ours and it wouldn't be a full picture of the work if I said that hasn't affected me. One of the more rewarding aspects is when I do a lecture or event and a parent comes up to me with their young daughter and tells me how our work has inspired their child to be brave, speak up, and want to be a leader. I want to make clear, there's nothing wrong with being scared or not wanting to take on a leadership role, but I think it's really important to show both sides. For far too long our field has only shown the one that feeds into a very old narrative.

"What I love about the paranormal field, that I hope we see more of when it comes to media, is that regardless of gender, religion, race, sexual orientation, age, nationality, status, etc. it brings so many people together based off of a shared interest or, in many cases, being affected by the unexplained and spending your time searching for answers. That's powerful and I hope we see more of that varied representation moving forward."

She's right; interest in the paranormal can be a unifying draw and can still honor individuality and deeply personal moments.

I have over twenty years of experience working in and guiding people through many haunted places around this beautiful country. The only things each site has in common is a hook of historical interest and people who come with unanswered questions in their hearts.

I too love the question. As one of my favorite poets Rainer Maria Rilke said in his *Letters to a Young Poet:*

> *I beg you . . . to have patience with everything unresolved in your heart and try to love the questions themselves as if they were locked rooms or books written in a very foreign language. Don't search for the answers, which could not be given to you now, because you would not be able to live them.*

> *And the point is, to live everything. Live the questions now. Perhaps then, someday far in the future, you will gradually, without even noticing it, live your way into the answer.*

I think that lingering question may extend after death too. Happy haunting . . .

Carnations numbering the dead laid out in front of the former Triangle Shirtwaist Factory on the anniversary of the fire. Photo by Leanna Renee Hieber

PART 1

Death and the Maiden

INTRODUCTION

LEANNA AND ANDREA

EDGAR ALLAN POE FAMOUSLY SAID, "THE DEATH OF A BEAUTIFUL woman is, unquestionably, the most poetical topic in the world." In Poe's defense, quite the melancholiac, this may have more to do with conceptualizing and memorializing the loss of women he loved than something a woman should aspire to. By poetry he means the topic is one to be explored with careful words, that death is an antithetical state to the young and beautiful. Still, the emphasis on *beautiful* women implies the bias toward youth and beauty that has been around since the dawn of time. As if were she not young and beautiful, it would not be worth notice.

Some took that poetry quite seriously, and a sort of tuberculosis chic look became popular in the nineteenth century, romanticizing wasting away. Modern fashion still covets too-thin models and whole industries revolve around the sale, marketing, and idealization of women's body image, a consistent topic of media obsession. The very idea of what's prized as beautiful changes through time, and women must keep up. In the rush to do so, society's structured gender binary again resets the distinct parameters of what's "acceptable" and what is "ideal." For femme-presenting folks and trans women, there is an additional layer of scrutiny, gatekeeping, and marginalization levied upon them; the societal hoops to jump through remain in flux and entirely conditional. The creation of an ideal is used as a voracious sales pitch to those who wish to be seen as beautiful, the standard of beauty being determined by societal law and in the context of a given era. But that beauty is, of course, fleeting. Part of the chase also races against the clock.

The spirits who are stopped in time retain their youth, mystery, and beauty. They might also still hold their pain, eternally, a cycle of revisiting their final moments or haunting the place where they died or had their most emotional impacts.

The following stories bring Poe's quote to spectral life as we see how idealization set in as an inherent part of their ghost stories and they become the perfect poetical subject, an eternally beautiful young wraith who can neither grow old nor break out of the idealization they have been placed into.

Considering the expectations placed on women through the years, to put it too bluntly: these women died before they could become a disappointment. Their life being cut short places them in a realm of endless possibility and eternal romanticization. For The Don CeSar, the idealization of an opera singer led to the construction of an elaborate hotel in honor of a star-crossed love, while Kate Morgan, who died by suicide at the Hotel del Coronado in 1892, was dubbed by the press "The Beautiful Stranger," and a race to identify her captured the nation in the throes of the Gilded Age.

There are several references in this book to *Angel in the House*, a sprawling, overwritten poem published in two parts by Coventry Patmore in 1854 and 1856. It was held as the standard bearer for women's existence in the middle of the nineteenth century. The poem creates a rarefied, limited sphere for a woman, where she is simultaneously belittled and placed on a pedestal. The maidens of this chapter would have been expected, in their time periods, to adhere to the conflicting expectations laid out in this poem, one that had an extraordinary cultural influence that would outlast its century.

As influential of a poem as *Angel in the House* was to nineteenth-century attitudes regarding women, so too was "Of Queen's Gardens," a conservative essay originally given as a lecture and published in *Sesame and Lilies* in 1865. This essay—the mere thought of which still makes Leanna furious over twenty years after her first collegiate examination of the text—essentially posits that a woman should be kept behind walled gardens, tending the beautiful flowers she herself represents. In doing so, she may remain a pure, innocent, and civilizing force to tame the beast of man, who goes out into the wild world as the "doer." The author, John Ruskin, famously had his marriage annulled by his wife, Effie Gray, for lack of consummation. Essentially, it seems Ruskin was revolted by the reality that his wife had pubic hair and was a full-grown woman. His sense of an "idealized woman" was at a profound disconnect with reality, to put it mildly. The annulment was a huge scandal at the time. But Ruskin's ideas about women, their place and their purpose, his evident desire to keep them forever children, still scurry into modern thought.

There has always been an expectation of women that they perform their societal roles, a purview which is wide-ranging and must be done without complaint. It is no coincidence that several of the women in this book are performers, actresses, singers, or women reinventing themselves, where their identities on- and offstage were a subject of interest, intrigue, and expectation, well after their deaths.

Those who have bucked the narrow window of "femininity" through history have often been punished or additionally marginalized. How we think of such women as ghosts often carries on those burdens. However, if a "maiden" has not progressed to her next level of "purpose" as defined by the limited maternal and matrimonial social mores our modern society still grapples with, she is additionally trapped in an "unfulfilled" state. That tension then adds to societal perceptions of her ghost story and any mythmaking surrounding it.

Beginning this book with the tragedy of the Triangle Shirtwaist Factory Fire of 1911 throws the doors of trauma wide open. The shock of so many lives cut short by greed, negligence, and egregious lack of consideration lingers on beyond historical fact, haunting us with the terrible reality of people who were thought to be disposable.

The women of dark academia straddle a nebulous void; spirits moving toward progress and expansions of mind and intellect and yet perhaps moving farther from that idealized "house" and its resident "angel." The college years represent a time when women are straying further from their domestic role and closer to the traditionally masculine territory of the intellect and the professions; perhaps it is for this reason that the trope of the murdered coed remains so popular: it is bloody revenge upon the maiden for daring to seek fulfillment in these arenas. Precisely at the moment the young woman dares to break away, she is violently struck down. Threats of sexual and physical violence haunt the college campus and are reflected in the ghost stories handed down in American collegiate ghostlore. Not only are young women violently dispatched in these tales they are also often suicides, or accidents, caused usually by broken hearts or excessive alcohol consumption. Either way, these maidens serve as warnings, and cohere to the essentially conservative impulses that underlie this type of folk tale: beware, and do not stray from your assigned role, for that way death and madness lie. Female faculty members serve as a mirror to the "maidens" of college ghostlore, and we find teachers, administrators, and librarians serving the role of "eternal maidens" in these tales. Educated beyond eligibility, these women took their academic impulses too far and failed to heed the warnings; having failed to get their "MRS" degree, they are doomed to a spectral existence in shadowy hallways, dormitories, and carrels, cloistered away to haunt dim and dusty schools and libraries evermore.

Idealization is not reality; it is a dream, an expectation, and a projection that does not need a woman to be alive to still be beholden to its trappings. The following are tales of potential cut short and the ghostly aftereffects of that loss. They are eternally innocent; all the possibilities of what these lives could have been and what they may have done in better circumstances charge these stories and their afterlives with a distinct, unliftable weight.

INDUSTRIAL MONSTERS

Ghosts of the Triangle Shirtwaist Factory

ANDREA AND LEANNA

NEW YORK, NEW YORK

GREENWICH VILLAGE, MARCH 25, 1911. THE AIR WAS BRISK, the sky a bright, crisp blue.

It was a Saturday, 4:45 in the afternoon. In Washington Square Park, New Yorkers scurried in the early spring chill. On nearby Greene Street, a block east of the park, sewing machines hummed in the Triangle Shirtwaist Factory, a square and solid ten-story brick edifice that daily churned out hundreds of the most common long-sleeved women's garment of the nineteenth and early twentieth centuries. It was almost closing time, and the nearly two hundred workers inside the Triangle were eyeing the clock and looking forward to collecting their pay packets and going home, when the first black columns of smoke marred the air.

The chaos was instantaneous. Within minutes, screams joined the smoke to fill the air. Fire alarms were pulled and fire wagons raced to the scene. A reporter strolling in the park ran to the burning factory, beginning to jot mental notes even as he ran. Scores of passersby crowded the scene and watched in horror. For one surreal moment, as bright frills of fabric fluttered and fell from the top-floor windows of the Triangle, these witnesses imagined that factory owners Max Blanck and Isaac Harris were preserving their inventory. "He's saving his best cloth," one man declared.

It took bystanders a moment to realize those were no bolts of cloth falling from the windows.

Those were women.

BY THE TIME THE FIRE AT THE TRIANGLE SHIRTWAIST FACTORY had run its course, 146 factory workers, 123 of whom were women, had died.

These were mostly immigrant women: Jewish, Italian, and Eastern European, many living on the Lower East Side. They were young, mostly between fourteen and twenty-four, many hoping to be married, all dreaming of better things to come: the promise of New York, a place where they'd been told the sidewalks shone with gold. They had worked in the grinding, clanging noise of the factory six days a week for bosses who saw them as interchangeable parts of a machine to be hammered into productivity and submission. Whenever murmurs of protest began to ripple through the ranks, the bosses quelled them and locked the doors of the factory to keep their workers firmly inside. *You will sit at your machine and sew,* they commanded, *and punch buttons, and labor until your fingers are raw,* because that was the way of the world.

The tensions between the city's garment workers and the factory owners had been high, but the largest strike by female American workers up to that date had just made a few strides. November of 1909 saw the "Uprising of the 20,000," when garment unions, led by young women just like the Triangle employees, followed the words of Clara Lemlich, her bruised body beaten on a picket line, as she hobbled up to stand before an audience at Cooper Union and called, in Yiddish, "for a general strike." Thousands poured into the streets to protest myriad injustices and extreme hazards. The International Ladies' Garment Workers' Union, supported by the National Women's Trade Union League of America, settled with factory owners in February of 1910.

Excepting the owners of the Triangle Shirtwaist Company.

Nobody knows with exact certainty how the fire got started. It was likely a stray match or cigarette butt alighting atop a bag of greased cloth. It hardly matters; there were so many potential disasters simmering in that building. Scrap bins located under the long tables of sewing machines held thousands of pounds of highly flammable cloth (cotton burns notoriously quickly).

The building's developer had been allowed to construct his edifice without the required third stairway, substituting instead a flimsy fire escape in a narrow air shaft, which acted essentially as a chimney flue when the fire broke out. The Triangle bosses designed the factory floors to slow the egress of their workers, who were stopped and their bags inspected every night to prevent theft. And the exits were kept locked during working hours to prevent both theft and wildcat strikes or walkouts.

By the time the workers realized what was happening, they ran for the exits, only to be crushed and pressed against locked doors and panicked bodies.

Those who worked on the tenth floor had the best chance of getting to one open door or skylight to the rooftop. The stairs between the levels were made of wood and were quickly engulfed. Telephone communication between the floors was lost, one floor wasn't warned until the fire was upon them, and even then, nearly every door was locked.

The limited fire escapes were rusted and poorly maintained. They buckled under the weight of the women, who then crashed to their deaths on the pavement below. Fire trucks did arrive, but their ladders reached only to the sixth floor. The firemen had safety nets, and some women jumped into these; some missed the nets; some nets broke from too many jumping at once. Imagine seeing one's rescuers only two floors below, just out of reach. The city was climbing higher by the year and those charged with rescue couldn't keep up.

A single brave operator ran the last working elevator up and down again and again as long as he could, until the heat and smoke made it impossible. Some workers leaped atop the elevator shaft, attempting to hitch a ride, flaying their hands on the elevator cables in the process.

One brave New York University law professor, Frank Sommer, commanded his students to scale the roof of the adjoining building to help bring workers across to safety.

The truly desperate threw themselves from the windows. Clasping hands with a coworker or friend, they jumped to their deaths as the fire seared their backs.

Police had to keep throngs of hysterical observers from throwing themselves into the building in vain attempts to help, while others fainted away at the sight of the piling bodies and the gore pooling in the street.

A newspaper reporter on the scene, William Shepherd, dared to describe the sound of a human body on pavement: "thud-dead." Not to be shocking for the sole purpose of shock, but to show a readership this grim reality, trying to describe the indescribable. He also recalled those girls at the forefront of the "Uprising" the year prior, marching to try to prevent this very atrocity. He suddenly grieved for what they'd been pleading for, what they'd told the city would happen if they weren't heeded. A dread prophecy had come to pass in one of the worst industrial accidents this nation had ever seen.

By the end of the day, an ad hoc morgue had to be opened across the street from the factory on an open floor soon filled with bodies. Many women were identifiable only by their engagement rings, small sparks of gold amid the ash.

THE CITY'S OUTRAGE WAS INSTANTANEOUS AND AS FURIOUS AS the fire itself. But the factory owners had broken no laws. They went to trial and were acquitted. The fury mounted.

Frances Perkins had been having tea on Washington Square North when the fire broke out and stood watching the horror unfold from across the street. The disaster prompted her to abruptly change the course of her life and, with New York mayor Al Smith, begin work on the nation's first labor laws. Perkins would serve as the first secretary of labor and the first female cabinet member. She was quoted as saying the day of the Triangle Fire was "the day the New Deal began."

But it didn't change soon enough for the dead.

Contemporary reports in leading newspapers counted several unnamed dead. The *New York Times* account of March 26, 1911, noted, "The victims who are now lying at the Morgue waiting for some one to identify them by a tooth or the remains of a burned shoe were mostly girls from 16 to 23 years of age." But those English-language newspapers hadn't thought to go looking at the Yiddish-, Italian-, Ukrainian-, or German-language newspapers for the list of the dead. The power of the name is the same across all people, and this tragedy was further haunted by anonymity. Since then, thanks to interest and scholarship, almost all the names have been found. Every year on the anniversary of the fire, volunteers from the New York City Central Labor Council (AFL-CIO) lay 146 carnations on the sidewalk where so many bodies fell.

WHEN WE SPEAK OF THE TRIANGLE ON OUR TOURS, WE CENTER that discussion around the idea of residual hauntings.

In current parapsychology, a residual haunting is often defined as the energy left behind in a location by a traumatic event.* Sir William Barrett of the Society for Psychical Research first wrote of it back in 1911, the same year the Triangle burned: "In certain cases of hauntings and apparitions, some kind of local imprint, on material structures or places, has been left by some past events occurring to certain persons, who when on Earth, lived or were closely connected with that particular locality; an echo or phantom of these events becoming perceptible to those now living." Some paranormal researchers have gone so far as to try to prove these psychic residues or echoes are literally imprinted in the materials of objects and places—the so-called Stone Tape theory—and that residual hauntings are actually these recorded imprints being replayed. People who possess a degree of psychic sensitivity sometimes speak of physical locations having an "impression" or a "stain" on them.

A residual haunt makes no attempt to communicate with the living; they merely repeat whatever they were doing in life, usually at the moment they died. This type of haunting is sometimes described as metaphorically resembling a record stuck in a groove, playing the same note over and over: ghost trains that cross the same trestle at the same time every day, ghost ships that sail the same waters at low tide, ghost battles that rage at sunset, and so on. The residual haunt possesses a repetitious, looping nature. Disaster sites, battlegrounds, hospitals, and prisons are often the sites of high levels of residual energy, otherwise known, somewhat poetically, as place memory.

Today, the building where the Triangle occurred has been repurposed by New York University. The renamed Brown Building contains undergraduate biology classrooms; the sewing machines have long been replaced by microscopes and lab equipment. It is

* Some parapsychologists, such as Loyd Auerbach, acknowledge a distinction between ghosts, which are apparitions who can sense and communicate with the living, and residual hauntings, which are the psychic echoes or imprints of past events and appear as phantasms who do not communicate or seem to sense the living.

the original building, the actual walls in which it happened. (Ironically, the building itself was fireproof.) People do report sensing something palpable when they stand in this location; it is hard not to. NYU's blog quotes Dennis Kroner, a public safety officer who works on the site, as saying, "I know the building is haunted, because you can feel it. But I've never seen ghosts or anything." Kroner speaks to the idea of residual haunting, but stops short of claiming to have had any apparitional experiences. Almost anyone lingering long enough at the Brown Building would, we think, come to agree with the SPR's William Barrett that there is "an echo or phantom of these events [perceptible] to those now living." It is the same feeling anyone gets when in the presence of any place that makes them a witness to history: Gettysburg, Auschwitz, Flanders Fields, the Freedom Tower.

Residual haunting remains writ large here, as if emotion became a kind of flash paper capturing the silhouettes of falling women who held hands as they jumped, and there that memory still falls, a shadow out of the corner of one's eye. The story of the jumpers does tend to bring to modern mind the stories of the World Trade Center, and an old, early twentieth century horror is instantly made more personal. The ache of this residual psychic scar is felt every time these stories are told, and yet retelling them is precisely how human beings metabolize such tragedies.

Whether or not there really are ghosts at the Brown Building, or even a residual haunting in the parapsychological sense of the term, this is absolutely a building haunted by history and memory, as all disaster sites are.

Legends do abound, as perhaps is inevitable, ranging from wisps of smoke in the air, to NYU coeds feeling choked or struggling to breathe, to vague apparitions of disordered, sooty women staggering down the street or floating down the hall, charred.

Stories are told of formerly locked doors suddenly and mysteriously unlocking themselves, ephemeral faces appearing in bathroom mirrors, and coeds feeling vaguely pressed to flee the building with no real reason why.

Body-shaped shadows have been said to appear, falling from windows. The sounds of screams. The echoes of crackling fire. The smell of smoke. Worse, burned flesh.

But first-person accounts of ghost stories are notoriously hard to pin down, and this is one locale where it doesn't do to be glib. When discussing a tragedy of such seriousness, how does one then turn around and declaim, wide-eyed, that *you can still smell the charred flesh of the burning bodies!?* How can one in good conscience repackage this suffering for profit, particularly in the absence of any concrete evidence that a single living person anywhere has actually experienced these ghosts and apparitions? Because here is the interesting thing about the Triangle ghost sightings: it seems they have been manufactured by those with a vested interest in profiting from them.

When researching ghostly accounts involving the Triangle Fire, there is a dearth of plausible primary sources to choose from. Most of these tales come from books and websites that cite no sources for their ghost stories. A search for Triangle ghost stories online takes you to the SquareUp store of American Hauntings Ink, a company whose online bookstore boasts an impressive 130 titles, including *And Hell Followed with It*, a recounting of American disasters and their subsequent hauntings, among them the Triangle Fire.* Other paranormal accounts can be found on the blogs of local ghost tour companies. These retellings are characterized by abrupt tonal shifts that veer off into the ghoulish: *Their screams often shatter the night, as if they are still trying to escape from the terrible blaze. So powerful is their paranormal panic that it infects the living. So don't be surprised if you suddenly feel the urge to flee during your visit!* There is money to be

---

* Authors Troy Taylor and Rene Kraus have created a veritable factory of haunted Americana.

made in these wisps of smoke and smells of charred flesh. Tales of residual hauntings like Dennis Kroner's aside, we have yet to come across a single highly sensory or graphic apparitional encounter written by anyone who could be described as "unaffiliated" with the paranormal industry. And it *is* an industry, filled with haunted hotels, ghost hunts, guided tours, and cities competing for the title of "America's Most Haunted."

In fact, almost every single printed ghost story associated with this site can be traced back to someone with something to sell. In an irony so thick you'd need a cutter's knife to slice through it, the women of the Triangle perform the ultimate invisible labor.*

Cultural critic Alicia Puglionesi wrote for *Baltimore City Paper* that "haunting originates in the structural violence of capitalism," an idea that becomes quite literal when writing about the ghosts of the Triangle Shirtwaist Factory.[1] The ghosts of the Triangle workers—who were barred from unionizing, whose demands for better, fairer, safer, and more humane working conditions went unmet—are one example of Gilded Age excesses haunting America's ghost stories. Collective anxiety about a system riddled with endemic inequality suffuses every retelling of the Triangle. Ghost stories bring to light the repressed and troubling parts of our history, and our society, those we have difficulty talking about any other way. Far from being mere morbid voyeurism, the discussion of these ghosts potentially gives us an outlet to confront the darker chapters of our past and what they mean for us today.

Of the many stories we tell on our tours, the Triangle most connects emotionally with guides and customers. Our customers, who are, as a group, very astute, sensitive, and intelligent people, immediately recognize their own complicity in a modern global economic system that still exploits workers—who among us has not bought a

* A cutter's knife was an 1870s innovation that allowed a garment worker to "cut the pieces for dozens or even hundreds, of identical garments in just a few strokes" (David Von Drehle, *Triangle*, 39).

"fast fashion" item in the last decade or so? And, as guides, we can reflect for a moment on our own place in the industry of tourism. Tour guides themselves are, as we will tell you at the end of a tour when soliciting tips, members of the service industry. It is an industry that, like many others in our current age, is rapidly becoming decentralized, one where benefits and a social safety net are disappearing and being replaced by the "gig economy," the modern version of piecework (the paid-by-the-piece sweatshop sewing so many women performed for pennies, working long hours in cramped, stuffy tenements).

How much does a human life cost? Companies around the world decide on an arbitrary number, life reduced to ticking numbers in growth portfolios. People still perish in garment factory fires, as evidenced in 2012 in Bangladesh. To this day, women across almost all industries remain underpaid for their labor (women in the global south are even more badly compensated for the work they continue to perform in the modern garment industry). Behemoth industrial monsters still churn, chew, and rend raw material like all the old mills, but many of the substances mined, manufactured, and commercialized have changed.

Perhaps we all, on some level, identify with the precarious lives of the Gilded Age underclass. The obvious, even if unspoken, parallels between the average American worker in the twenty-first century and the garment workers of 1911 seems to resonate with nearly everyone. Incidentally, the term for the type of invisible, automated, gig-based labor that drives the current internet-based information economy is "ghost work." A telling term if there ever was one.

When done properly, ghost tours have the potential to serve a very serious purpose. Ghosts can be presented not as frivolous fun, but, as historian Tiya Miles writes in her examination of plantation ghost tours in the South, "messengers from another time that compel us to wrestle with the past, a past chained to colonialism, slavery and patriarchy, but a past that can nevertheless challenge us and commission us to fight for justice in the present." By keeping this imperative in mind, and by being careful to present the spirits of the Triangle in an honest and forthright manner, we are capable of leading responsible, ethical, and nonexploitative ghost tours, and reminding people of their responsibility to honor the spirits of the Triangle by continuing to fight for justice in the world of the living.

We memorialize the lives of the women and men who worked and perished here. We must, encouraging our audiences not to take labor laws for granted, and to fight against any efforts to weaken them. The Triangle's litany of injustices are cautionary tales that *should*, then, haunt us all—an eternal warning. A spectral demand for vigilance.

The ghosts of capital are still here on Washington Place, not far from the thousands of bones below the surface of Washington Square Park, where a long-hidden eighteenth-century potter's field lies secretly beneath some of the most valuable real estate in the country.* Here in the NYU buildings that ring the park, in the hallways of what is now a staggeringly expensive private university, young minds are molded and shaped, taught to earn their keep to repay their student loans; here adjunct professors toil without safety nets. Outside on the streets, taxi and delivery drivers, waitstaff, performers (and tour guides) are all surviving. The push and pull of capital and labor continues as the ghosts move between two worlds, in the endless dance of profit and loss.

* From 1797 to 1825, the City of New York buried roughly 10,000 to 20,000 bodies in the area that is now Washington Square Park (no exact numbers exist). After 1825, the city turned the land into a public park and lined it with expensive real estate. The human remains were never reinterred and are there to this day. The people buried there have been commemorated with a small plaque set into the pathway near the public restrooms.

THE BEAUTIFUL STRANGER

Kate Morgan and the Hotel del Coronado

LEANNA

SAN DIEGO, CALIFORNIA

THE HOTEL DEL CORONADO, NEAR SAN DIEGO, IS A STUNNING relic from a bygone era. In the nineteenth century, beautiful spa and resort hotels made of dark wood and lavish detailing arose in coastal areas and sightseeing hubs around the nation. Being wooden, not many survived, whether due to changes in architectural styles or devastating fires. But the Del still reigns on the coast of Coronado Island—*coronado* meaning "crowned" in Spanish. The hotel's dark wood interior is such a deep contrast to the bright sun, the sparkling water, the clear blue sky, and the sweep of white beaches beyond. When one enters the Del it's a dramatic shift of temperature, hue, and time.

A grand stair leads up to a second-floor clerestory walkway that looks down over the entrance and reception area. It begs to be climbed and walked. One is compelled to gaze down from above, surrounded by dark wood rafters and bygone energy.

When visiting the Del in 2011, I found myself asking the usual question in any building of interest, especially one built in my specialty area of the 1880s: "I wonder if it's haunted?" There was a slight chill in the air, but that was likely the air conditioning, a twentieth-century addition to the nineteenth-century construction. Still in contemplation, I turned to the hallway behind me and came face-to-face with a picture of Kate Morgan in a glass case and a display created by the hotel to reference her story, alluding to her mystery, tragic death, and lovelorn, unanswered questions.

Kate Morgan, described in every article ever written about her as a pretty woman in her mid-twenties, checked into the Hotel del Coronado on Thursday, November 24, 1892, under the name Lottie A. Bernard of Detroit, carrying only one small bag. She would be found dead on the morning of November 29 on an exterior staircase leading to the beach. A pistol lay on a stair near the body, and blood was described at the scene. Her clothes were wet, and it was determined her body had lain there for at least six to eight hours. None of the witnesses who found her directly mentioned her wounds in inquest transcripts, but the San Diego County coroner determined she died by a self-inflicted gunshot wound to her temple.

It wasn't "proper" for a woman of any means to be traveling alone, but the situation was common enough for the Del and other hotels of the era to have a discreet "ladies' entrance," by which an unescorted woman could check in without entering through the showcase of a grand entrance. There was also a ladies' dining room, should a woman prefer not to be seen dining alone in "mixed company." Kate likely used this side entrance and made sure to say that her brother would be joining her with their trunks of luggage as the clerk signed her in. She frequently asked if there had been any word from her brother, almost desperately, right up until her death.

The newspapers began reporting about Kate immediately, widespread press dubbing her "the beautiful stranger." For the next three weeks, speculation, falsehoods, and mistaken identities would flourish in press reports nationwide. But the following, from the *Seaport News*, written on December 3, 1892, was mostly true, the papers having no idea her name was an alias:

> *Mrs. Anderson-Bernard, twenty-four years of age, arrived at Del Coronado alone last week. She was reserved and mingling not with the other guests, made few acquaintances. It was known, however, that she was an invalid. On Monday she resolved to end her sorrows and sufferings, so crossing the bay purchased a revolver and cartridges. Soon after dark on that evening, she deserted the warm, cheerful rooms of the hotel for the darkness outside, and on the steps at the rear in the cold, drizzling rain, took her own life.*

November was off-season for the Del, but there had been enough staff that Kate interacted with in the days she was there to paint the picture of a polite, well-dressed woman who moved slowly, in pain, clearly ill and increasingly distracted.

From the accounts of the bellboy and the druggist at the shop inside the Del, she refused any attempts to call a doctor, eventually declaring that she had stomach cancer and that the doctors had concluded her a "hopeless case." In addition to asking if her brother had sent any word for her or had sent along word of her trunks after a miscommunication at a train station, she asked for matches, as she wished to burn papers in the fireplace. When a staff member, seeing her ill health, asked if she needed funds, she gave a name and a bank, and a Mr. Allen in Hamburg, Iowa, wired twenty-five dollars.

The day of her death, taking a trip out of the hotel that she claimed was to check in at the train depot to claim her trunks in person, seeming physically weak but determined, she arrived at Chick's Gun Shop on Fifth Street in San Diego instead. There, she purchased a pistol and rounds, returning by streetcar. Hours later she ended her life on a side staircase leading toward the beach.

Her body was found by an electrician, who explained that he had been "trimming" the exterior lights in the early morning. The Del was one of only a few electrified edifices in San Diego and one of the first fully electrified resorts, but workers of the time still utilized gas lamp terminology. He went to get the manager and met the groundskeeper along the way; together the men examined the scene but did not move her. Just placed a canvas over her and sent word to the coroner's office to make his assessments and take the body, and the electrician continued trimming the rest of the hotel lights.

The coroner pronounced her death a suicide, but then there was the matter of who would come to claim her body.

One of the most unsettling things about Kate's case is that her body lay out for viewing in the coroner's building for *days,* still waiting to be identified and claimed by a relation. A constant parade of people—almost entirely women—came to see the dead woman. She was a sensation, her body becoming an instant, morbid attraction.

A coroner's inquest was held with a jury of men. The coroner called hotel staff, those who found her body, any witnesses, and the gun shop owner to testify about their interactions with Kate. Who she was and what troubled her remained a mystery. The papers in the fireplace of her room were all ashes. But it did seem clear from the evidence that she died by her own hand.

It would take some time to unravel that Lottie A. Bernard was an alias. Several mistaken identities were announced, then ruled out, and the nationwide press was rushing to catch up.

A man came forward to state that he'd been, supposedly, on the same train as Kate, and witnessed her with a man with whom she'd had a very bitter and public quarrel. After some time, she apparently beseeched him to forgive her, but he seemed obstinate and left the train at Orange. This third-hand account provided some clues as to the idea of missing trunks and a male relation of some kind, but Kate was still shrouded in mystery.

Finally, the *Los Angeles Times* reported on December 8, 1892, that Mrs. Katie Logan had been missing since November 23, and that the description of the beautiful stranger in all the papers was a match for her. Under the alias of Katie Logan, Kate Morgan had been working "as a domestic" for the Grant family in Los Angeles for the past two months. Kate was described as a model employee who tended diligently to her duties and never went out at night. The Grant family and Kate's fellow staff relayed that she refused to discuss her past, saying only that she'd married a gambler and "was not happy with him" and didn't know what had become of him.

On the twenty-third of November, Kate had said she was merely going out for a brief trip and would be back in time for Thanksgiving dinner preparations, carrying only a small "gripsack" and a shawl. It was said she'd been anxious to get some papers signed and seemed to be worried about something, but no one knew what.

When Kate didn't return, police departments had been notified. But the various aliases used in each situation delayed what truths could easily be pieced together.

The trunk Kate left behind at her Los Angeles workplace provided a clue to her identity, but what she was trying to conceal, and the papers she wanted signed, and those she burned in the Del fireplace, remain a mystery. Names and mailing addresses had been scratched out from any letters or pictures in the trunk. Only her wedding license was unaltered, noting that she had been wed to Tom Morgan in December of 1885. It's possible that Tom's professional gambling career had taken on one too many risks and Kate was trying to escape a morally gray life.

If the fight on the train was a true account, it is widely presumed he was a lover and either "ruined" her or simply deserted her after their quarrel. Kate did not have a brother, so whoever she was asking after at the Del was some other sort of relationship, one that required a lie.

That she'd said she had stomach cancer, in addition to bottles and medicines found in her small bag, including others she'd asked for, could be indicative of her trying to induce a miscarriage. While speculation ran high that she'd been pregnant, no autopsy or procedure was completed to determine the fact one way or another.

That the housekeeper who had attended Kate while at the Del was not questioned is a startling omission by the inquest. The male bellboy was questioned and gave testimony, but the (presumably female) housekeeper did not. Was this a slight of not thinking a woman capable of appearing in court, or did she simply, as did many ancillary figures in this tale, not wish to get involved? Mr. Allan, who had wired Kate twenty-five dollars, evidently out of sympathy as her husband had been his school friend, refused to answer any further telegrams.

Kate's supposedly well-to-do family said absolutely nothing. A terse telegraph reply from Kate's grandfather, J. W. Chandler, once his relation to Kate was made clear by a letter from an extended family member, ordered the coroner to bury Kate and bill him for the expenses. Her plain marker in San Diego's Mount Hope Cemetery reads: "KATE MORGAN ALSO KNOWN AS LOTTIE A. BERNARD DIED NOV. 29, 1892 AT AGE 24 YEARS."

Perhaps marrying a gambler had ostracized Kate from the family. If he deserted her, or she didn't want to continue in that itinerant lifestyle, she was entirely on her own. Finding work in Los Angeles, she was able, at least briefly, to create a new life for herself. She had knowledge of the fine hotels of the nation, perhaps having traveled there with her husband, as would befit his career. Presumably this was how she, reportedly well-dressed, navigated a resort that was above a domestic's station. What drove her specifically to the Del and to the depths of suicide remains unknown. What's perhaps saddest about Kate Morgan is how alone she was in the end, without a friend in the world to comfort her in a time of extreme distress and need. Now, her gravesite draws hundreds of visitors a year.

The beautiful stranger had captivated the nation. She was idealized, pitied, and morbidly celebrated by a nineteenth-century society that would never have accepted her as a single woman, a single mother, a ruined creature. The hand-wringing of the newspapers didn't address the restrictive society that placed such burdens and shame upon women who had suddenly found themselves distinctly cursed by becoming an "unfortunate." It's clear Kate felt she had nowhere to turn. She was hardly the only one in that time period driven to drastic depths.

In Gothic fiction, setting is character.

The Del, completed in 1888, is a character in and of itself, a darkly beautiful grand dame of an old age whose architecture has long gone out of fashion (but was, thankfully, protected and designated as a National Historic Landmark in 1977).

Kate Morgan wasn't a famous woman; she was clearly trying to live in those dark, wooden shadows due to societal shame or myriad sorrows. But as she wanders the halls of the Del, a true gem of the Gilded Age, Kate lives on, in various retold facts of dubious provenance that took on wild alterations through the years. She is a hotel attraction, as one will find with The Don CeSar and other historic hotels that boast ghosts as an additional part of your travel package. It is perhaps kindest to think that she matters in this capacity in a way she clearly couldn't feel she did in life. Her room is often requested and she makes her presence very known.

For quite some time, the Del, much like The Don CeSar, downplayed and denied its spectral phenomenon. But a good ghost story simply won't die, and Kate's story was the best kind: a mystery and tragedy all in one. Her press tagline of "beautiful stranger" is irresistible. No truly haunted property can suppress its ghost stories indefinitely. Wilder and wilder stories about Kate's death began circulating—that she'd been pushed from the roof to her death, that there had been direct witnesses to the gunshot, and other larger-than-life details that bore no resemblance to what the coroner had found.

In *Beautiful Stranger: The Ghost of Kate Morgan and the Hotel del Coronado,* a book authored and published by the hotel's heritage department, the Del is trying to clarify what became runaway narratives about Kate. The book includes the full coroner inquest transcripts and lays out a careful, meticulous timeline of every fact that is known and can be documented about her time there. It also offers a teeming set of ghost stories.

The Del website gives the briefest summation of Kate's known history, but invites a mystery, adding that "some skepticism still surrounds this finding."

Today, Kate's spirit seems to have remained at the Del, where she tends to occupy and haunt her former guest room. But her beautiful vision—and ghostly pranks—can be experienced throughout the rambling resort and grounds. As described in *Beautiful Stranger: The Ghost of Kate Morgan and the Hotel del Coronado,* Kate is a relatively harmless ghost. "She generally limits her activity to fleeting appearances and inexplicable antics. . . . Guests in Kate's room report everything from breezes that come from nowhere to having to deal with a television set that turns on and off by itself."[1]

Room 302 was Kate's room at the time, with a present number of 3327. Kate rests in her guest room, regardless of other company. Hotel staff have repeatedly seen and felt the sunken impression of a body on top of the bedcovers that cannot be removed, no matter how the covers are shifted and tucked. It's made some witnesses run from the room, and other staff won't come near the door.

Those who have stayed in or next to Kate's room have often seen her. Some see a transparent woman in the hall or at her door, some see a full, solid figure in period clothes, so real that only the dated fashion is any indication of something unusual. She is always wistful and sad, but she is not violent. Kate does, however, like to pull the bedclothes off in the middle of the night, either appearing as a figure at the edge of the bed or an unseen hand flinging the covers aside.

Kate is known to toy with electricity, the electronic room keys, and various technological devices. Sometimes the phone rings in the middle of the night with no one on the line, or she'll bat a tassel hanging from the fan when no breeze is there to explain the movement.

One hotel guest noticed a woman in "period clothing" walking down an exterior staircase toward the ocean. The guest knew nothing of the ghost or her tragedy. The woman outside eerily turned to the guest watching and seemed to gaze right through her with a piercing, harrowing stare. Only when the guest made an inquiry with the hotel did she find out about Kate and realize the spirit's movement down the stairs matched Kate's last moments.

As a spirit, Kate seems to have some kind of sense that she is known. That she is asked for. That she is a point of curiosity and fascination. She does not seem to mind it. That does make her less alone, in the end.

DARK ACADEMIA

Ghosts of College Campuses

ANDREA

IN 1910, AT HUNTINGDON COLLEGE IN ALABAMA, A GROUP OF FEmale students saw the form of a ghostly lady in red walking down the hallway. They shivered in terror as they listened to her hollow, echoing footsteps. The ghost's eyes were vacant, staring into the middle distance. The red phantom, twirling a crimson parasol, promenaded up and down the hallways until dawn, when she promptly disappeared beyond an avenue of trees on the lawn outside. It was said that some of the female students became mentally unhinged at this point, nervous and prone to fainting, refusing to sleep with the lights off. While this red lady ghost was never seen again, a few years later another red ghost moved in.

This one had a backstory. Her name, according to some sources, was Martha. She was a shy and lonely student, a transfer from New York City, who was rich and aloof and shunned by her housemates. After many months of ostracism, Martha killed herself. It is said that her room was all decorated in red, and red light shot out from the transom of her dormitory doorway just at the moment she wrapped herself in her red comforter and slit her wrists and bled to death.

The definitive account of Huntingdon's Red Lady comes from *13 Alabama Ghosts and Jeffrey* by Kathryn Tucker Windham, a folklorist from Selma, Alabama. Windham's account is acutely detailed and vivid. Describing the first Red Lady of 1910, Windham writes with the flair of a gothic novelist: "Looking neither left nor right and uttering no sound, the lady clad in a red evening dress and carrying a red parasol was visible through a crimson aura of light which surrounded her and cast a lurid glow over her unearthly features." One student is so unhinged by the spectacle that she "would not retire without a lighted taper burning at her bedside." Windham's account of the second Red Lady's suicide continues in this vein as she describes Martha's prone body: "[there] lay Martha, dressed in her red robe and draped in her red bedspread, with blood around her in the floor."

The Red Lady story contains Poe-esque ties—the color red, the hints of madness, the possible transference of identity—and the reader wonders if the first Red Lady ghost in some way possessed Martha. In Poe's short story "Ligeia," the titular character dies and then possesses the body of the narrator's second wife, Rowena. Rowena actually seems to become Ligeia, even beginning to resemble her physically. And of course, Poe's short story "The Masque of the Red Death" is instantly evoked by the color motif of the Red Lady. Huntingdon's Red Lady seems to meld Poe's grotesque imagery into a new tale—into a new academic Gothic.

Windham was a Huntingdon grad, and she coauthored the book with her former English professor. It would seem, then, that the story comes from those who knew it intimately. Windham graduated in 1939 and likely heard the story at school. Her retelling has the feeling of a campfire ghost story, the way the best campus lore usually does.

Huntingdon College moved a few years after the appearance of the first Red Lady ghost; the second ghost appeared in the new location. The fact that there are two ghosts mirroring the two places—and that the school color is crimson—makes it likely there never was a Red Lady ghost, but that the story is a reflection of the school itself. School spirit, if you will. Windham offers no sources for any of the stories in her books, so it remains likely that the Red Lady is likely pure folklore, designed to lend a little Gothic splendor to Windham's alma mater and nothing more. But like most campus lore, there is a meaning and a purpose to this tall tale. The Red Lady is often cited as a story about the dangers of not fitting in. You hold yourself aloof at your peril; in the turbulent years of undergraduate dorm life, isolation can be deadly. But the Red Lady may also caution us about other perils of campus life; it is worth noting that it was likely a fairly rarefied group of women who attended college in the 1930s, when Kathryn Tucker Windham went to school, and the social anxieties about a woman leaving home to live among strangers would have been intense. Perhaps this is a parable about the dangers of seeking higher education in general.

The dangers lurking at college, when a woman first lives on her own, are legion; they include alcohol abuse, eating disorders, isolation, depression, suicide, and the threat of sexual violence. Campus ghostlore reflects these fears and anxieties. Other, less fraught anxieties also come into play, as college life reflects the changing roles of women in society. College ghost stories abound throughout the United States, a country that is uniquely intense in its campus culture. While university experiences around the world are, naturally, emotional times of sometimes exciting, sometimes painful growth, it is only in America that Campus Culture merits its capital Cs, for it is only here that nonacademic aspects of higher education, such as fraternities and sororities, hazing, homecoming, astronomical tuitions, elite-level college sports, and intense expectations blend together to create a specific atmosphere. College is a liminal space, partway between adolescence and adulthood. The move to one's freshman year involves a transition of identity, a new and exploratory phase, when old selves can be furtively sloughed off and new personas can be tried on for size. These years are an intellectual and emotional maelstrom to which young women are particularly vulnerable, and so, perhaps unsurprisingly, some of the most compelling campus ghost stories are female-centered narratives. Many of the "most haunted" colleges in America that have embraced their haunted identities are women's colleges. Smith is one of the nation's most notable women's colleges, and rather adorably maintains an ongoing list of its various ghost sightings on its website, Smithipedia.*

In terms of American ghostlore, college stories are among some of the least likely of all ghost story types to be verifiable, history-based, or true in any way.† These are less ghost stories than on-campus urban legends, mirroring back the emotional upheaval and insecurities students face. It is perhaps fitting, given the age and liminal identity of a college student: just as these ghost stories are not quite true, but in between myth and legend, so is a college student in between young person and adult. Whether or not the stories

---

* The ghost page on Smithipedia is a delightful work of amateur folklore. It is an endearingly earnest list, primly footnoted and peppered with first-year-term-paper vocabulary such as "endemic," and goes house by house, noting any spirit activity. It even takes pains to point out when a house is not haunted ("There are no ghost stories in Albright House"). There is a gravitas to this list, with its painstakingly scholarly citations and links to historic facts. The section on Sessions House contains no fewer than six citations in its 255 words, and describes the story of one of the oldest houses in Northampton, Massachusetts. The house dates from 1751, and the ghost story dates, naturally, from the Revolutionary War because we are, after all, in New England. The story is an eye-glazingly dull affair of a soldier in love with a girl from the opposite end of the political spectrum, a British soldier named Burgoyne and an American girl named Lucy, ending, as expected, with the ghostly star-crossed lovers maintaining an eternal ectoplasmic rendezvous. To their credit, the students maintaining the Smith website concede that there may never have been a "Lucy," and that the only female living in the house at the time was likely the happily married matron, Martha Sessions. They also note the seasonal ritual of the hidden staircase where the ghostly lovers purportedly met: Freshmen are tasked with finding it on Halloween, a game invented by Sessions's first housemother. The girls at Smith are smart enough to realize that ghost stories are, at heart, acts of creative nonfiction.

† The other type are the "witch grave" stories we outline in the introduction to our section, "Witches," in this book.

are true perhaps matters little in this context; what they signify and how they function is of more importance. Campus ghost stories can potentially create community through supernatural legends, bonding students to the traditions of their schools whether as legends told on freshmen orientations, or as Halloween rituals, in the case of the Red Lady Run of Huntingdon College, Alabama, where sorority sisters dress up in honor of a legendary campus ghost. According to Elizabeth Tucker, author of *Haunted Halls*, ghost stories also serve an initiatory function, helping college students transition from the world of childhood to the world of adulthood.

The spirits that float through American campuses can range from cautionary to comforting. Other notable female college ghosts include those of Flagler College in St. Augustine, with a pregnant woman, a woman in black, and Flagler's wife and mistress among the ghosts; the Faceless Nun of Saint Mary-of-the-Woods; Condie Cunningham of the University of Montevallo, also in Alabama, who caught fire on the Bunsen burner while engaged in the very traditionally feminine activity of making fudge or hot chocolate (stories vary); and at Drew University, Roxanna Meade Drew, the founder's wife. And at SUNY Cortland, we have Elizabeth.

If the Red Lady functions as a cautionary tale about the perils of being socially aloof at school, Elizabeth serves a more comforting function, almost a guardian spirit of a certain residence hall. Her story comes to us via "Ted," a freshman at SUNY Cortland in 2003, and is recounted in Elizabeth Tucker's *Haunted Halls*. According to Ted, a girl who may or may not have been called Elizabeth (he can't really remember) was murdered by her boyfriend on the fourth floor stairwell of Cheney residence hall in the 1970s or early '80s. She was apparently pushed over the railing. A lot of "weird stuff," Ted says, happens on the fourth floor. People say they see the spirit of a female ghost with her arms stretching out. Once a girl fell over that very same railing, and lived. "Makes you wonder," he writes, "if Elizabeth was protecting her."

Tucker points out the folk motifs in this spirit on the staircase, with her arms outstretched as though waiting to catch falling students. Tucker notes the similarity to a common folktale motif, "Ghost returns to protect living" (known in folklorist circles by the catchy moniker "folk motif E363.2"). The modern-day girl Ted writes about—the one who fell—wasn't pushed by her boyfriend and wasn't a victim of domestic violence; rather she got drunk and fell. Drinking too much is certainly a hazard of college life, one to which girls especially fall prey; while all genders have been known to drink to excess on campus, a woman's lower body weight combined with social pressures and anxieties, to say nothing of the notorious roofie, creates a particular set of vulnerabilities. The image of Elizabeth's ghost helping out a fellow student is rather a lovely one. Tucker draws parallels between Elizabeth's outstretched arms and the arms of saints and angels in Renaissance paintings, and notes that Cheney students have actually painted their own mural honoring Elizabeth; in this way she "functions as a secular saint." There is a resonant beauty to this story.

Residence halls are among the more usual places for college ghosts to haunt, and as we have seen, a staircase can be a particularly poetic site for a haunting. Collegiate architecture is inherently ripe for haunting, from its Gothic ghosts in their dark ivory towers to the brutalist cinder blocks of dated, 1970s missteps. Residence halls are also representative of the difficulties of coeducational integration, as they would often have to make a sometimes awkward transition from male to female residences or—horrors!—become coeducational. Residences were a focal point as many colleges struggled with transitionary periods in the early twentieth century after going coed. Housemothers functioned in loco parentis, and strict boundaries delineated the social lives of girls and boys. These pressures and anxieties—and unresolved sexual tensions—create an atmosphere that is ripe for hauntings.

In the early twentieth century, it was often joked that women went to school solely to earn their "MRS" degree, and scholarly study was a mere pretense to the real aim of landing a suitable husband. In this environment, then, the genuinely scholarly woman was an anomaly, an aberration; even, in some sense, a living ghost, doomed to stay in her lonely tower on Saturday nights. Here we see the archetype of the frigid, virginal spinster, the eternal frozen maiden. And here we find the ghost stories of librarians, teachers, and administrators.

At the Wesleyan University of Nebraska in Lincoln, a secretary named Coleen Butterbaugh entered her suite of offices and had a bizarre experience. The windows were open, the room was strangely hushed, and she smelled a powerfully musty odor. She looked up to see "the figure of a woman standing with her back to me at a cabinet in an inner office. She was reaching up into one of the drawers. I felt the presence of a man sitting at the desk to my left, but as I turned around, there was no one there." Coleen then looked out one of the large windows behind the desk and saw that the "street [Madison Street], which is less than half a block away from the building, was not even there, and neither was the new Willard House. That was when I realized that these people were not in my time, but that I was back in their time."[1]

Coleen Butterbaugh later told the professor she worked for, who upon hearing her description of the woman, identified her as Clara Mills, a teacher at Nebraska Wesleyan in the 1920s and '30s. She had died in her office of a heart attack on April 12, 1940. The case is, to this day, one of the school's most popular ghost stories, and was even written up in the *Journal of the American Society for Psychical Research.*[*]

---

* If you thought of the Moberly-Jourdain incident while reading this story, you're not alone. There are several parallels, from the woman-centered focus of the story to the time slip element. The Moberly-Jourdain incident famously involved two highly educated Englishwomen who claimed to have slipped into the era of Marie Antoinette while strolling on holiday at Versailles.

The story of Caroline Colvin also concerns an administrator, but this one has shades of the Red Lady, where there is possibly more than one ghost at work. Colvin Hall at the University of Maine is said to be haunted by the ghost of a weeping girl. When the dorm was all-female, students would hear the sound of crying on the third floor; there were only three bedrooms on that floor, and all were empty at the time the sounds were heard. Nobody ever figured out the identity of the weeping female ghost, but later clues began to emerge to connect her to another specter.

The 1970s was a time of upheaval for Colvin Hall, as the dorm went coed. According to a former RA, once the dorm went coed, students began having full-on apparitional experiences. Female students would see the form of a woman when they were in the kitchen making sandwiches. Tucker points out that the spirit who appeared before them while they were engaged in this traditional "women's work" seemed harmless, whereas when the ghost appeared before male students, it took on a slightly more threatening aspect. It would materialize, almost menacingly, before them, and address them by name. It seemed as though the ghost was warning these male students to behave themselves.[2]

Students began to attribute the ghostly sightings to Caroline Colvin, whose portrait hung in the dormitory's front hallway. Caroline Colvin had been the school's Dean of Women in the 1950s, and her portrait had a certain cool, refined, slightly stern quality. She seems calm, poised, and polished in her picture, with her hair elegantly fastened into a chignon beneath her mortarboard, gazing slightly over a shoulder draped in an academic robe. Miss Colvin functions as a sort of spectral housemother, warning students to maintain order; her presence, Tucker asserts, may hold more authority than that of young RAs close in age to the students themselves. For those who subconsciously miss the presence of an adult authority figure, Miss Colvin's ghost story and portrait may serve a soothing purpose.

Interestingly, Caroline Colvin was an undergraduate student prior to becoming the school's Dean of Women. In this guise she was connected to the wailing, weeping student ghost, and students often spoke of her having committed suicide or dying a tragic death. The fact that this doesn't mesh at all with her biographic reality doesn't deter those who like to tell thrilling tales. It gives Colvin's ghost a dual identity, that of a young, distressed student with whom young girls can identify, and an older, authoritative presence to whom these same students can turn for comfort.

It's interesting to see the dual nature of both the Red Lady and Caroline Colvin. Both ghosts reflect the duality of our light and dark, or shadow, selves. They are at once old school and new school, undergraduate and administrator, child and woman. Like many first-year female students, they harbor more than one identity, just as a freshman girl may be at once the girl she was to her friends and family in high school and a new and complete stranger to herself, her new peers, and even those same family and friends back home if she finds herself changed by her experiences at school. Ghosts and freshmen aren't just liminal, then; they are also dual, and these stories reflect that.

Sometimes campus life functions as a way to reinforce traditional female identities, for example in the case of the sorority, which is predicated on maintaining eternal femininity. That horror staple, the murdered sorority girl, draws from the eternal trope of the dead girl, and the dead coed is depicted in movies from *Black Christmas* to *Happy Death Day*. What is the cause of her appeal? Is it the contrast of death in the prime of life? Or the classic appeal of the death of a beautiful woman, or Eros and Thanatos, as you might say if you were an undergraduate? Are social anxieties, such as the aforementioned anxiety about campus violence and rape culture, at play here?

The Chi Omega sorority house at Florida State University is said to be haunted by two women killed by Ted Bundy; the spirits of

Margaret Bowman and Lisa Levy continue to make their presence felt among those who live in the house to this day, and, according to the National Directory of Haunted Places, "over the years it came to be accepted that the two murdered women were haunting the house.[3] The feminist blog Jezebel critiques the idea of the haunting, calling it "a conjured spectacle . . . a grotesque fantasy played out on the bodies of women," noting that the ghostly sorority girls "came with ready-made meaning." When Ted Bundy murdered Margaret Bowman and Lisa Levy, he "violated the concept of the sorority itself, a consecrated space in which a certain kind of femininity was safeguarded and reproduced."[4] The figure of the dead sorority girl, both real and fictional, continues to haunt our collective imagination.

The phrase "dark academia" is an aesthetic these days.* There are dozens more stories of female ghosts haunting various colleges and universities around the country, and their stories change and grow as needed, reflecting societal changes. What role do these ghosts and haunted dorms serve now? In a #metoo era, in a time when many campuses have gone online due to COVID, when on-campus camaraderie has been shattered? When the reality of the past half decade has been far more frightening than any specter? At a time when a woman's prospects post-graduation may be to ultimately drop out of the workforce as soon as the strain of childcare or a pandemic demands it? In most of these tales, the ghosts themselves have faded; some of the dorms aren't even active any more (Pratt Hall at Huntingdon closed in 2019). They exist only as memory, as the

---

* It started in the 2010s or thereabouts on Tumblr, then moved to Instagram and TikTok, an evolving hashtag that celebrates the sublime pleasures of the Goth side of school, the faint romance of autumnal, tree-lined quads, stone towers and named halls, the shades of Hogwarts, arcane knowledge, and an exclusive location in a faraway setting. Dark academia also has specific cultural roots in Donna Tartt's roman à clef of Bennington College life, *The Secret History*, with its stylish narrative of insular, sociopathic classics students and their murderous neopagan rituals. Bennington College, of course, boasts a connection to horror master Shirley Jackson, who lived in that milieu when her husband was a professor there, and who set her dark novel, *Hangsaman*, there.

ghosts of our younger, more ambitious selves, as bright young girls who once strove for acceptance and education, for professional status, who fought against the destructive threats of patriarchy, little knowing how quickly all these gains could be lost in a moment.

There is a striking story in *Haunted Halls* called "A Heavy Load of Laundry." A girl at a small Midwestern college was studying late at night when she heard footsteps falling—heavy footsteps—as though "someone were carrying a heavy load of laundry." Three days later, the girl mysteriously disappeared. In the spring, the remains of her body were found buried near the school; she had been raped and kidnapped. Today, it is said she can be heard screaming on the anniversary of her death.

Tucker notes that this story, which took place in the 1960s, reflects the tensions between the "woman's place is in the home" ethos, and the new attitudes regarding women's rights and capabilities. This student heard heavy footsteps like "someone carrying a heavy load of laundry" days before she was kidnapped, raped, and murdered—a reproach, perhaps, for her studying instead of performing more "traditional" duties, struck down in her prime the moment she deviates from her domestic role.[5]

This ghost, this wailing woman, warns us of something. Something we can't quite put our finger on, but that vaguely haunts the backs of our minds as we walk by our framed master's degree in the hall on the way downstairs to do the family laundry.

FOREVER, MARITANA

The Ghosts of The Don CeSar

LEANNA

ST. PETERSBURG BEACH, FLORIDA

"COME ALL YE WHO SEEK HEALTH AND REST FOR HERE THEY are abundant."

This is the quote originally above the entrance to the "Legendary Pink Palace," The Don CeSar Hotel in St. Petersburg Beach, Florida. A massive pink hotel in a Moorish style, its design based predominantly on the Royal Hawaiian in Waikiki, the building is a character in and of itself. Known fondly as the "Pink Lady," she presides over a beautiful stretch of ocean and beach. The 300-room hotel is an enormous labor of love completed in 1928, built to honor a star-crossed passion.

Orphaned at the age of four, Thomas Rowe was sent from his birthplace of Boston, Massachusetts, to his grandfather in Ireland. Educated in London, at some point in the 1890s he attended a performance of *Maritana*, a light opera. The hero of the production is

Don Cesar, a gallant man whose series of misfortunes are turned around by those who care for and admire him.

Maritana is a three-act opera including spoken dialogue and recitatives that is based on the 1844 French play *Don César de Bazan*. It premiered at the Theatre Royal, Drury Lane, in 1845, but the character of Don César de Bazan first appeared in *Ruy Blas* by Victor Hugo. Clearly, a character for the popular imagination. *The Victor Book of the Opera*, in 1915, called the *Maritana* "beloved for its tunefulness and its sentimental music."

The first time Thomas Rowe saw an 1890s revival of *Maritana* in London, he fell madly in love with the leading lady, an actress named Lucinda.

A young Spanish soprano with long, dark curls and mesmerizing dark eyes, Lucinda played the titular role of Maritana, a Roma street singer and dancer. Songs like "'Tis the Harp in the Air," "Of Fairy Wand Had I the Power," and the Rondo-Finale, "With Rapture Glowing"—sentimental music indeed—seized Rowe's heart and imagination. He would never be the same. The opera's plot twists and turns, but finally the titular heroine and the famed Don César emerge triumphant lovers. A rare operatic happy ending.

Thomas Rowe went back to see *Maritana* night after night. Eventually he was able to meet the star and managed to win her love in return. They would rendezvous after the show by a secluded fountain courtyard they called their "secret garden." As if it were a side plot in another opera, the two planned their escape together when the run of the show was complete. But on that fateful night, she never appeared at their secret garden. Lucinda's parents had other plans for her and she was whisked back to Spain. Life did not imitate art.

A heartbroken young man moved to Virginia and began a career in real estate. He did marry, but unhappily. It wasn't long before Rowe and his wife, Mary, were estranged. Poor health, a heart condition, and asthma had Rowe moving to Florida for better weather and new real estate prospects.

Rowe wrote Lucinda countless letters over the years that were all returned unopened. A note arrived in the early days of the twentieth century, along with an obituary. In her final moments, Lucinda reportedly wrote:

> *Tom, my beloved Don CeSar. Father promised he will deliver you my message. Forgive them both as I have. Never would I despair. This life is only an intermediate. I leave it without regret and travel to a place where the swing of the pendulum does not bring pain. Time is infinite. I wait for you by our fountain . . . to share our timeless love, our destiny is time. Forever, Maritana.*[1]

Rowe was going to rebuild that fountain, their secret garden, as if it were a summoning spell, determined to evoke her spirit.

And it worked.

Rowe, managing to overcome his poor health, had a vision for The Don CeSar Hotel when others thought it was madness. He spent $100,000 ($1.6 million today) to purchase eighty acres on the barrier island of Long Key. He divvied up the land to be sold into lots, saving a narrow slice along the beach for his labor of love. By the time of its January 1928 completion, the Pink Lady had cost $1.5 million, three times its original budget (more than $24 million today).

Thomas Rowe recreated his and Lucinda's "secret garden" fountain exactly as he remembered it. It would serve as the hotel lobby courtyard and fountain, the first impression of the Pink Palace, fashioning a familiar and sacred place for Lucinda's spirit to find him, a rendezvous decades in the making and only accessible to them both after death. Having lived in the hotel since its opening, Rowe later died in the hotel, refusing to be taken to the hospital. Emergency equipment was brought into his ground-floor rooms; he was a man unable to be separated from his monument. After his death a man in his signature white suit and hat was often seen promenading about the premises, a dark-haired lady on his arm.

One of the hotel's former executives had direct experience with Thomas and Lucinda. His office in the executive suite was on the south-side ground level of the building and his was the only key. One early morning as he put his key into the lock, he was disturbed to hear voices from within. He could tell it was a specific kind of intimate conversation, a passionate exchange between two longtime lovers.

"The moment he turned the key in the lock, the voices ceased. With a trembling hand he opened the door. He later said, 'I actually heard them leave. I could hear every step she made. I could even hear the crinoline on her skirt rustling. Every pore on my body had the goose bumps. It was bizarre.' When he walked into his office, it was totally empty."[2]

Perhaps the sentimental, operatic backstory of the hotel attracts phantom lovers.

Some of F. Scott and Zelda Fitzgerald's last happy moments were spent at The Don CeSar. Their infamous, complex, sometimes volatile relationship was the subject of intense fascination within their own lifetimes and continues to this day. Shortly after their visit to The Don, Zelda's mental health deteriorated and she was eventually institutionalized, where she later died in a horrific fire.

The ghostly Jazz Age couple seen dancing in the courtyard and ballroom spaces of The Don CeSar, when described by those who have glimpsed them, are not of Thomas and Lucinda's era or dress. It must be F. Scott and Zelda, surely; sentiment would lead one to believe they have been reunited, all horrors, trauma, and pain healed by time and supplanted by a spirit's happier memories.

Perhaps "Come all ye who seek health and rest for here they are abundant" over the door was a magical spell drawing in those beyond the veil who needed it. Yet we know so little of Lucinda as a person. She was idealized then and now, never a full person or a complete name. An opera formed her and Thomas Rowe's understanding of each other. Certainly the performer and her beau knew truth from fiction, but they still used character names for each other long after the stage lights had dimmed. The building erected in honor of that opera's happy ending holds those character names, not their given ones.

It is surprising that *The Don Ce-Sar Story*, a history of the hotel written by June Hurley Young, who was the key figure in saving the legendary Pink Palace from destruction in 1971, doesn't mention Lucinda at all. One would expect more than a few ghost stories with an opening line such as this: "A mysterious charisma clings to the Don Ce-Sar, giving it a unique personality, forging an almost supernatural link with its indomitable builder, Thomas J. Rowe." But the book contains not a single mention of a ghost. It is an exceedingly curious omission. Perhaps June Hurley Young didn't want any phantasms stealing the show from the building's storied history. The Don CeSar narrowly evaded demolition several times, even after it had offered the country commendable service as a military hospital in World War II.

The hotel website, however, does discuss its ghosts.

"Built as tribute to his lost love" is the only mention or reference Lucinda gets on the main pages of The Don CeSar's official website. She is the raison d'être of the building, but to get more than a footnote in their named history, you have to sift and search to find a brief mention of Thomas and Lucinda's star-crossed history in one of the hotel's blog entries: "The Haunted Ghosts of the Don CeSar":

> *The Don CeSar, whose lobby courtyard and fountain are an exact replica of the one where Thomas and Lucinda rendezvoused in London, is Thomas' tribute to lost love. Since his*

passing, staff and guests report otherworldly sightings of a gentleman sporting an old-fashioned Panama hat and white summer suit strolling the grounds and even greeting guests. Yet when approached, he disappears.

Hotel staffers report strange happenings throughout the hotel and especially on the floor where Thomas lived. Housekeepers hear mysterious knocking at doors while cleaning rooms, yet find no one there. Swinging doors open by themselves to accommodate staffers laden with trays, perhaps Thomas still helping his team as the gracious hotelier he was. To this day, sightings continue of a young couple strolling the grounds, wearing a white suit and traditional Spanish peasant dress.[3]

The entry urges readers to come stay at The Don CeSar to see if the ghost stories are true. Much like Kate Morgan and the Del on the other side of the country, a lovelorn ghost story has become a part of hotel advertising.

Lucinda's family name doesn't turn up in any of these accounts, just her first name. Denied agency and choice by her parents in life, she is denied full personhood even in her own ghost story. She is merely an idea of a woman, a coveted but still unknown thing, lifted up into that romanticized and saintly place reserved for the concept of beautiful women who die young.

Forever, Maritana.

The Bewitched Statue in Salem, Massachusetts. Photo by Leanna Renee Hieber

PART 2

"WITCHES"

INTRODUCTION

ANDREA

Witches are powerful women. Like all powerful women, they have been maligned, persecuted, hated, desired, feared. They are eternal, mythical subjects, a source of endless fascination. In American history, they occupy a unique place where folklore blurs the lines of reality; we remember the "witches" of Salem, Massachusetts, who were not actually witches. They have become totemic figures in television, movies, books, and pop culture, and their appeal shows no signs of waning: as of this writing, the Peabody Essex Museum in Salem is devoting a full-scale exhibit to the power and imagery of the witch.

But where and how does the witch intersect with the ghost?

The witch has an interesting relationship to ghostlore; she is both part of it and separate from it. Though some lump the witch into the category "all things supernatural," her status is somewhat distinct due in part to her complex and specific history, symbolism, and relationship to defined spiritual and cultural traditions. Yet where there are points of contact, the witch emerges as a curious but recognizable type of ghost. There are a few defining traits when it comes to the ghost-witch: first, she is generally the ghost of a woman who was accused or executed for witchcraft, whether she practiced it or not (usually not), coming back to seek revenge or draw attention to the injustice visited upon her. Second, she is often associated with a curse, and her powers transcend the grave. She is so strong, she bursts through the boundaries of death and comes back to wreak vengeance on the living. The witch as ghost, then, is defined by pretty much the same qualities as the witch as a living woman: she is powerful, fearsome, and not to be trifled with. The living witch can, however, be put to death; the real terror of the witch as ghost is that nothing can stop her.

Another thing these ghostly witches have in common? Rumor. They probably were never witches at all, and have been so dubbed due to some confluence of coincidence, circumstance, and urban legend—or, as it happens, rural legend, for most of these tales take place in small towns and rural or semirural locations. Aesthetics and appearance have a lot to do with it, whether it's the appearance of the "witch's" grave, or the appearance and demeanor of the woman herself. Every town is haunted by the idea of the old woman in a ramshackle house, even if one doesn't exist there. Fear of the crone is fundamentally at work here, and single, outspoken, or old women are always suspect.

In rare cases, the witch's "curse" can at least somewhat be corroborated with local history, as with the witch of Yazoo City, an unpopular old crone whose deathbed vows surprisingly came true when the entire city burned to the ground a few years after her demise. An outcast old woman cursed the city to burn in a fire on May 25, 1904; after she died, her prediction came true, and a chain around her grave was found broken (the interpretation being that she escaped and got her revenge). This woman was dubbed a witch merely for her age and supposed but unsubstantiated supernatural powers, alleged mainly in hindsight and rumor. Attributing the fire to her curse merely solidified the legend, making it easy to believe that the witch continued to exert supernatural agency after her bodily death. Even if these stories are, for the most part, pure fabrication easily disproven, there is a collective desire to believe them.

A surprising number of so-called witches have in common one specific element: their graves look a particular way. The likeness on the grave of "Witch Bonney" in Lowell, Massachusetts, has piercing black eyes, outstretched hands, and a salaciously low-cut robe drooping low to nearly expose her breasts. It is said that her top falls lower and lower each day in October, until she is completely exposed by Halloween. Teenagers love legend-tripping at her grave, and Wiccans regularly pay Witch Bonney tribute on Samhain night. In Tallahassee, Florida, the grave of Elizabeth Budd-Graham, nicknamed "Bessie," evokes witchy symbols in its design, placement, and epitaph, leading locals (usually, again, teens) to ponder in awe this supposed "white witch" and her benign spirit, who appears to her grave's visitors in their dreams. Her mysterious epitaph refers to a woman "doubly dead in that she died so young," which some point to as evidence that she was a witch, because you "have to kill a witch twice." But the quote is from Edgar Allan Poe's "Lenore," a poem about a grieving husband mourning his young wife, and not a coded or veiled reference to witchcraft. In both these cases, and in nearly every similar case, the most cursory historic research reveals not a shred of evidence linking them to any witchy activity. But the power of myth mightily and easily outmuscles the more prosaic truth.

Sometimes such stories can actually end up damaging the very graves and cemeteries they feature. The sad story of Mary Jane Terwillegar is one of these: The woman interred at Loon Lake Cemetery in Lakefield, Minnesota, is said to be an accused witch who was beheaded. So many legend trippers visited her grave, including members of Megadeth (who wrote a song about her, "Mary Jane"), that the entire cemetery ended up being repeatedly vandalized and her tombstone stolen. The tombstone is now in a local historical society, but many others have been irrevocably damaged or lost. The fact that Mary Jane was a domestic worker who died of diphtheria and not a beheaded witch doesn't deter local legend.

Why do so many of the vaguest and most circumstantial stories end up getting pinned on "witches," and why do so many involve exotic or unusual-looking graves? Is it a reflection in death of what happens to witchy women in life—that is, they are pigeonholed because they (or their graves) look a certain way? Maybe. It's an intriguing question, and we've chosen one example of the preceding type of story to examine in closer detail here: the story of Ida Black and the "Witch's Curse" of Bucksport, Maine. In this case, a witch was entirely invented to explain a strange mark on a powerful man's grave. The story involves so many commonly repeated tropes, conjured in the fires of urban legend, that it becomes instantly familiar and readily adopted, regardless of easy debunking. A vague "truth" immediately becomes taken for granted. As with most of these tales, the "facts" of the stories are patently false, or at best unverifiable, but the ghostly legends are remarkably persistent, due perhaps to the unending allure of the witch. These are stories nobody seriously believes, but they are worth examining nonetheless, as they demonstrate the imaginative power the witch still exerts over us all.

The other type of witch-as-ghost story deals with accusation and injustice. In these stories, an accused or executed witch haunts the site of her injustice, reminding us of the repercussions of scapegoating and fearmongering. Grace Sherwood, the last woman ducked for witchcraft in colonial Virginia, still haunts Witch Duck Pond; Mary Tyler, one of the Salem accused, haunts her family farmstead in Boxford, Massachusetts. Both outlived their accusers, but nevertheless return in spectral form to protest their wrongful accusations. Moll Dyer, accused of witchcraft in seventeenth-century Maryland, ran away from her accusers into a frigid night and was later found frozen to death near a rock; you'd better believe her spirit comes back to haunt that site. And in Stratford, Connecticut, where Goody Bassett was hanged as a witch forty years before the

Salem witch trials, poltergeist activity at the nearby Phelps Mansion was attributed to her angry spirit. In these stories, the accused witch laments injustice after her death. One such story is that of accused Salem witch Bridget Bishop, whom we've taken a closer look at in this chapter.

The reality of Bridget's life and death is a maddening tale of paranoia and cruelty, but her spirit remains, quietly reminding those who are paying attention that something unjust happened in that town—it doesn't matter how long ago—and that they sit on land wrongfully seized by those in power.

Another witch we've examined in detail here is the "Bell Witch" in Tennessee. This story is an anomaly, a local oddity more evocative of a poltergeist than a witch. This witch isn't a wrongly accused or particularly troublesome woman. She is a disembodied spirit essentially endowing a powerless teenage girl with surprising psychokinetic abilities, giving her the kind of power that has driven countless teenage girls in modern times to dabble in Wicca. Thus the witch comes full circle.

In the end, the true allure of the witch rests in the concept of power. When in the historical narrative that power is stripped away from her—by being falsely accused or even executed, or by virtue of being a teenager, a minority, or the voiceless dead who cannot defend her reputation against slander—she comes back from beyond the grave to prove that nothing can stop her. This is a satisfying fantasy to consider. No wonder it is teenagers who continue to carry the torch of these tall tales. These witches display all the fantastic power the powerless ultimately crave.

If nothing else, the witch is never forgotten, always remembered. Of all the female ghost tropes we have encountered while researching this story, the witch is one of the strongest. Nothing can silence her. Not accusation, not punishment, and certainly not death.

A RED PARAGON BODICE

Bridget Bishop

LEANNA

SALEM, MASSACHUSETTS

BRIDGET BISHOP FIT THE PERSISTENT STEREOTYPE OF A WITCH: elderly, alone, defiant. Thrice a widow, she was no longer "of use" by society's standards and so was the first to hang in a harrowing circus of injustice that was the Salem "witch trials" of 1692.

The infamous Salem, Massachusetts, outbreak began innocently enough, late in 1691, when a group of Salem girls and young women began experimenting with "magic" via an improvised crystal ball, wanting to know something of their beaus and their futures. A spectral, coffinlike form was seen, and soon several of the girls in attendance began having "fits," exhibiting writhing physical manifestations that were thought to be possession by demons, by the devil himself, or by his agents, the accused witches. Possession was said to have spread like a contagion through Salem and the town gave over to the disease.

The belief in witchcraft and the dangers therein was so pervasive among the Puritan New England settlers of the seventeenth century that it created a self-closing circle, the same sort of process that makes conspiracy theories so hard to break; disbelief in itself is suspect.

In puritanical belief structures, a distinctly named "spectral sight" would lead the possessed to name witches in their midst. While the possessed were at times suspect themselves, more often than not they were given an unprecedented voice and agency. During these trials, the girls became the important authorities they never would have been otherwise.

The girls and young women of Salem who, perhaps like the Fox sisters, were maybe just caught up in playing games, soon found themselves at the center of an inferno, one that just kept consuming. Those in power found accusations, trials, and subsequent executions politically and socially advantageous, using their most vulnerable as targets, while incendiary accusations distracted attention away from power, land, and monetary grabs. Young Ann Putnam, for example, was quick to name two women whose families were engaged in property disputes with her own.

Witchcraft suspicions in colonial New England generally began as conflicts between people who knew one another. Any difficult or angry encounter with a neighbor could become fodder for accusation. Researching the interconnected disputes, grudges, and family matters of Salem at the time is a dizzying association matrix.

The fervent belief in witchcraft—and an ongoing, paranoid assumption that the devil was out to get everyone—supercharged small-town petty grievances into a maelstrom that led to a flood of accusations and, ultimately, the execution of nineteen people, fourteen of whom were women, with many more dying in prison awaiting trial. Of the 185 witches identifiable by name, more than 75 percent were female. Half of the accused men accused were husbands or relatives of the accused women.

The girls' "second sight" became weaponized as a destructive tool; their own limited status turning on others of limited status, the circle fed by gossip and defamation.

Despite the few husbands who were also accused, husbands could prove a measure of protection against accusation, whether by being able to appeal to authority figures on behalf of their wives or by bringing about proceedings of slander against the accusers, allowing witnesses to testify to the character of their spouses. A number of women caught up in the Salem horrors were formally accused within a year or two after they became widows. If they'd had the misfortune to be accused of witchcraft charges and cleared while married, once widowed, they found themselves again in danger and a target.

The puritanical idea of women's limited purpose gives root to society's greater anxieties about women alone.

"In the eyes of her community, the woman alone in early New England was an aberration: the fundamental female role of procreation was at best irrelevant to her. At worst, of course, she might be performing this function outside the institution of marriage. Moreover, women alone no longer performed—perhaps never had performed—the other main function of women in New England society: they were not the 'helpmeets' to men Puritans thought women should be."[1]

Bridget Playfer (later Bishop) was born in the 1630s in Norwich, England, and married her first husband, Samuel Wasselbe, in 1660. It is unclear whether Samuel died before or after immigrating to Massachusetts, but a child from that union died in infancy in Salem, as one had died before in England. Bridget married widower Thomas Oliver in 1666. They had one daughter, Christian. Thomas Oliver maintained property and an orchard. Thomas and Bridget were known to have fought publicly, even so far as to have been fined for it. Thomas's daughter from a previous marriage paid her father's fine but did not do so for Bridget, who was made to stand in the public square as punishment. This woman had already been painted as unruly in the public eye, an easy target when fomenting further accusations.

Charles Wentworth Upham, mayor of Salem in 1852 and a Massachusetts state representative in 1853, notes in his own in-depth history of the Salem trials:

> *Edward Bishop had resided, for some seven years previous to the witchcraft delusion, within the limits of Salem, near the Beverly line. His wife Bridget was a singular character, not easily described. She kept a house of refreshment for travellers, and a shovel-board for the entertainment of her guests, and generally seems to have countenanced amusements and gayeties to an extent that exposed her to some scandal. She is described as wearing "a black cap and a black hat, and a red paragon bodice," bordered and looped with different colors. This would appear to have been rather a showy costume for the times. Her freedom from the austerity of Puritan manners, and disregard of conventional decorum in her conversation and conduct, brought her into disrepute; and the tongue of gossip was generally loosened against her. She was charged with witchcraft, and actually brought to trial on the charge, in 1680, but was acquitted; the popular mind not being quite ripe for such proceedings as took place twelve years afterward. She still continued to brave public sentiment, lived on in the same free and easy style, paying no regard to the scowls of the sanctimonious or the foolish tittle-tattle of the superstitious. She kept her house of entertainment, shovel-board, and other appurtenances. Sometimes, however, she resented the calumnies circulated about her being a witch, in a manner that made it to be felt that it was best to let her alone.*[2]

The idea of a red bodice inevitably, like summoning a spirit, conjures up thoughts of *The Scarlet Letter.* Author Nathaniel Hawthorne was inspired and horrified in seemingly equal measure by the harsh cruelties of Puritan society, and sought to distance himself from his own family's involvement.

Bridget's manner clearly ruffled the feathers of the dour, pious community where modesty—albeit often performative—was valued above all. Her colorful manner of dress was noted several times as a reason for her guilt. Societally, we're hardly over that particular detail. If a woman is assaulted, you still see people attempting to use what she may have been wearing as justification.

After the death of her third husband, Edward, Bridget Bishop found herself once more accused, this time by the "afflicted" girls. The gossip of the town had already set her up. A parade of accusers from the town spanning age and gender noted myriad improbable details of her spectral form doing all manner of eerie deeds, placing blame upon her for any random accident. All her accusers had some sort of bone to pick with her, whether the sale of a hog that had fallen ill or fowl that had gotten onto their lawn or the unfortunate circumstance of a sickly child who happened to have been present when Bridget paid a visit, and then the child worsened.

Then there was the matter of property, hers being so centrally located. Property "held" for her by Edward Bishop during her marriage to him *from* her marriage to Thomas Oliver would have been technically hers, for use only for maintenance of herself. Any uses of the land had to be approved, and with no male heirs, Bridget's own authority was extremely limited. A great deal of understanding the witch delusion is understanding the property and inheritance battles that were ongoing through the town. At the height of the Salem outbreak, an attainder law was passed by town legislators that barred civil, inheritance, and property rights from being passed along to children, effectively seizing property outright. Bridget's possessions became, due to the accusations of the "possessed," fresh assets of the town and those in power.

Bridget was hanged, pronounced dead, and her body hastily thrown under the rocks below the gallows. The only precise death record that managed to survive noted unceremoniously that they "buried her on the spot."

It was only when the "possessed," "bewitched," and "afflicted" began naming those in increasing and broader positions of power or public favor, as the outbreak went on, that the zeal for persecution waned and the Age of Enlightenment began to take hold.

Representative Upham has a connection with Bridget Bishop—and the site that she haunts—that he reveals in his endnotes of *Salem Witchcraft:*

> *The reader may judge of my surprise in now discovering, that, while writing the "Lectures on Witchcraft," I was owning and occupying a part of the estate of Bridget Bishop, if not actually living in her house. The hard, impenetrable, all but petrified oak frame seems to argue that it dates back as far as when she rebuilt and renewed the original structure. Little, however, did I suspect, while delivering those lectures in the Lyceum Hall, that we were assembled on the site of her orchard, the scene of the preternatural and diabolical feats charged upon her by the testimony of Louder and others. Her estate was one of the most eligible and valuable in the old town, with a front, as has been mentioned, of a hundred feet on Washington Street, and extending along Church Street more than half the distance to St. Peter's Street. . . . It is truly remarkable, that the locality of the property and residence of a person of her position, and who led the way among the victims of such an awful tragedy, should have become wholly obliterated from memory and tradition, in a community of such intelligence, consisting, in so large a degree, of old families, tracing themselves back to*

the earliest generations, and among whom the innumerable descendants of her seven great-grandchildren have continued to this day. It can only be accounted for by the considerations mentioned in the text. Tradition was stifled by horror and shame. What all desired to forget was forgotten. The only recourse was in oblivion; and all, sufferers and actors alike, found shelter under it.[3]

Upham speaks of a tension that is still palpable in Salem today, long after he wrote those words. My frequent visits to Salem for work, family visits, and research have always felt like walking a tightrope of historical fact and kitschy overcompensation. Salem tried to reject the sordid period that made it so famous, but eventually embraced it in an entire reversal, branding the town as "Witch City" (replete with a broom-riding witch icon on the local police cars), though none of the people *executed* would have identified as a witch or practiced witchcraft. Only walks along Salem's peaceful harbor and waterfront seem to have a quiet and solid identity in an area still psychically scarred.

Colin Dickey describes his own impression of this duality in *Ghostland: An American History in Haunted Places*:

We know Salem—we know it to be a tragedy, we hold it up as a cautionary tale about mass hysteria and persecution—and yet we're also confused: we conflate the dead with actual witches, we attribute supernatural powers to those killed, we revisit their deaths for comedy and entertainment. Above all, we fail to apply the lessons we've supposedly learned from 1692, for by no means was this the last time in American history when a powerless minority was scapegoated, persecuted and killed by an ignorant mass. We recall the events of Salem, but we can't quite remember why they matter.[4]

There are numerous ghost stories in Salem, inexplicable things that continue to happen, demanding an audience that, in turn, demands that we see them.

Noted Salem ghost tour guide Sebastian Crane leads his guests through the heart of Salem, and his narrative along Essex Street and beyond is full of sharp facts, genuine pathos, and uncanny accounts of spectral activity. He notes that the Great Salem Fire of 1914 consumed almost all of the last traces of Puritan architecture. But even though the buildings that housed the tormented, accused, and executed are gone, their energies are no longer bound to those bleak confines.

Turner's Seafood was built on top of what would have once been Bishop's land. It has gained the reputation as being the most haunted restaurant in Salem.

Describing the paranormal details that have been noted and documented through the years, Crane replied to my query:

> *There are rumors of inexplicable electrical difficulties, flying glasses, and silverware quietly vanishing off of tables. However, as active as her ghost is said to be, it is also notably shy. Paranormal activity never occurs on the first floor when it is bustling with guests. Given how her community turned on her during the hysteria, it reasons that her spirit is reclusive in the afterlife. Many of the paranormal enthusiasts [dining] there in the hopes of experiencing something leave Turner's unsatisfied.*

Crane goes on to discuss the nature of the hauntings relating to the trials:

> *These are not the malicious ghosts that people flock to Salem for. They are not wreaking blood-curdling havoc. They*

want to be remembered. Much like infants who don't have the words for what they need or young Puritan girls living seen-but-not-heard under the tyranny of the Christian patriarchy, poltergeists act out in order to be acknowledged. They are the supernatural embodiment of the deeply human need to be understood, to be fully witnessed. Salem is packed with them.

So much has been said *about* Bridget Bishop. But what did Bridget have to say?

"I am no witch. I am innocent. I know nothing of it. I am innocent to a Witch. I know not what a Witch is."

Let Bridget Bishop's own words here, as documented by the court proceedings against her, be the final witness in the matter, here and across the veil.

TUGGING AT YOUR HEM

Dorothy Good

LEANNA

SALEM, MASSACHUSETTS

THE SALEM WITCH TRIALS OF 1692 WERE A HARROWING FARCE of justice. The more one looks into the matter, the more incredible it seems that anyone could have believed in the accusations, let alone added to them—an entire town consumed by murderous paranoia. But unfortunately, our modern era has shown us that people still all too easily get sucked into dangerous conspiracy theories that tear families apart.

It isn't just the executions of the nineteen victims, the several additionally accused who died in jail awaiting trial, or those who were exiled or had to flee due to the hostile environment even if acquitted who beg redress; it was what happened to their families too.

Dorothy Good, the youngest prisoner of the witch trials, was just four years old.

Four years old.

Certainly, this fits no one's stereotypical image of a witch. The

Salem trials proved that no one, no matter age, gender, or social status, was immune from accusation.

When an entire village has abandoned reality, how can a four-year-old know what is true? A four-year-old repeats what they've heard. And Dorothy had heard her mother was a witch.

Sarah Good was one of the first to be accused of witchcraft by a group of young women who had begun experimenting with "magic," and the situation escalated into what was common in puritanical society: belief that the devil was at work. Through "possession" and "second sight," a state in which it was thought that the afflicted could see the witches in their midst, Sarah Good was announced to be a witch, a woman who made an easy target. A woman who was known to be poor and often distraught, Sarah insisted upon her innocence to the end. Sarah happened to be several months pregnant with another child when she was arrested.

Dorothy Good was named as Dorcas on her arrest warrant by John Hathorne, and that name is what she came to be known by, even though the name Dorothy appears in the rest of the court documents and proceedings. John Hathorne, incidentally, was the only judge who did not repent his involvement in the trials. (He was an ancestor of author Nathaniel Hawthorne, who added the "w" to his name to distance himself from the stain of the witchcraft trials when he became a celebrated American novelist in the nineteenth century.)

The "possessed" girls who began expanding their field of accusations soon named Dorothy as attacking them with bites, the child presumably taking supernatural revenge for the arrest of her mother.

Mob mentality in Salem was fueled by *absolute* belief that the devil was constantly trying to undermine the overtly pious, puritanical regime. For an already zealous religious community, seeking out the devil's agents became a fervent mission that swept up the entire area in a vise grip.

It's clear that Dorothy said what she must have felt her captors wanted to hear. In cases where reality and fiction are already so painfully blurred, Dorothy added to the storytelling, explaining, during her examination by the magistrates, that she had a snake familiar, given to her by her mother. She showed her inquisitors a red spot on her finger where the serpent drank. For the young child, it may have all seemed like a game, and all the attention may have been interesting at first, if not bewildering. If her mother was said to be a witch, then perhaps she was too, and she wanted to be with her. The consequences of actually being imprisoned for it would likely not have been understood by an overwhelmed four-year-old who just hoped for comfort and acceptance.

While imprisoned, Sarah Good gave birth to a child, Mercy, who soon died from malnourishment and the harsh conditions of the prison. It is staggering to consider how deeply robbed this family was by these events.

Adding insult to injury, it was Dorothy's "confession" that ended up "proving" the case for her mother's guilt, and Sarah was taken away from her daughter and hanged on July 19. This innocent four-year-old would spend another five months alone in jail.

Massachusetts legislator Charles Upham wrote about Sarah Good's character, her execution, and the shocking curse that followed in his thorough accounting of the trials, written in the mid-nineteenth century:

> *Sarah Good appears to have been an unfortunate woman, having been subject to poverty, and consequent sadness and melancholy. But she was not wholly broken in spirit. Mr. Noyes, at the time of her execution, urged her very strenuously to confess. Among other things, he told her "she was a witch, and that she knew she was a witch." She was conscious of her innocence, and felt that she was oppressed, outraged, trampled upon, and about to be murdered, under the forms*

> *of law; and her indignation was roused against her persecutors. She could not bear in silence the cruel aspersion; and, although she was just about to be launched into eternity, the torrent of her feelings could not be restrained, but burst upon the head of him who uttered the false accusation. "You are a liar," said she. "I am no more a witch than you are a wizard; and, if you take away my life, God will give you blood to drink." Hutchinson says that, in his day, there was a tradition among the people of Salem, and it has descended to the present time, that the manner of Mr. Noyes's death strangely verified the prediction thus wrung from the incensed spirit of the dying woman. He was exceedingly corpulent, of a plethoric habit, and died of an internal hemorrhage, bleeding profusely at the mouth.*[1]

The curious circumstances of Noyes's death added the inevitable possibility of a witch's curse fulfilled, a deserved supernatural revenge. Despite there being no *actual* witches involved, Sarah Good's condemnation became a palpable truth. Her final words in court proved prophetic, casting their own spell into the future and somehow making people wonder if there was witchcraft involved after all. Mythmaking will often double back on itself, and wild accusations might try to prove themselves.

Dorothy Good, imprisoned in March of 1692, was held in prison until December of that year, when she was released on a fifty-pound bond—a huge sum of money in that era—that her poverty-stricken father managed to gather. William Good noted that his daughter was significantly altered after her imprisonment, saying that she could not "govern herself." Grave, irreparable psychological trauma had taken place.

Dorothy died as a teenager, around fifteen or sixteen years old, the circumstances of her passing unknown.

Defiantly, her spirit has not let the violence done to her and her family define her. Instead, her spirit goes on about the business of being a curious, even playful child, a state cut all too short.

The concept of a psychic mark or residue is often ascribed to haunted places, the impact of something particularly powerful or traumatic leaving a spectral impression. The site of a particularly gruesome death, for example. In Salem, on the grounds of the old jail, the destruction of Dorothy's childhood at the hands of inhumane cruelty, is a spectral impression. It seems that when innocence was stolen from her, it remained as an echo on the land instead.

Modern Salem, an admittedly charming town, walks a difficult line of truth, history, pain, and sensationalism. Salem takes in tens of millions in tourist dollars every October, a sort of paranormal playground that grates against the historic reality of an imprisoned child and her executed mother.

Acclaimed Salem ghost tour guide Sebastian Crane is very aware of the pit and the pendulum of Salem history and its attractions. In an interview query, he stated the following regarding his understanding of the modern landscape of Salem and a spirit caught therein:

> *The Great Fire of 1914 transformed downtown Salem Massachusetts, consuming almost all of the last traces of bleak, Puritan architecture. What was once The Old Salem Gaol is now an office building, an ice cream parlor stands on the foundations of the courthouse where The Witch Trials unfolded. And tourists are often disappointed when I escort them to the paranormal epicenter of the city, a sprawling parking lot behind Witch City Mall. This is where the spirit of Dorcas Good has lingered for three centuries.*
>
> *Full disclosure: On night zero of my training as a ghost tour guide, when I heard about the tragedy of her brief life for*

the very first time, I made the wrong assumption about her haunting. I suspected that her spirit might be one of the most righteously vengeful in the city. Looking back, I can understand why. The harrowing injustice of her history made me want to raise Hell on her behalf. But the paranormal activity involving her ghost is profoundly gentle, actually. It always takes place in the strange hours before dawn, when the city is still and silent, and the story is always the same. Someone will be walking alone under the lamplight across the parking lot until they are stopped by a very disconcerting, very distinct yank, yanking at the hem of their coat. Upon turning around, they find no one is there. Dorcas's restless spirit is still searching for comfort in the one place she found it in life; at the hem of her mother's skirt.

A playful innocence, captured through time. Tugging at your hem for notice. Defiant in the face of misery. Recapturing a childhood violently ripped away. This haunting exists as pure and uncomplicated sentiment, desirous of a connection with modern adults unconnected to the horrors surrounding that child. A child reaching out is so understandable, so universal through any era. The heartbreak of it should serve as a cry, a demand into our modern era to beware the pitfalls that befell Salem. Beware a zealous, paranoid mob. No innocence can survive it, only a ghostly echo can remain.

Guide Sebastian Crane comments further:

Yes, there are entire wax museums flooded with the fog of dry ice devoted to sensationalized versions of their histories, but how much truth is actually being told here in Salem? The lives of the victims are obscured by melodrama and misinformation, Dorcas Good is often forgotten entirely. Could this be why their poltergeists still, after three hundred years, interrupt dinner, tug on our sleeves, catch us off guard? Perhaps they are reaching through the veil to beg us to do more than spin spine-chilling tales about their spirits, to reckon with the raw tragedy of their lives, to see them for all that they were; as so much more than the horror of their deaths.

OUR FAMILY TROUBLE

The Bell Witch

ANDREA

ADAMS, TENNESSEE

THE BELL WITCH HAS BEEN CALLED THE "GREATEST AMERICAN ghost story."[1] It's been written about and recounted extensively, been made into several film adaptations, inspired fiction and songs, and even become the name of a doom metal band. For those not already familiar, the bare facts of the case are these: In 1817, in Adams, Tennessee, a supernatural entity tormented a farmer named John Bell and his family. The haunting centered mainly on John and the family's pretty, pubescent daughter, Betsy. An entity who called herself "Kate" tormented the girl, slapping and scratching her, pulling her hair, and otherwise afflicting her. The entire family ceased to sleep at nights as the torments continued, eventually attracting the attention of the neighbors. The entity continued in her harassment of the family for years, finally culminating her career in the outright murder of John Bell. The mysterious case was never adequately explained.

In 1894, newspaper editor Martin Van Buren Ingram published *An Authenticated History of the Famous Bell Witch,* containing a chapter supposedly based on the diary of John Bell's youngest son, Richard, who was six years old when the haunting began. Richard Bell titled his account *Our Family Trouble.* Most of what is now known about the case comes from this book, and from Richard's putative memories.* Bell and Ingram's material is repeated in nearly every account of Tennessee ghostlore, and in many other compendiums of the Southern supernatural.

Let's examine, for a moment, that word again: "witch."

In the case of the Bell Witch, the word is employed in an archaic way, to describe a sort of discarnate version of a living person. It's used in the sense of a disembodied spirit of a real, living person who somehow manages to travel freely, unbound from the fleshly body. The entity tormenting the Bell family claimed to be "the witch" of a neighbor's stepmother before eventually declaring herself "nobody else and nothing but *'Old Kate Batts' witch.'*"† Kate Batts was a living woman and a neighbor, who was naturally enraged and embarrassed when she heard this announcement. Bell writes, "the matter made Mrs. Batts very mad, causing a lively sensation in the community." Though many folk sources claim Batts was a local outcast, or that she had quarreled with and cursed John Bell, none of this is true.

---

* Some argue that the chapter was a forgery (see Grady Hendrix, "Little Ghost on the Prairie"), and claim Ingram's entire book a work of fiction. No contemporary newspaper records of the event exist, which seems strange considering the length of the case (the entity tormented the family from 1817 to roughly 1821) and its scandalous nature. Many secondhand accounts place General Andrew Jackson (later president) at the scene as a curious visitor, but none of these tales can be proven, and nothing of the kind is mentioned in any official histories of Jackson's very well-documented movements during those years. The Jackson angle was likely a fabrication or exaggeration of Ingram's. Yet Ingram didn't make it all up out of whole cloth: Though the first newspaper accounts only appear after the publication of Ingram's book, *Goodspeed's 1886 History of Tennessee,* which mentions the case, predates Ingram's book by a half decade.

† A trickster, the entity had also previously claimed to be a "disturbed spirit hunting a lost tooth," and a spirit that had returned to reveal the hiding place of a buried treasure. John Bell's attempts to hunt the tooth and the treasure provoked intense mirth for the spirit.

Kate was not only very much alive during the incidents she was also Mrs. Bell's niece. (Talk about awkward family dinners.)[2] Despite Mrs. Batts's rage, "ever after this the goblin was called 'Kate,' and answered readily when addressed by that name."* Significantly, Batts's witch, by functioning as a spectral double of a living human being, creates a sort of "second self," as it were.

It is interesting to note how slippery Bell's language is here; throughout *Our Family Trouble,* he variously refers to the entity as "goblin" or "spirit" and numerous other terms, even at times calling it the "wizard" or "warlock," the "seer" and the "mage." At one point he refers to it as "the invisible." His use of language, in terms of naming the entity, is the vocabulary of someone groping in the dark. This is a man struggling to name something for which he has no words. And part of the reason for that is very likely because the term "poltergeist" had not yet entered the popular American lexicon when he ostensibly penned his account of the Bell "Witch."

But to modern readers, this entity—who throws, punches, kicks, slaps, howls, whistles, laughs, and pulls bedsheets—is instantly recognizable as a poltergeist. Anyone who's ever heard JoBeth Williams tell Carol Anne to run to the light understands this immediately, and even if you haven't seen the 1982 blockbuster, you've likely absorbed the concept through cultural osmosis. It is in this category that most paranormal researchers recognize the Bell Witch, and it is here that she should rightfully be categorized.

The tale of the Bell Witch is also well accounted for in the annals of parapsychology, having been famously studied by the legendary psychical researcher Nandor Fodor. It was under the heading of "poltergeist" that Fodor first classified her. It is his conclusion regarding the case that is the most thought-provoking.

---

* Bell seems a bit rueful and apologetic here, writing, "for convenience [*sic*] sake I shall hereafter call the witch Kate, though not out of any disregard for the memory of Mrs. Batts, for after all she was a clever lady, and did not deserve the cruel appellation of 'witch.'"

Fodor's great contribution to the Bell Witch canon was to suggest one possible explanation of *why* the entity tormented the father and daughter of a large, prosperous, upstanding, well-liked, religious family with nine children, and in particular, why it focused so violently on the father.

He somewhat hesitantly offers, with the caveat that this is speculation, and there is by no means any evidence to prove this accusation against John Bell, the theory that Betsy was allegedly sexually abused by her father in childhood, and the onset of puberty triggered a trauma-based response.* Betsy's psychic split was a subconscious defense mechanism, and the Bell Witch was an entity that came forth from Betsy herself, from her troubled and tortured mind. Betsy's hatred of her father could only be expressed if sublimated through the entity of "Kate," who allowed her to lash out. Fodor admits that the psychological explanation can't really account for the intensity of the supernatural manifestations, but concludes such things may be possible if the force of a psychic rupture is strong enough.

Poltergeists have always been allied with the female from the earliest days. An eighteen-year-old nun named Antoinette de Grolée was haunted at Saint-Pierre, Lyon, France, in 1526, "enduring levitations and rappings."† These supposedly supernatural manifesta-

---

* There's a lot of pushback on the "obvious Freudian interpretations" (see Lloyd Rose, "Night of the Hunter") underpinning the Bell Witch case, mainly from people who hated the *American Haunting* movie. As with most paranormal cases involving females with a strong father figure, e.g., Lizzie Borden, there is at least one self-professed psychic (see Nicole Young, "Psychic: I Know the Real Bell Witch Story") willing to come to the fore to verify absolutely that such accusations are true, having personally spoken with the spirits about it, and at least twice as many people willing to come forward pronouncing such claims of sexual abuse to be pure hogwash. What's really interesting for our purposes are the implications here about teenage girls, abuse, and power that manifest in cases of poltergeists, multiple personality disorders, psychic abilities, and telekinesis, all of which are demonstrated in the Bell Witch case as it is currently documented. The symbolic meaning is far more interesting than the literal meaning.

† See Roger Clarke, *A Natural History of Ghosts*, page 89. Clarke also notes that a 1979 study of 200 poltergeist cases in the UK and North America found that around 75 percent of poltergeist cases center on a female protagonist, and 78 percent center on individuals under the age of twenty.

tions seem like a natural outgrowth of women's innately terrifying power. Teenage girls, with their particularly intense maelstrom of hormones, sex, and raw emotion, are associated with poltergeist activity. Fodor's psychologically based theories of the poltergeist were virulently rejected by his fellow psychical researchers, but eventually gained a foothold in twentieth-century parapsychology. Psi researchers now acknowledge the likelihood of the connection between adolescent emotional states and the telekinetic phenomena witnessed during poltergeist events, and now accept that such occurrences are more likely the result of powerful telekinetic forces emanating from a profoundly troubled and possibly traumatized mind, and less likely the result of a disembodied spirit entity. The current preferred term for poltergeist in the world of all things psi is RSPK, or "recurrent spontaneous psychokinesis."

One well-known contemporary case of RSPK is that of Tina Resch. In Columbus, Ohio, in 1984, fifteen-year-old Tina was plagued by poltergeist-type activity, including levitating objects. She was from a troubled home, with histories of mental illness and abuse. William Roll, a parapsychologist at the Rhine Research Center, then located at Duke University in North Carolina, championed Tina Resch's case, defending her against charges of fakery and writing a book about her, *Unleashed*. In 1992 Resch was arrested on murder charges after the mysterious death of her three-year-old daughter, whom she had left in the care of her boyfriend. Resch remains in prison to this day.*

William Roll's sensitive handling of Resch's case underlies one important factor that many poltergeist stories have in common: They often center on teenage girls in less than ideal family situations. Though these girls are often accused of fraud, they don't really benefit from all the attention their poltergeists bring them. They are not calculatedly vying for attention and wealth: their manifesta-

* Tina Resch was denied parole in October 2021.

tions of RSPK are desperate acts born of haunted minds. They are screaming for help the only way they can.

Few people are denied agency as much as a teenage girl: She is dismissed, belittled, cut down to size at every turn. Her pleas for help are derided as "attention seeking," and Heaven help her should she dare come forward with stories of abuse at the hands of someone who has power over her—namely, nearly everyone. Cutting, eating disorders, and other types of self-harm are some of the more earthbound cries for help, and at the other, extreme end of the spectrum dwells the poltergeist.

When this world robs them of power, teenage girls may slip over to the spirit world for aid, sometimes unconsciously, sometimes deliberately. A powerless teenage girl may turn her pain inward: anorexia mirabilis, or mystical fasting, has been another way for teenage girls to achieve a sense of control, perform self-inflicted punishment, and to cry out. The "fasting girls" of the nineteenth century often laid claim to psychic powers, including one girl named Mollie Fancher, who was known as "the Brooklyn Enigma." She had profound trances during which she "traveled to heaven and back," exhibited multiple personalities, and subsisted for months at a time on almost no food except crackers and water. These fasting girls were the secular descendants of saints and mystics such as Catherine of Siena, who notoriously starved themselves to achieve heavenly visions (and make themselves unappealing to men).* They were untouchable and unearthly, removed from the material and bodily world that denied them power over their own bodies and minds.

There is a vast body of literature about teen girls and RSPK, particularly as it relates to trauma and revenge. Betsy Bell fits

---

* Fasting girls would starve themselves in part to achieve psychic powers and in part to remain unattractive to men; modern rape victims often develop eating disorders from anorexia to overeating. "One analysis of 57,000 women found that those who experienced physical or sexual abuse were twice as likely to be addicted to food." See Olga Khazan, "The Second Assault," *The Atlantic*, December 15, 2015.

squarely into this pattern, the spiritual foremother of Steven King's Carrie White. Carrie, as we know, exacted revenge through her telekinetic powers, and perhaps so did Betsy Bell. It may have been her only outlet. The vengeful telekinetic girl is a trope in horror movies as well, from *Firestarter* to *Lucy, The Lazarus Effect, The Fury,* and *Thelma.* The girls react to being bullied, abused, and undermined; they were "not born monsters but made that way by worlds that demanded they be dominated [until their] denied, repressed power becomes explosive."[3] Rage is an emotion women are typically forbidden to express, and it is repressed until it become unleashed in ways that seem supernatural to those who cannot fathom how it feels to be so violated.

Many have argued that any poltergeist activity centered around a teenage girl necessarily involves deception and fakery; noted psychical researcher Frank Podmore baldly stated as much in the nineteenth century, dismissing all such cases out of hand.[4] Others, such as Guy Lyon Playfair, who investigated the Enfield poltergeist in 1977, claim that poltergeists are in fact real entities, but ones that feed off the sexual energy and general turmoil of adolescence.[5] William Roll seems to inhabit the third path, arguing that poltergeists do emanate from teenagers themselves, but they are neither fraud nor supernatural, being rather the psychokinetic force of the child's mind itself. All theories are possible, even plausible.

Regarding the connection between teenage girls, trauma, and psychokinetic activity, psychologist and psychoanalyst Carol Gilligan notes that puberty is traditionally a time when girls cast their most assertive natures "underground," replacing them with societally approved "feminine" personalities. She calls this process dissociation, noting that it can be a traumatic experience, and that girls who go through it often experience depression as they are expected to become young ladies, docile and "silent in the name of feminine goodness." Gilligan notes that "it is not surprising . . . that [times] in development when children are initiated into the codes and scripts of patriarchal manhood and womanhood . . . are marked by psychological distress."[6]

Whether Betsy Bell suffered torment at the hands of a genuine spirit or merely the torment of a fractured mind doesn't really make a difference if the end result was still torment (with a measure of release). The incredible manifestations supposedly witnessed at the Bell farmhouse certainly make one wonder how a teenage girl could ever have pulled such things off. The "witch" was highly loquacious, meaning Betsy would have had to become very adept at "throwing her voice"—but, according to Richard Bell's account, the spirit became audible by degrees, beginning at first as whistles and growls and gradually working its way up to speech. These are exactly the techniques used in learning to throw the voice. Perhaps Betsy figured it out for herself. In any case, it's impossible to know, but the most likely scenario is that it's a mix of reality—something strange *was* going on there—and the usual game of "broken telephone" that accompanies such events.

We may never know what really happened in Tennessee in 1817, but we must surely be able to imagine, if not (hopefully not) know, what it feels like to be angry and powerless and voiceless, and imagine the relief of being able, somehow, to unburden oneself. As Emily Arsenault writes in her discussion of the Tina Resch case, "the question of whether [these stories] are real or fake has never been the primary draw for me. Rather it is the emotional power—and simultaneous feeling of pure powerlessness—of being a lonely young girl in need of love and attention that is the source of my fascination . . . I feel drawn to these girls' stories because their suffering is so clear—and because I believe the line between real and fake is fuzzy when it comes to adolescent emotions."[7]

Of course, the word "poltergeist" (much less telekinesis) wouldn't have been in Bell's vocabulary, which is part of why he seems to be groping for something to call it. The other reason he can't seem to find the words to name this phenomenon, besides the fact that words like telekinesis didn't exist, is this: If Fodor's theory is correct, what happened to Betsy is unspeakable. Even if Bell had had the vocabulary, the idea that the entity was a split self of his own sister would not likely have been accepted by him. Neither would have the idea of his father as abuser. Richard takes pains to emphasize his father's upright nature, wondering repeatedly what John Bell had done to deserve such torment.

At one point, John Bell is tortured by the feeling of an invisible stick wedged in his mouth, preventing him from speaking or eating for days. He is rendered mute by this bizarre apparatus. At another point, "Kate" sings a hymn to the mother, Lucy, when she is ill, and the lyrics of the hymn reference a longing to speak out:

Speak and let the worst be known
Speaking may relieve you.

Both Betsy and John seem desperate to reveal some secret but are, of course, prevented by the deeply repressive culture of the day, and the profundity of the sins allegedly committed against Betsy. John's longing to break his silence suggests a feeling of profound guilt. He is keeping the dark secret of "their family trouble" locked deeply away. There is no way of knowing, but there is so much symbolism in this case, particularly about speaking out, that it really seems to give credence to Fodor's theory.

Another possible theory is that John Bell was shielding a close friend of his: James Johnson, who seemed ever-present in the Bell house, and was referred to sardonically by "Kate" as "Old Sugar Mouth." Johnson seems singled out here; the entity originally identified herself as his stepmother's "witch" before settling on Kate Batts for reasons unknown. Is it possible Johnson was the alleged perpetrator and John Bell a silent witness? Again, this is all speculation. Whether or not Richard Bell's account unconsciously reveals more than he could say, we'll never know. If it was written by Richard Bell at all, and not by his publisher, Ingram—either way, the patterns, the language, the word choices in the document seem to lend themselves extremely readily to Fodor's interpretation.

John Bell died on December 20, 1820. His death was unusual, even for the Bell family. It is said that he died from a drop of poison poured between his lips while he slept. No one, not even the family doctor, could identify this poison, but when the contents of a mysterious bottle were administered to the family cat, "the creature whirled around, sprang crazily into the air, keeled over, and died. And the witch's taunting laughter filled the room."[8] The witch made a triumphant cameo at John Bell's funeral. In the words of Richard Bell:

> *It was a bright December day and a great crowd of people came to attend the funeral. Rev. Sugg Fort and Revs. James and Thomas Gunn conducted the services. After the grave was filled, and the friends turned to leave the sad scene, the witch broke out in a loud voice singing, "Row me up some brandy O," and continued singing this until the family and friends had all entered the house.*[9]

After John Bell's death, "Kate" focused her energies on breaking up Betsy and her fiancé, a local boy named Joshua Gardner, alternately begging her, "Please, Betsy Bell, don't marry Josh" and threatening "If you marry Josh Gardner, you will both regret it to the end of your days." When Betsy broke off her engagement to Josh, the witch finally disappeared.[10] Richard Bell writes that the broken engagement "was of such a delicate nature that it was kept a secret as much as possible in the family and ignored when talked about. But it never ceased its tormenting until her young dream was destroyed."[11]

In the first half of the nineteenth century, a world where

psychology was unknown but where victimization and trauma were certainly real for many young girls, it seems inevitable that poltergeists would be one outlet for a shattered mind. Fodor suggests that "Kate" was able to salvage Betsy's fractured psyche, enabling her to live to a ripe old age. This brings us back to the "witch." In this context, she was the spirit of a living, embodied person. This second self, this split self, is the one that floats freely while the body remains in place (a common motif among rape victims). The "witch" is a spiritual cousin of the telekinetic teen girl, taking back her agency to avenge her wronged self. Interestingly enough, Carrie White, who we discussed above as an example of an iconic "troubled teenager with telekinesis," has also been called a witch; in the 1973 movie version by Brian de Palma, Carrie's mother refers to her twice as a witch, prompting some critics to draw parallels between Carrie and medieval witch trials (the film's final inferno underscores these parallels).[12] In the essay "Woman as Witch: Carrie," Barbara Creed writes that Carrie is "a divided personality. On the one hand, she is a painfully shy, withdrawn, child-like girl who just wants to be 'normal' like every other teenager, while on the other hand she has the power of telekinesis which enables her to transform into an avenging female fury."[13] Film scholar Heather Greene adds, "In Carrie's case, it is the liminal state of the teen girl as she loses her prized innocence and gains the fearsome power of female sexuality."[14] Perhaps there is no need to get so hung up on literal uses of "witch" and "poltergeist" here, as we can see many points of contact between the two—particularly in a case like Betsy Bell's, where psychokinesis is prompted by sexualized adolescent emergence, a nucleus of fear and power in cases of poltergeists and witches alike.

For better or worse, whether persecuted for it or celebrated, the witch is and always has been a woman with power. Without "Kate," Fodor surmises, Betsy may have ended up in a madhouse. How many other girls have? How many of these saints and fasting girls and witches and poltergeists' victims were, in fact, traumatized girls lashing out? How many cases of telekinesis have been triggered by trauma? Where does the pain and rage go when there is no earthly outlet for it? It goes to visions, and mystic manifestations, screams, and shattered glass. These are not the demons of hell; they are our own demons. These are not ghosts and spirits from another world, they are our fierce, troubled, raging spirits, knocking and rapping and howling and desperate to scream, to speak, to reveal, and to be heard.

GRAVEYARD DANCE

The Witch's Curse

LEANNA

BUCKSPORT, MAINE

A GRAND GRAVESTONE IN BUCK CEMETERY BEARS AN UNMISTAKABLE mark.

Bucksport, Maine, is named for Colonel John Buck, a local Revolutionary War hero. His gray, stately, obelisk-styled monument rests behind an iron fence. A curious image descends directly from beneath Buck's carved name on gray stone, impossible to miss.

The mark gave rise to instant, wild folk legend that popularly persists to this day. Regardless of the thin premise of believability, there *is* an uncanny image on that headstone. Ghost stories often rely on things that can't be verified, seen, or heard by everyone. But in Buck Cemetery, the image of a foot is clearly dancing on a man's grave.

Born in Massachusetts in 1719, Colonel Buck became a soldier of steadfast, unwavering will who died in 1795 at the age of seventy-seven. His original tombstone was a simple one with name, dates of life and death, and a bit of scripture. In 1850, the Buck family installed the stately obelisk in the family plot to honor the colonel.

That's when the "curse" began.

A curious image appeared on the stone soon after its completion. Distinctly shaped, blackened against the gray stone, a calf descends to an ankle and to a pointed toe. Any attempt to scrub the stone clean saw the image reappear within a day, undaunted.

Where there is a curse, there has to be a witch: the inevitable momentum of folk legend logic.

Maine is a beautiful state full of proud people, a land of natural storytellers. (I've found my visits to Maine absolutely enchanting.) It's easy to see how the oft-misty, atmospheric landscape can give rise to tall tales, offered with a wink and a bit of self-deprecatory humor. In the words of famed Mainer Stephen King, "the primary duty of literature is to tell us the truth about ourselves by telling us lies about people who never existed."

Matching a lurid tale—and a witch—to the mark on Buck's grave flourished in the decades after its placement atop a cemetery hill, despite Maine's having no documented witch trials.

The first time this witch appeared in dated print was in the *Haverhill Gazette*, March 22, 1899, though the *Gazette* itself referenced an undated quote from the *Philadelphia Inquirer*, proving the concept of an uncleanable stain on a powerful man's grave had already been making its rounds and likely merging with other Eastern lore along the way.

The general through line for the curse and the grave blemish is the same: a woman is accused of witchcraft and executed for it by Buck, who would have been serving as justice of the peace (never mind that such a title wouldn't have carried the capacity for execution orders).

As this woman is about to hang, she pronounces a curse. The *Haverhill Gazette* writes it as such:

The hangman was about to perform his gruesome duty when the woman turned to Col. Buck and raising one hand to heaven, as if to direct her last words on earth, pronounced this astounding prophecy: "Jonathan Buck, listen to these words, the last my tongue will utter. It is the spirit of the only true and living God which bids me speak them to you. You will soon die. Over your grave they will erect a stone that all may know where your bones are crumbling into dust. But listen, upon that stone the imprint of my feet will appear, and for all time, long after you and your accursed race have perished from the earth, will the people from far and wide know that you murdered a woman. Remember well, Jonathan Buck, remember well."

A tale like this has a tendency to become exponential in its subsequent versions. Author J. W. Ocker begins his *New England Grimpendium* entry on this curse with the declaration that he is *not* a fan of this story:

In one version, instead of hanging her he has her burned, and her leg falls off and rolls out of the fire at Buck's feet. In another, she wasn't a witch at all, just unfortunate enough to be pregnant with his child in a socially unacceptable situation, the burned-at-the-stake-as-a-witch bit was just an easy fix to his inconvenient problem. In yet another version her already born and deformed son grabs the leg when it falls off his mother's burning body and runs away with the relic, never to be seen again.[1]

Still, the image and this legend have an impressive *persistence* of narrative.

Poet Robert Tristam Coffin of Brunswick, Maine—a Rhodes scholar and Pulitzer Prize–winning poet, wrote about Buck's tombstone in his poem "The Foot of Tucksport," naming the witch Ann Harraway and substituting a T in the town and surname.

Over the course of his romanticized poem, several townspeople speak out against the supposed witch in examples clearly taken from the template of Salem's wild accounts. Perhaps Coffin had something to say about small-town hysteria and rumor-mongering leading to violence and curses. Perhaps he simply found the image on the stone too compelling not to prompt verse. The stone attracts hundreds of tourists a year. The town has to reckon with the popular legend and it, like many of the sites in this book, has to walk a fine line between truth and tourism dollars.

A Globe Mini entitled *Haunted Places*, one of those small magazines once sold on grocery-store checkout lines alongside horoscopes and lurid tabloids, tells the tale of "The Witch's Footprint," and this edition uses the name Ida Black. Author Merlin Jones notes myriad versions of "Ida's" story, and while the magazine admits there is no consensus on the details, that this woman *existed at all* is repeated as an unquestioned fact. It also trades out the idea of a darkened footprint for a more sensational color, transposing the mark as rusty and "bloody." In this edition Ida pronounces her curse much more pointedly: "Though you may slay me now, my colonel," she croaked, "I shall come back and dance upon your gravestone while you roast in hell."[2]

During the nineteenth century, the context of this grave's construction, the ankle was considered one of the most scandalous parts of a woman's body. It was *not* to be revealed. That this Ida Black version of the curse goes so far as to *dance* upon the gravestone, dancing being another taboo of the time, and the mark forever bares her ankle; these are two societal restrictions that Ida's tale has managed to buck. The revelation of the foot and ankle, like a dangling stocking coming down from the colonel's surname, would have had a more shocking effect than in our modern context, where neither dancing nor ankles are considered the epitome of scandal. But the historical context of the image as *deeply risqué* offers insight into why people felt such a need to justify it.

The reasonable explanation of the mark credits some flaw or mineral vein in the stone that has oxidized and weathered into its shape, an unavoidable watermark. The legend declares several headstones predated the current one, each scrubbed repeatedly and then entirely replaced. A sort of *Macbeth* moment; an "out, damned spot" that keeps returning.

Some people in Bucksport will tell you that the entire monument was replaced once and that the foot returned to the very same spot on the new monument; others will say that the monument was never replaced and that the foot is simply an imperfection in the stone known as an inclusion, or knot. If this last assessment is true, however, why didn't the stonemasons notice it originally? Inclusions are readily apparent when the stone is cut; they do not gradually bleed through the rock.[3]

The placard next to Buck's headstone, installed by the cemetery in hopes of getting a handle on yet another one of America's runaway spectral narratives, states, yes—the all caps are a transcription: "There is no record of ANYONE being executed for witchcraft in the state of Maine. Stories that the monument has been replaced are simply untrue. This is the original." The placard goes on to say: "Notably, the witch's curse was unheard of before the flaw in the marker appeared."

Buck was born twenty-five years *after* the Salem murders that made that town so infamous.

However, suspicion, ostracism, accusations, and leveraging power against those accused or suspected of being a witch didn't vanish after those "trials" ended. While no area saw the same levels of violence as Salem, there have been plenty of accounts involving "witches" even into the twentieth century. (Helen Duncan was a Scottish medium and the last person to be imprisoned under England's Witchcraft Act of 1735 for fraudulent claims. She was arrested in 1944 and again in 1956.)

In the century following Salem's murders, many of which carried their own talk of lingering curses, the popular consciousness seemed to beg the question: What if an accused witch could truly leave her mark beyond the veil? The idea of a woman having the last, grisly word upon the grave of someone who had unjustly accused her and leveraged power over her does have a redemptive satisfaction. But if she was really serious about it, one would think she'd have come up with a better revenge than a stocking-shaped grave rubbing.

While the mid-to-late nineteenth century would have liked to think itself far more civilized and rational than the horrific hysteria that gripped Salem, it was an era voraciously interested in all manner of paranormal happenings and communication. Women were at the core of Spiritualist circles. Across the nineteenth century there were changing, expanding anxieties about women's bodies, freedoms, and attitudes. Our modern shorthand and iconography of witches riding brooms with pointy hats is taken directly from nineteenth-century illustrations, a diabolical, reactionary counterpoint to the domestic tranquility the *Angel in the House* was supposed to provide.

Women are often confronted with societal identities as a mere summation of parts, not of a whole. In this case, a perceived part of a *presumed* woman became a wildly expansive story of brutality and pain. In each version of this witch's tale, the woman is humiliated, tortured, ostracized, murdered. Folk legends do not spare women from grisly details; more often than not, their suffering is the crux of any given story. Mythmaking traffics heavily in women's suffering, treating it casually in pursuit of a salacious story. The image of her foot becomes fetishistic. A sexualized (in nineteenth-century norms) body part revealing itself—in a graveyard, no less, a space we as a society have a complex and ongoing relationship with—remains a push and pull of the sacred and the profane.

Colin Dickey makes the point several times in *Ghostland* that ghost stories and urban legends have the capacity to be instructive—a warning to take care, to pay attention—but in the case of Ann/Ida, it's hard to see any moral of the story, other than perhaps a prompt to question power and how it may be leveraged. But the stories are so over the top that this legend would have been popularized to sell magazines and papers, not to provide words of caution.

This particular witch is an invention of the penny dreadful attached to a local monument, and a historic figure, drawing on those all-too-real abuses of power in Salem as a template. Bucksport historians have their work cut out for them in dispelling these inventions.

But perhaps considering a tale such as this, however spun throughout history, could prompt society to take a look at who they may be scapegoating and why, and what indelible mark may be left into the future.

Valerie Van Winkle wrote about the legend for Bucksport's bicentennial celebrations, the text of which is archived on the town's official government site, and while it's clear the city seeks to debunk falsehoods and bite back against lascivious accusations born in legend, there is a fascination that can't be discarded. She writes: "Writers who have researched the legend seem to conclude that it is a fiction concocted after the appearance of the image on the monument. No records have been discovered suggesting that any version of the legend predates the appearance of the leg. It all seems very reasonable, unless you have seen the image of the leg firsthand. It has a vitality, a naughtiness, which seems to laugh at rational data."[4]

A melancholy stone maiden in Poughkeepsie Rural Cemetery.
Photo by Leanna Renee Hieber

The Farmer's Wife, Johnson, Vermont, by Arthur Rothstein. Library of Congress, Prints & Photographs Division, FSA/OWI Collection LC-DIG-fsa-8a08629

PART 3

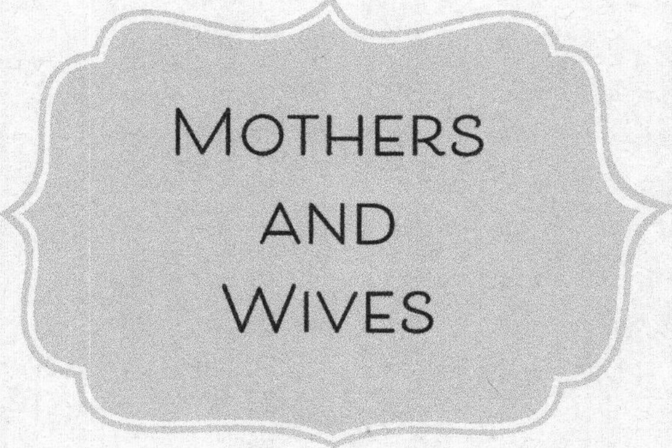

Mothers and Wives

INTRODUCTION

ANDREA AND LEANNA

There are many ways to be a mother. Mothering is simply nurturing and raising, caretaking and loving; it is not a strictly biological process. The terms "childless woman" and "mother" are a "false polarity," as poet Adrienne Rich has observed, noting, "there are no such simple categories."[1] There are many types of mothers. All readers of modern horror stories share in common one great mother, Mary Shelley; all inhabitants of planet Earth share in common the Great Mother who provides for us all. Mothers, biological and otherwise, are complex creatures; they can be frightening, indifferent, unhappy, wretched, spiteful, violent, and sad; they can be overbrimming with pure love and encouragement; they can be your soft place to land when the world batters you. They bring you into the world and sustain you in it, even amid trauma, strife, and ambivalence. Mothers are powerful, yet consistently stripped of power. Motherhood in its truest form is glorious; motherhood as an institution can be nightmarish.

Mothers are also easy targets, especially in ghostlore. They often are maudlin, stripped of any other personality or points of reference, existing only in relation to their children, with no identities of their own outside motherhood. A common, repetitive trope involves such a mother whose child dies, and so she dies of grief. We have tried to avoid these types of stories here, because they are fairly uninteresting and there isn't much to say about them: the biological mother as tethered to her child, the mother with no outside life or personality. This trope has been examined before, and it is not very productive. These ghostly mothers are absented, faceless, interchangeable, keening wraiths who fulfill conservative societal roles of complete, unalloyed maternal devotion. Stories of angry, vengeful, ambivalent, or sometimes even humorously over-the-top ghost mothers are far more satisfying than sorrowful stories of dead ghost moms who usually killed themselves or died of grief because their children died. On a personal level, it is also unbearable to read these stories closely when one is the mother of a young child living through a pandemic. Let us not dwell among the sad wraiths who have lost little ones; let us only mourn for them briefly, honor their pain, and then move on.

And let us not idealize mothers. There have been bad ones, and sad ones. Mothers driven to murderous rage by the sheer forces of exhaustion and frustration. Mothers who have been ignored and dismissed by the dominant systems and institutions. Ghostly mothers like La Llorona who are wailing still, angry mothers still boiling with rage and fury. At times they exist as allegories or warning fables; La Llorona is both an allegory for the destructive patriarchal forces of colonialism and a warning fable for small children, designed to keep them away from deathly waters and dark streets. In this way, La Llorona is as much a protective force as a dangerous one, for fear of her keeps living children safe. Like most mothers, La Llorona has both a loving and a terrifying side.

As much as mothering is about life-giving, motherhood is also inseparable from death. Outside of calamity or grave illness, a woman is never closer to the line between life and death as when she gives birth. Historically, childbirth is the number one killer of women; to this day maternal mortality rates remain disgracefully high in the developing world and the United States. America has terrible maternal mortality rates, particularly for women of color.[2]

And if you happen to survive labor and delivery, you are promptly plunged into a zombielike abyss. To be a mother in the United States—and we won't write "working mother," because *all* mothers are working mothers—is to operate entirely without support. At the time of this writing, there is no other developed country on earth that offers zero legally mandated paid family leave, *not one*. America is a hellscape for mothers, who suffer from extreme unwanted government scrutiny and intervention during their pregnancies, then are dropped into a void the minute they're discharged from the hospital. Hypocrisy, that yawning gap between the lip service paid to motherhood and actually wading through the literal pile of shit that is reality, adds insult to injury. (The originator of Mother's Day eventually disavowed the holiday and spent the latter part of her life trying to get it stricken from the calendar.) And dare you voice your dissatisfaction with the institution of motherhood, you are greeted with irritation and derision because, after all, *you chose* to become a mother. The discourse surrounding motherhood, which seems so endless and dominant, is essentially impactless because it is generally ignored by all non-moms, including men in power. Want to talk about affordable day care? Have fun screaming into the void.

Early motherhood—the sleep-deprived kind where you suddenly realize how *stacked against you* are the patriarchal forces of motherhood in the United States—is an exercise in hallucinatory rage. The impassioned, infinite love for your infant combined with deep insecurity, terrifying identity loss, and smoldering bitterness is the very definition of maternal ambivalence.[3] (One begins to feel more understanding for the ghostly mothers with no identities of their own; many mothers of newborns have felt equally spectral, invisible, identity-less, walking the corridors at 3:00 a.m.) This two-sided coin of love and anger is just Motherhood 101. Such ambivalence is a natural part of the process of "matrescence," as it is now called in certain circles, but it is rarely acknowledged as normal in the mainstream.[4] Instead, maternal anger and ambivalence are seen as monstrous. The reductive flip side of a benevolent mother goddess is a death-bringing destroyer.

The murderous mother is a figure of great interest in mythology and lore. Ghost stories love to linger on the figure of the unnatural mother who kills her own offspring. These tropes are given permission to delight us because we are able to see them as anomalies. They exist in contrast to normal, human, living mothers, who definitely aren't supposed to be simmering with barely repressed fury almost all the time. The aberrant, disagreeable, "domineering," or even murderous mother is the inheritor of outdated traditions from olden times. She comes from dusty tales of Rhea, Medea, and Clytemnestra, whose stories were forged in the misogynistic sexual politics of fifth-century Greece, which worked hard to move the center of spiritual and material power from the female to the male. A so-called domineering mother is just a woman whose needs have never been met, and who has no other outlet for her pain and rage. For a society that has a lot of sympathy for serial killers, we're pretty harsh on moms.

These mythical, monstrous, or one-sided reductive ghost mothers allow us to conveniently forget that most real-life mothers are emphatically *not* seen. She is the first to wake, the last to sleep, the invisible hand who refills soap dispensers and washes the comforters.[5] Her labor is invisible; she is the unseen ghost in the house.

So, rather than retell the same old stories, let us discover and celebrate those other, less-expected kinds of mothers. In the following pages, we relate the story of Ma Greene, steamboat captain, who loved her ship and steered it stoutheartedly with a great, expansive love, and who haunts it still. She is her vessel's caretaker and its mistress; she is our mother at sea who refreshes us all with her undaunted spirit.

And, in these pages, we remember the bio moms, too. In the following stories you will find devoted mothers. You will find loving mothers. You will find tragic mothers, like Margaret Garner, who slew her daughter rather than deliver her back into slavery. The spectral mothers who haunt these pages run the gamut of emotion from joy to fury to ambivalence to grief, just as living mothers do—whether we see them or not.

The role of wife has been the one that women, through history, have been "supposed" to fulfill—almost above all else. Even if a woman wasn't a mother, if she was an adult, she was *supposed* to be a wife. Marriage was the sole vehicle, until the mid-nineteenth century, by which women had any rights or status whatsoever, although her name was entirely subsumed and she was Mrs. First and Surname of Husband.

There was a Victorian adage that a woman's name should appear in print only three times: at birth, marriage, and death. This is dehumanizing and wholly reductive of human experience. So it should come as no surprise, then, that the same era that popularized such an adage of invisibility birthed the New Woman: more independent, educated, worldly wise, and fighting for her rights while she questioned the institution of marriage entirely. Maybe she was even so bold as to wear pants, ride a bicycle, and demand the vote.

But to this day, many single women still face an uphill battle being accepted as a whole person in their own right. It wasn't until the 1970s that a woman could own a credit card in *her* name. The business and legal paperwork of modern marriage are still full of the transactional language that created the institution in the first place.

Many women in this book are wives in addition to other tropes or roles we highlight, but with the examples we've chosen for this section, we'd like to examine the transactionality of marriage and unpack some of the expectations involved, whether these women felt free to marry or whether they felt they had to.

The ghostly wives of West Virginia bring us rich folklore alongside lives of toil and resilience. They transcend the concept of standing behind a husband as a meek "helpmeet" or submissive partner, and range from righteously vengeful spirits to the torchbearers of ancestral knowledge and power.

Self-educated and ambitious, Eliza Jumel came from nothing and became one of New York's wealthiest women in the 1830s. She was never accepted into the New York society she longed to be a part of, nor did she ever become a mother. But she utilized marriage as leverage, and her shrewd business acumen turned real estate ventures to her advantage when no woman dared such a thing, and her presence remains a force of nature in the house that she kept in her name with an iron fist.

These women, these mothers and wives, deserve a far greater mention than mere birth, marriage, and death. Their ghosts want to tell us infinitely more.

STILL CAPTAINING HER SHIP

The Ghost of Ma Greene

LEANNA

CINCINNATI, OHIO

CINCINNATI, OHIO, IS KNOWN AS THE QUEEN CITY. LIKE ANY good ghost story, how a city gains its nickname has more than one source, more than one truth, and plenty of opinion. Growing up outside Cincinnati, I always remembered hearing that it was the glimmering crowns topping the steam stacks of the city's famed Ohio River steamboats that had given the city its crowning title. This may be partly true, but the nickname dates back to around 1819, when it was first used by prominent locals. It was further cemented by a stanza in the poem "Catawba Wine" by Henry Wadsworth Longfellow, first published circa 1858. The poem extolls the virtues of Nicholas Longworth's winery and delivers a coronation in his final stanza:

And this Song of the Vine,
This greeting of mine,

The winds and the birds shall deliver
To the Queen of the West,
In her garlands dressed,
On the banks of the Beautiful River.

Cincinnati's placement along the picturesque Ohio River, and indeed the river's crown-topped steamships, the city's culture, the grand music hall, and its considerable wealth due to enormous industry, made the Queen City an international draw. Cincinnati was the top honeymoon spot in the United States for a great deal of the nineteenth and early-twentieth centuries.

The city also represented freedom during the horrors of slavery; Cincinnati was a powerful city beacon in the southernmost part of a northern state. Just across the river from Kentucky, a slave state, Cincinnati was a huge, vital stop on the Underground Railroad. From Cincinnati, travelers would continue north toward Cleveland and Lake Erie, at the top of the state, representing additional pathways of northern freedom.

It is admittedly refreshing to write about a celebrated, beloved trailblazer of a woman rather than a victim. And it is also a delight to write with pride about one's hometown.

During the height of steamboat shipping and leisure travel, thousands of steamboats were winding their way up and down the Ohio. Navigating these waters before locks and dams was a learned art. Mary Becker Greene had an eye for this art, having been interested in weather, boats, and water since she was a girl, having been born in Marietta, Ohio, in 1868, near the Muskingum River.

Mary was introduced to a riverman named Gordon Greene by a mutual friend, and once they were married in 1890, they cofounded Greene Line Steamers in Cincinnati. While they did have a land-based residence in Newport, Ohio, they were a more hands-on family and immediately took up residence on the *H. K. Bedford*, a steamboat where Mary always helped, working around the ship and learning how to navigate while watching intently in the pilothouse.

By 1892, Mary's experience and aptitude in steamboat navigation paved the way for her to obtain her master pilot's license, making her the only female captain on the Ohio River and the first woman ever licensed to pilot a steamboat in the United States. Undaunted by being a woman captain in a man's world, her presence and achievements helped pave the way for other women pilots. As she herself said, "When you marry a riverman, you marry the river too. That's the code of steamboatin'."

It was a happy marriage.

She looked at the riverboat industry in a more holistic and commercially savvy way than other packet boat companies of the time. Rather than thinking of the boats as purely functional, she added touches of warm and elegant décor, comfort, meal services, amenities, and reliable customer service that garnered a fiercely loyal ridership as the couple's fleet grew. It was said when she wasn't steering one of the company's steamers, she was sewing fine curtains for the guest cabins. It helped that Ma was her own best investment; sometimes people would buy tickets just for Ma's company. *Wheeling Heritage* heartily celebrates her:

> *A successful company also made for a successful marriage and one that was also filled with fun-loving antics and competition. One such occasion was when Mary and Gordon decided to race their own steamers from Pittsburgh to Cincinnati in 1903. Taking the lead and winning the race by arriving into the Queen City, the five-foot-tall feisty lady's already rising fame skyrocketed to new heights.*[1]

Ma understood her boats and her business top to bottom. There wasn't really anything she couldn't do on board. She gave birth to her son, Tom, who would grow up to help helm the family business, while the company's side-wheeler ship, the *Greenland*, was stuck in an ice jam. The early 1900s proved successful for the Greene Line as the family continued to add additional boats—and children—to their fleet. Mary's fame and charm led to Greene Line boats enjoying sell-out cruises on the Ohio, Mississippi, Cumberland, and Tennessee Rivers for decades.

When Gordon died in 1927 and it came time to return her late husband's body home for interment in the family plot in Newport, it was Mary who was at the helm of their steamer, the *Tom Greene*, named after one of their sons, upon arrival. Captain Chris Greene took on the reins of the company alongside his mother.

The Great Depression spelled uncertainty for all steamboat companies. The Greene Line was down to only two steamers in the 1930s, and Mary and her sons were facing a wavering future. But Mary soldiered on in the business, a steadfast optimist, quoted as saying, "Once you ride between two stacks, you're doomed to ride upon a river craft until you're tombed."

Her determination was rewarded. In 1935, the family purchased the steamer *Cape Girardeau* and renamed it after their late patriarch. The new *Gordon C. Greene* was renovated to provide accommodations for 175 passengers and 60 crew. The large main cabin served as the social hub, where dining was enjoyed three times a day. Mary, expert captain and hostess, went table to table to greet fond passengers. She also liked to dance.

Music and dancing were plentiful and joyful on board all Greene Line boats. But as Ma was a fierce backer of the temperance movement, there was no alcohol served on board her ships.

Captain Chris Greene died suddenly in 1944, and operations for the company shifted to Ma's remaining son, Tom. By 1946, with Mary in her late seventies, Tom made a daring decision to put a bid in for an iconic ship.

One of the great gems of riverboat history was, and remains, the *Delta Queen*, built in 1927 alongside the *Delta King*. Luxurious boats, they were valued at more than one million dollars apiece, and the *Delta Queen* had been used for transport and medical facilities during World War II. Tom managed to place the only bid for the *Delta Queen* at her auction in 1946, paying $46,250, a mere fraction of what she was worth. Next followed the epic adventure of getting the 285-foot steamer from the California coast to the Ohio River. Boarded up for an ocean journey, the *Delta Queen* was towed down the coast of California, Mexico, and Central America. It then passed through the Panama Canal, through the Gulf of Mexico, and finally to New Orleans, LA, where it could be un-boarded, ready to journey north on her own.

Once the *Delta Queen* was finally moored in Cincinnati, and after a six-figure renovation, Ma was quick to take up residence in stateroom 109, adding a "G" to the room number to denote it as her own.

She helmed and presided over this grand boat until the very end.

Ma died quietly in her stateroom on April 22, 1949, having piloted top-tier steamboats for more than fifty-two of her fifty-nine years in the industry. A mere two days before her death, Mary had happily joined the guests, who had come for her famed hospitality, in dancing the Virginia Reel Mary was on the twelfth issue of her pilot's license, out of fifty-six years of renewals, at the time of her passing.

After her death, the boat was returned to Cincinnati and was docked on the Ohio. Her son Tom died of a heart attack at the wheel of the *Delta Queen* just a year later. The *Delta Queen* is presently moored in Chattanooga. In 1989 it was designated a National Historic Landmark, and in January 2004 it was inducted into the National Maritime Hall of Fame.

It is fitting that such a famous boat had been run by such a well-loved woman, herself a queen of the Queen City. A force of nature in life, so too does Mary preside in death, still at work and still steadfastly watching over her ship and its guests. *Ghosts of Cincinnati* describes quite the meaningful encounter:

> *In 1982, First Mate Mike Williams was sleeping alone on the ship during annual repairs. He was awakened by an urgent-sounding whisper in his ear. He began hearing what sounded like a door slamming. Williams followed the sound to the engine room thinking that someone had boarded the ship. When he arrived, he discovered water pouring in from a broken intake pipe. The steamboat would have been in serious trouble if not for him being awakened by something—or someone.*

On a trip overnight, a new employee working as a purser spoke with Williams about a pressing concern. An older woman had rung her from the stateroom, saying she didn't feel well. As Williams had medical training, the purser sought him out. Investigating, they found the stateroom empty. But the purser got quite a fright when she turned to see an old woman staring at her through a window.

> *Williams offered to walk the employee to her cabin. As they passed a painting of Captain Mary Greene, the purser became more frightened because the woman staring out of the painting was the same woman who had stared at her disturbingly through the window. The two were later married and often tell people that Ma Greene introduced them.*[2]

Pictures of Mary Greene evidently captured a great deal of her spirit, so much so that during the filming of a documentary, the cameraman was shooting footage in the Betty Blake Lounge when he screamed and recoiled, pointing frantically to the camera. When he was able to speak again, he explained that while filming Mary's picture, *she* had come to life before his eyes.

Phyllis Dale, an entertainer aboard the ship, often spoke about seeing a small, distinguished woman in a 1930s dress who disappeared just as she looked up. When comparing it to Captain Mary's portrait, the singer exclaimed that was the woman she'd seen.

Sometimes, Ma will forgo her finery for more comfortable attire, as guests have seen her roaming the corridors in a long green robe, only to disappear when turning a corner.

Just after Ma's death in 1949, a few changes were made on board. Ma had been so strongly against alcohol it wasn't even a subject to be broached during her lifetime, but after her death, plans were made to open a new saloon on the ship.

Mere days after opening the new bar, a barge crashed into the side of the *Delta Queen,* destroying the renovated area in a direct hit.

Once the barge was dislodged from the steamboat, the name on the prow shocked the crew.

It was the *Mary B.*

Long live Mary Becker Greene and "Ma's" eternally skilled watch.

MAMA TRIED

ANDREA

ON A COLD, GRAY NOVEMBER EVENING AT THE TURN OF THE last century, a tired mother named Dolly Pauls Messick went outside to fetch her cows. Dolly wasn't looking forward to the walk to the commons, a pasture of short, scrubby grass where collectively all the neighbors' cows grazed during the day. The night threatened snow, it was already late, and her bones were tired from a day of work. Her teenage daughters sat by the flickering orange warmth of the fire, refusing her entreaties of help, and with a heavy sigh Dolly settled herself into her scratchy wool shawl and trudged forth. The last of the daylight was thin and pale on the horizon, and Dolly brought a lamp. All around her the marsh glimmered and the sounding tides mirrored her weary sighs as salted water swelled onto the shore before once more retreating to sea. She picked her way carefully among the stubby plants lining the sandy cow path; this narrow, winding way dotted with rocks and broken shells was fickle and prone to disappearing into high grass from time to time. It took a seasoned native of Virginia's Tidewater region to find her way through this tentative pathway, always in danger of being swallowed back into the ocean, but Dolly *was* a seasoned native and she considered herself sure-footed.

But it was cold that night, and the light faded fast, and marshes are always deceptive even at the best of times. Perhaps the flurry of snow disoriented her, or perhaps, disheartened by her daughters' recalcitrance, she became distracted by a blurred veil of infuriated tears. At any rate, she lost her way, and as the night wore on and no cows came home and no supper appeared on the table, even her daughters noticed she was gone. When morning came, the neighbors were greeted by a terrible sight: a thin leg stuck out of a patch of quicksand like a broken twig, and attached to the leg was Mrs. Dorothy "Dolly Mammy" Pauls Messick.[1]

Dolly Mammy, as she was called, began haunting her ungrateful daughters almost immediately. Her retribution came in various forms: She pinched them and slapped them, angrily moved furniture around them, kept them awake all night with terrible scratching and other hideous sounds, and when the girls did finally manage to fall asleep huddled in their shared bed, they would awake to find their long hair had been braided together during the night.

Dolly's daughters suffered for several years from the torments of their mother's ghost, and eventually the tale became local legend. The road at the water's edge where their mother met her death is said, nowadays, to be one of the most haunted byways in America, and the coastal town of Poquoson, Virginia, which is to this day still filled with Dolly Mammy's descendants, remembers her name.[2]

If you look up the story of Dolly Mammy, an old newspaper clipping comes up.[3] It shows a gray-shingled, weather-beaten cabin, and is captioned "Dolly Messick's house." Other articles emerge, seasonal local interest pieces about séances and Halloween parties hosted by local historic societies.[4] The legend of Dolly Mammy's ghost lives on, even if—as with most ghost stories—the facts of her case are pretty fungible. L. B. Taylor, a careful chronicler of Virginia ghost stories, noted that Dolly Mammy's origin story was said to take place either in the 1850s, or in 1904, but nobody was really sure which.[5] A Poquoson man named Bill Forrest claimed that Dolly Mammy was his great-aunt, but he wasn't exactly sure either.[6] Another one of the Forrest family, a woman named Jessie Fay Forrest, was an avid genealogist and local historian, but as she followed Dolly Mammy to the grave a few decades ago, she can't be reached for comment, at least not by this writer.[7] Jesse Fay and Dolly also seem to be distantly related; Forrest was the maiden name of one Dolly Messick—a Dolly Elizabeth Forrest Messick—but it's unclear which branch of the family tree *that* Dolly belongs to.

Confused yet?

L. B. Taylor lists the names of Dolly's daughters in one of his books, and the names match Dolly Elizabeth Forrest Messick's family records, but according to other online records of their family tree, they might be daughters of a *different* Dolly Paul. According to her obituary, *that* Dolly Paul died peacefully in the home of her son in 1937, and *her* funeral was widely attended by numerous people, including a whole cadre of "honorary pallbearers," among whom was yet *another* Dolly Paul.[8]

Calls, emails, and other entreaties to Poquoson historic societies and research librarians have so far gone unanswered, possibly because nobody can sort out the cascade of Dolly Pauls. Accounts of the ghost story all invariably mention that her funeral was "well attended," and it's easy to see why: She seems to have been related to everyone in town. Dolly Mammy really seems to be a mother in a larger sense, a great presence looming over the entire locality where she once resided as a (probably) real person. Yet at the same time she really is a ghost—her true identity is lost to time and legend and she drifts ephemerally on the margins of local lore.

As far as ghostly mothers go, Dolly Mammy is actually pretty refreshing (despite her exhausting genealogy). In the annals of American ghostlore you will mostly find a preponderance of sorrowful mothers, devoted souls mourning departed children. There are dozens of them, and their stories seldom vary. These typical sorrowful mothers are easy archetypes for two reasons: First, they play into Christian notions of the sacrificing mother, a trope that has been prevalent in the Western world for two millennia. Secondly, they are a fairly accurate reflection of the experience of motherhood. Matrescence, the process of becoming a mother, is fraught with mortality; it was particularly so in the nineteenth century, when most of these stories originate, and it remains so to this day. Scores of ghost stories involve mothers who either killed themselves or died of heartbreak when their children and babies died, and these stories reflect the very real emotional response to the loss of a child. Even if, in the less dramatic world of daily life, mothers are not apt to commit dramatic acts but are far more likely to simply soldier on, the loss of a child is a kind of living death for any parent, a wound that never really heals but only scars over. Child and infant death is emotionally crippling, and it often leads to the breakup of marriages and a life of semipresent constant mourning. The reams of ghost stories about sorrowful ghostly mothers exist for a reason, then. Any mother would die for her child in a heartbeat, and any mother would struggle to go on living after the death of a child. The impulse toward Spiritualism in the mid-nineteenth century was prompted in significant part by the high child mortality rates of the era, so it is no surprise to see that American ghost stories of the last two to three hundred years are littered with these sad spectral mothers mourning their beloved departed children. It makes for poignant reading, and is difficult and depressing to wade through pages and pages of these accounts.

But there are more kinds of ghostly mother stories than just the sad ones. Just as mothers in the world of the living run the gamut from serene to psychotic, there is a variety of maternal experience in the spirit world. Besides the rather cathartic story of Dolly Mammy really sticking it to her ungrateful daughters—the wonderful image of their braided hair alone makes the story worth the price of admission, particularly if you've ever threatened to shave your daughter's head as she wriggles like a demented trout while you try for the fifth time that morning to run a Wet Brush through her goddamn tangles—there are angry mothers, frightening mothers, entertaining mothers, dire-warning mothers, and absent mothers.

The ghost of Joan Crawford, for example, remains highly entertaining. Everyone knows that Joan was never mother of the year, no matter how we feel about *Mommie Dearest* (we personally think she was right about the wire hangers), so it's somewhat delightful to read that, after she died, her bed would spontaneously burst into flames, and her house required an exorcism.[9] Then there's the ghost of Mary Ball, George Washington's reputedly "extremely possessive" mother, who continues to steadily interfere in her historic house, puttering around her kitchen and generally being underfoot. She sometimes walks the boxwood path behind the house near the meditation rock where she was buried; it is said that some of the boxwoods are the original plantings that were on site in Mary Ball's day, which is a nice testimony to the tenacity of grumpy mothers, boxwoods, and other thorny plants.[10] Eugene O'Neill's mama apparently haunts Monte Cristo Cottage in New London, Connecticut, the setting for *Long Day's Journey into Night*. Presumably she is irritated that her son wrote about her morphine addiction, or maybe she's still annoyed at the slipshod renovations performed by her cheap, incompetent husband.[11]

These spirit mothers are entertaining; they are women whom an average mom (whose mood generally hovers somewhere between "mildly irritated" and "brittle with resentment" on any given morning) can certainly identify with. They speak to us in the way Dolly Mammy speaks to us; any mother of reluctantly unhelpful, screen-attached teenagers (i.e., any teenager) immediately cheers them on. In fact, "If you don't clean your room now, I will haunt you when I die," is something most moms can hear themselves saying, or possibly have already threatened before.

Spirit mothers also issue warnings. Motherhood is at its heart a fairly dark enterprise (just ask Shirley Jackson), and early motherhood especially is an incredibly frightening experience.[12] The ghost of the White Lady of Stow Lake in San Francisco epitomizes every mother's worst fear. Though the experience of motherhood is wildly diverse, a few things are truly universal. Every parent harbors the ever-present fear of something happening to their child, and one of the most common parent fears is the very real terror of losing your child at the playground. According to lore and the Golden Gate Park website, the White Lady of Stow Lake is the ghost of a Gilded Age woman who turned her back for a split second to chat with a friend while her small child played near the lake, and then realized, to her horror, that her child was gone.[13] The mother ended up drowning in the lake as she searched for her child. There have been some accounts of park patrons witnessing her pale form, but historical records are silent as to whether such an accident ever occurred. Many records from the era were destroyed in earthquakes and fires, so no death certificate can be found, and no news coverage seems to have existed in local papers either, according to researchers.[14]

The White Lady of the Lake remains a symbol, a cipher, and a warning—and typical of most warnings aimed at parents, particularly mothers, there's a shade of nagging in there, too, the slight hint that if anything happens to your child it's probably your fault and you're a terrible mother. You shouldn't have turned your back for a split second to talk to a friend. How selfish of you for putting your own needs before your child's! This typifies the tone of most parenting advice, which puts 100 percent of all responsibility on a mother's shoulders, thus maintaining the dominant capitalist heterocentric model order, i.e., fathers go off to work while mothers mind the babies, a conservative fantasy of a world that has never really existed.[15]

The White Lady of Stowe Lake also contains shades of La Llorona, perhaps the most famous ghostly mother in the Americas. Appearing in Mexico and in the American Southwest, where large Mexican communities dwell, La Llorona is a famed symbol of tragic motherhood, a cautionary fairy tale for children and a metaphor for colonialism's destructive forces. Like most mothers, she contains multitudes.

The famed Mexican folktale of La Llorona is typically told this way: A young Indian woman fell in love with a Spanish conquistador. He did not marry her, but put her up in a beautiful, big house by a rushing river. She bore him two children, but over time his affections waned. His visits grew less frequent and he eventually spurned her completely to marry a Spanish noblewoman. In rage and despair, she drowned her children in the river and then killed herself. To this day she wanders in the world in search of her babies, weeping. Her name, La Llorona, means "the crying one."

It is a tale told to young children. Because La Llorona is often found near water, it is a way to keep little ones from straying too far into the depths; because she walks at night, it is a way to ensure they get home before dark. It is every mother's worst fear personified—the fear not only that something dreadful may happen to her children, but that *she* may be the one to do it. It is also a larger parable about colonialism, the possession and abandonment of the motherland by the foreign invader. The symbolism of the cast-aside Indigenous woman and the subjugating Spaniard could not be clearer or starker.

The White Lady of Stowe evokes La Llorona by sharing a watery grave, along with her child. The symbolism of water is also prevalent in Dolly Mammy's shimmering marshes; all mothers have in common the symbol of water, of fecundity and life-giving properties whose flip side is death; mothers of the breaking waters whose fetuses float in natal oceans and rise from "the amniotic salinity" of the maternal sea.[16]

In Dolly Mammy's case, it is interesting to note that she died in the muck of quicksand in a marsh, which is similar to a telluric or swamplike environment that evokes imagery of the chthonic; female sexuality is mired in this swampy imagery, at least in strict patriarchal cosmogony.[17] In none of the stories does Dolly have a husband; perhaps the fact that she was mired in quicksand speaks to society's mistrust of sexually active single mothers, who dare fulfill their needs outside the boundaries of traditional marriage. Her death in quicksand, then, would be an appropriate punishment, and her failure to raise obedient and industrious daughters would be a reflection of her morally dubious mothering.

These mothers' stories also share a fairy-tale quality; their stories are dreamlike, migratory legends filled with picturesque images: the braided hair of Dolly's ungrateful daughters is an image that could have come from the pages of the Brothers Grimm, whose mother, by the way, was reportedly a "devoted and caring housewife, even though she tended at times to be melancholy."[18] Again, these stories evoke a subterranean, subconscious, oneiric quality, represented by "darkness, unconsciousness, and sleep," and by sleep's close companion, death.[19]

Rain and snow (all precipitation, in fact) evoke the feminine, and snow figures prominently in another ghost story, the tale of Catherine Sutter. Like Dolly Mammy's, her tale is blanketed by snow, again invoking the symbolic quality of a fairy tale. In the 1870s, a settler family stopped at Fort Leavenworth, Kansas, on their way farther west. The Sutter family sent their two young children out to look for firewood, and they never returned. Catherine Sutter stayed at the fort the whole winter, heading out every day to look for her lost children. She wandered through blizzards, squalls, and snowstorms, and died of pneumonia before she ever found them. She is buried in the cemetery near the fort, where her pallid ghost is often spotted floating over the ground and crying, still looking for her lost children.[20]

According to some versions of the story, her children fell into a creek while out looking for firewood that day. They nearly drowned but were rescued by a group of Fox Indians who nursed them back to health and returned them to the fort as soon as the snows of winter subsided. They were too late, however, and apparently their mother ghost "never got the message" that her children were safe and sound. The obvious thing to do in this case, it seems, is to hire a psychic medium to convey that message and put Catherine's ghost to rest, but there is no record of anyone ever having tried.

Far more interesting is the relationship between the Fox Indians and the white settlers, particularly in the setting of Fort Leavenworth. This Kansas fortification was central to the genocidal tragedy that was the Indian Removal Act, and carries a heavy, location-specific symbolism.[21] What are we to make of the story of this spirit of a white woman who has no idea a group of Indians actually saved her children's lives? How can this story be read? Is it significant that in a story in which Native Americans play an important role, the focus of the story is only on the distraught white woman?[22] (Surely there must be heartreading stories of Fox mothers and their missing children, but these have not been recorded.) There's already been a fair amount of analysis on the idea of ghostly encounters between Indigenous and settler communities, from discussions of the trope of the "Indian Burial Ground" to commentary on the presence of the spectral Native in American ghostly lore generally, but nothing specific to the ways it might connect to notions of motherhood.[23] For this, perhaps, we might look to Queen Esther.

Queen Esther was a half Iroquois, half French woman who lived during the days of the Revolutionary War in what is now western Pennsylvania. Her family, the Montours, were prevalent throughout the area, and in the part of upstate western New York near Ithaca. Esther served at times as an interpreter and a translator between the Six Nations and settler communities, and was once received by high society in Philadelphia. During the Revolutionary War Battle of Wyoming in 1778, she achieved notoriety by scalping seventeen soldiers in a rage of revenge-induced fury following the death of her only son in a previous battle. Some versions of the story hold that she was promptly lynched and executed, and that her ghost haunts the site of her death to this day. Other sources say she lived to a ripe old age by the shores of Seneca Lake. That she lived, and that she likely committed intensely bloody acts during the Battle of Wyoming, is a matter of fair certainty in the historic record.[24]

Queen Esther's ghost isn't very well known these days. Though as a folk figure she achieved some renown around the same time Rip Van Winkle and Hiawatha did—namely, in the first half of the nineteenth century—her story hasn't been as enduring. It's a shame, because she's a rare female folk figure who embodies so much about the experience of motherhood—the rage, the fierce love, and the shifting between these. Her intense love for her son is a grounding force in her story, and her "mama bear" reaction to his death makes her actions, if not forgivable, then immediately comprehensible. Meanwhile she embodies, in her mixed-race heritage, a unique position that demands further analysis; she is one of the few Indian mothers represented in American ghostlore, at least settler-centric ghostlore. Corn Mother, Cave Mother, First Woman, and myriad other mother figures are placed high in the diverse pantheons of Indigenous spirit stories throughout the continent; they are not ghosts per se—at least not in the way settler culture understands supernatural beings—but they are hugely important presences. Much more work remains to be done regarding the encounters of settlers and Indigenous spirit mothers, and the ways these stories inform each other.[25]

Perhaps unsurprisingly, most popular collections of ghost stories intended for wide audiences omit any mention of non-white spirit mothers. If ghost stories hold up mirrors to the societies in which they are told, then our predominance of ghostly white mothers is a reflection of larger societal tendencies. It takes a fiction writer to remedy this error, but a fiction writer who took her ghosts directly from history. Toni Morrison's *Beloved* is perhaps the last word in American ghost stories. And at its center is a mother.

Morrison's novel takes its central character from the true story of Margaret Garner, who escaped slavery in Kentucky and resettled in Ohio in 1856. When her family was apprehended under the Fugitive Slave Act, Garner murdered her own daughter rather than see her forced back into slavery. In the novel, Sethe, the mother based on Garner, is haunted by Beloved, the spirit of the daughter based on Garner's real-life child. According to sociologist Avery Gordon, Beloved is "one of the most significant contributions to the understanding of haunting."[26] While Garner's story is seldom spoken of as a ghost story, Morrison's adaptation is absolutely one: "the story is about a haunting, and about the crucial way in which it mediates between institution and person."[27] We often speak about understanding haunting as the specter of history, and *Beloved* reflects that: it is a ghost story in the sense that Beloved literally haunts Sethe; at its heart it is a haunting in that Sethe, along with the author, the reader, and everyone in this country, continues to be haunted by the specter of slavery itself. It is a specter we birthed.

THE EVERLASTING FAINT

The Ghostly Wives of West Virginia

ANDREA

THE CULTURAL AND ECONOMIC REGION OF APPALACHIA stretches like a long, broad ribbon through several states along the Eastern Seaboard, from northern Georgia, Alabama, and Mississippi in the South up through the western edge of the Carolinas and the eastern border of Kentucky, tucking in a little corner of Virginia, all of West Virginia—the only state contained entirely within Appalachia—and a generous swath of eastern Ohio and western Pennsylvania. It is a massive, mountainous slice of land, surprisingly heterogeneous, and far bigger than most people imagine. It is a region rife with decay and cliché, reviled by many as poor, ignorant, and backward, and romanticized by others as rugged, rural, and stuffed with the heritage of old-time Americana.

In part due to the remoteness of its mountains, Appalachia has a rich tradition of ghost stories woven into its folklore. Folklore is undeniably, for better or for worse, a staple export of Appalachia. Forbidding even today, as anyone who's ever driven on a winding mountain highway on a foggy night can understand, this landscape was almost otherworldly at the beginnings of European migration to the Americas. The forests were impenetrably thick, deep hollows and valleys were shrouded in nearly ever-present darkness, and ancient trees grew to forty-five feet in circumference. This incredible landscape was already acknowledged as a haunting one by the Indigenous people who dwelt there, and early Scotch-Irish settlers picked up at once on the strong spirit presence in the land, melding it immediately with their own beliefs and superstitions from back home. They carved out a life for themselves in this forbidding fairyland of hidden hollows (or hollers), and so it has remained even to this day, for almost no one is fonder of a weird tale than a West Virginian. (Just ask anyone at the Point Pleasant Mothman Festival!) Whether told in seriousness or jest, a good ghost story remains part of the legacy of Appalachia and a strong component of its folklore. Add to that the genuinely uncanny and sublime natural setting, with a little dash of fright for other, more material reasons (high poverty levels have made for some sadly burned-out towns; cell service is spotty, adding to the feeling of remoteness; and have we mentioned the roads?) and you've got a recipe for a seriously haunting region.

Much wonderful West Virginia ghostlore comes to us via the work of folklorist Ruth Ann Musick, who recorded these stories in her fieldwork and published them in *Tales from Coffin Hollow* and *The Telltale Lilac Bush*. Musick was a one-woman WPA Writers' Project, recording Appalachian ghostlore for posterity. And many of the stories she collected center around tales of wronged and murdered wives; *The Telltale Lilac Bush*, in fact, devotes an entire chapter to them. Some of these women are innocent, others not so much. Many submit quietly to their deaths, but others fight back with a vengeance from beyond the grave.

It's not surprising there are so many ghost stories in Appalachia, and the stories told there reflect the history, values, and demographics of the region. What was being a wife like in rural Appalachia, and how did that lend itself so strongly to the creation of these tales? If you were a young girl, you would begin your journey to the new world through a forbidding forest, and things grew more perilous from there:

> *Young girls who had first crossed into the region by foot with their parents would become brides of one of the few boys they had ever known. And naturally, not long after this, another generation of fearsome and rugged mountain people would be born [provided] they could make it past that most crucial hurdle of all, childbirth. Though there are no official counts, we know that the birthing process often resulted in tears of great sadness in the dank woods of yesteryear, leading a countless multitude of young women to early graves.*[1]

Marriage was pure drudgery, and that was a best-case scenario—if you were married to a violent man, you were in for a dangerous and dreary life. After the terrifying ordeal of childbirth, always shadowed by the specter of death, life was unremitting toil, leavened only by yearly church camp meetings. How desperately hard was the life of a mountain wife! No wonder she wanted to believe in life after death.

The specter of domestic and sexual violence loomed large in those old marriages, and at its most extreme end was the spousal murder that permeates the region's folklore. These fears are reflected in the stories of *The Telltale Lilac Bush*. Most ghost wives, writes author Ruth Ann Musick, "were in life mistreated, sometimes murdered, women, and their return is usually prompted by a desire to revenge themselves upon their former spouses." In the titular story, a nameless "old man and woman" lived in isolation near the Tygart River. It was known among their neighbors that they didn't get along, and nobody made any remarks when the wife disappeared.

The husband began living a "gay life" after her disappearance. One night as a group of friends gathered on his porch, talking of all his recent, wonderful parties, a nearby lilac bush began suddenly to stir, its branches beating on the windowpanes—strange, because there was no breeze. His friends dug up the bush and found its roots were growing from the palm of a skeletal hand. The old man "screamed and ran down the hill towards the river, never to be seen again."

Other ghost wives in the collection are similarly ill-used and disposed of and return to punish the perpetrators. Bill White's wife, whose first name is unknown, was used to his ill treatment. She was a hard worker and handled most of the labor on the farm alone; he was a shiftless wife beater. One summer it was said that Mrs. White "took a fever and died," and not long after, Bill White took another wife. Undoubtedly, they were lining up for this gem of a man. Not long after he remarried, strange things transpired around the farm. Two workers claimed to see the ghost of Mrs. White around a well, others heard her in the milking barn or heard the sounds of pots and pans rattling in the kitchen. One night, writes Musick, "as Bill was coming in from the fields and walking under the apple tree in the backyard, his dead wife seemed to come right up to him and say, 'Here Bill is where you knocked me down with a chair.'" After that the cows went dry, the new Mrs. White got sick, and eventually Bill sold out and moved away. Mrs. White's ghost was never heard from again, having presumably finished her business on the farm.

A similar story tells the tale of brutal Sam Walton, who kept his young, timid wife, Emily, "a bride of three summers," in a state of perpetual terror until he finally slit her throat after she found him lolling in the tall summer grass with the neighbor girl, Hilda. He buried her next to a spring-fed pool, but was driven nearly to madness by the continued presence of her ghost patiently going about her daily domestic duties in the kitchen. Within a year the spring ran dry and Emily's body was found. Sam made a hysterical full confession and died in a mental institution. Unlike the ghost of Mrs. White, Emily continued to quietly and meekly perform her wifely tasks, taking care not to scare the cows or rattle the pots and pans—perhaps the difference between a young bride who still thinks she can please her irredeemable husband and an old woman who knows better.

In one tale, "The Face on the Wall," a wife does manage to successfully redeem her husband. Nick Yelchick, an alcoholic miner, got lost in the labyrinthine warrens of mining tunnels one day as he was about to leave work. He was new to the job, having only worked there for five days. Prior to that, he'd been unemployed for a long time, and had spent most of his time getting drunk and beating his long-suffering wife. On this particular day—a Friday—he'd asked his buddy to punch out for him so he could cut out early to go to the liquor store. Upon finding himself lost, he began to panic. Completely disoriented in the pitch-black tunnels for over ten hours, he'd just about given up hope—until he saw the face of his wife hovering on the walls. "Follow me," she said; "come this way." He found his way out after about two hours, and was told that his wife had been here the night before, looking for him. He rushed home gratefully only to find his wife had hanged herself and written a suicide note: "I thought you would stop drinking when you got this job, but now I know different." According to Musick, Nick became a model citizen of Grant Town after that, and never drank a drop again.

There is a type of woman in Appalachia known as a Granny Woman. If you were hardy enough to survive marriage and childbirth, and lucky enough to see all your own children raised up and become parents themselves, then you were venerated as an almost otherworldly being. Not only were you durable, you were considered wise too. Granny Women were part midwife, part herbalist, and all-around wise women. Almost witchlike in their knowledge of healing herbs and birthing practices, these women were venerated for their knowledge, strength, and wisdom, and consulted on all types of personal matters, from love affairs to childbirth and -rearing, to housework, farming, and general life advice.* Granny Women were a tough bunch, and they pulled no punches when it came to what they thought of the old-time Appalachian marriage. Taking a rather "dim view" of the institution, according to *Appalachian Magazine*, their advice to young women more often than not was, "Don't you never get married."

That marriage could be dismal, brutal work is never more evident than in country music, from Loretta Lynn's "Coal Miner's Daughter," which features a mother scrubbing on a washboard until her fingers bleed, to the plaintive "Single Girl/Married Girl" by the Carter Family, which contrasts the carefree life of a single girl spending her own income on pretty, store-bought clothes with the dreary, routine-bound anguish of the young mother tearfully rocking her baby in the cradle.

Even in our modern, much more equitable versions of marriage, most heterosexual couples continue to divide domestic labor unfairly, whether consciously or not. Women still do far more housework and child-rearing than men, even when both partners have full-time employment. And to imagine how an old-time Appalachian wife would have dealt with issues such as postpartum depression actually makes one shudder. One can't help but nod and agree with the Granny Women.

The brutal lives of country wives are expressed in these ghost stories in their most extreme form. Silenced and resigned to grueling labor at best and regular beatings and forced pregnancies at worst, a woman might be better off as a ghost. At least then she could get a little revenge, like the wife in the story "Uncle Tom Howe," who died when her husband was too busy farming to go for a doctor when

* This is one of the few, remarkable instances of women more or less openly practicing what would, in another place or time, have them condemned as witches. Witches were an accepted part of life in rural Appalachia, and there were plenty of resources for those who should encounter a malevolent one.

she was sick; after she died her spirit persisted in playing the family piano night after night until it drove her husband insane. "Good for you," one imagines the Granny Women cackling.*

But perhaps the most famous spectral wife in West Virginia lore is Zona Shue, the Greenbrier Ghost. In the southeast corner of the state lies the small town of Greenbrier, and it was there in 1897 that the ghost of Elva Zona Heaster Shue, known as Zona, came back from beyond the grave to solve her own murder.

Zona was in her late teens when she met "Trout" Shue. Trout wasn't from around Greenbrier; he claimed to be a blacksmith and showed up in town taking odd jobs and sweeping Zona off her feet. Like many charismatic first dates, he quickly turned sour. Less than three months into their hasty marriage, Zona had already discovered his dark side. Trout was a drinker, a wife-beater, a liar, and a poor provider. One night, it is said, Trout flew into a rage when Zona didn't serve meat at dinner. Not long after that, a chore boy came by the house and discovered Zona lying motionless at the foot of the stairs.

A bad fall, Trout said. Or maybe "woman troubles." Zona was being treated for "woman troubles" by the local doctor, and had presumably been trying to get pregnant. Because who wouldn't want a mini Trout around the house for company? The local doctor tried to assess the cause of death but was stymied at every turn by the hysterical Trout, who refused to even let the physician near his deceased wife's body. Trout had arrived on the scene well before the doctor and had already dressed and bathed the body. An oddly loving and

* Not all the wives in *The Telltale Lilac Bush* are long-suffering and virtuous. Sarah Garlow, who married the dull-as-dishwater Ezra Gordon, got her rocks off by sneaking out of her staid, boring husband's house at night and partying in the boomtown near their home. Ezra reported to the neighbors one day that Sarah had run off with an oil salesman, and he sold the house to his neighbors, a couple named Joe and Mary Blake. The Blakes were awakened their first night in the new house by the sounds of a chain dragging across the floor. Night after night the clanking continued; and one morning, following a heavy rainstorm, the couple found a depression in the grass near the house. They began to dig and soon unearthed Sarah's body, with its skull bashed in and a chain around the legs with which her husband "had tried to keep her at home." Clearly he had a knack for the fine art of subtle symbolism.

attentive act for such a lout of a husband. What's more, Trout had dressed her in a high-necked gown with a big, billowing scarf around her neck, claiming it was her favorite item of clothing. He lovingly cradled her head, sobbing constantly, and eventually the doctor gave up and simply attributed the death to woman troubles and somewhat poetically listed the cause of death as "everlasting faint."

At the funeral, Trout continued to guard Zona's body jealously, never letting anyone near it. He had propped the head up on pillows, as though to make his dead bride more comfortable, and he hovered near the head of the casket throughout the service and burial.

Meanwhile, Zona's mother was beginning to smell a rat . . . or a trout, as the case may be. A few weeks after the burial, she claimed to have seen the ghost of her daughter in a dream. Zona came to her and announced dramatically, "I have been murdered!" Zona's mother immediately requested that the body be exhumed and reexamined, and presumably it was a slow day at the coroner's office because her request was fairly swiftly granted. Sure enough, numerous fingerprints were discovered around the neck, and several vertebrae were broken. The country doctor looked a bit of a fool and quickly amended his report.

Before long, Trout was arrested and awaiting trial for murder. He kept muttering in jail, "They can't prove I did it," showing once again he wasn't exactly a subtle criminal mastermind. The prosecution did indeed use these incriminating ramblings against him in court, and when he took the stand he continued to ramble and rant, showing himself in a poor light indeed. The prosecution revealed that Trout had had two previous wives before Zona, each dying in suspicious circumstances. Things were looking bad for this Appalachian Bluebeard. In an attempt to discredit Zona's mother, the defense asked her about her ghost story when she took the stand. She firmly and calmly stuck to her story.

With less than an hour's deliberation, and with decidedly circumstantial evidence, the jury pronounced Trout guilty.

Now, every teller of this tale is quick to point out a few key things. The jury did not take the ghost story into account in their deliberation. They weighed the circumstantial evidence and went on that. Therefore, the ghost didn't technically solve her own murder. But it makes a good story, doesn't it? And that's what's printed on the historic plaque in Greenbrier, and that's what's written on Zona's gravestone. The story survives today in numerous forms, from print to oral retellings on ghost tours to movies and TV shows (a *Drunk History* episode gives an enjoyable version). Zona is a bit of a folk hero, and so is her plucky mother, who refused to let that no-good Trout get away with the murder of her daughter.

The other thing everybody points out when they tell this story is that Zona's ghost probably never did appear to her mother at all. Zona's obituary was printed in the Greenbrier newspapers next to a story about an Australian murder that had recently been solved with supernatural aid. It's likely Zona's mother saw the article and was inspired. Most storytellers note the irony that a mother's intuition likely wouldn't have resulted in the same quick action as a ginned-up ghost story, and some even go so far as to wonder whether Trout had a fair trial. Was he an innocent man too hastily tried and convicted? That seems a bit of a stretch, but it's worth pointing out the ironies about the ghost of a dead woman having more power than a living one. Zona's mom certainly realized it, and was pretty clever for using Appalachian superstition to her own ends.

Thus do the women of West Virginia use and interact with their ghosts and ghost stories in powerful and subtle ways. They have taken up the voice of the ghost and used it to create agency where their own was missing, and they have recorded these stories to remind us that the power to speak was and is still there.

IN 1970 A LOCAL RESTAURATEUR NAMED SHIRLEY DOUGHERTY founded West Virginia's original ghost tour company, Harpers Ferry Ghost Tours. She conducted ghost tours for over twenty years; was featured in the *Washington Post* in 1980; and published a book, *A Ghostly Tour of Harpers Ferry*, in 1993. By the time she passed away in 2011 at the age of eighty-three, she was a local celebrity. Shirley would enthrall her customers with her lively, suspenseful oral retellings of the town's ghostly tales and haunted legends, regaling them in true Appalachian style. Those willing to go along with a few tall tales, like the legend of Screaming Jenny—a poor young woman who lived in a shack by the railroad, who ran screaming onto the tracks one night after her dress burst into flames when she drew too close to the fire—would be richly rewarded with a couple of genuine shivers. Photos of Dougherty leading her tours reveal a grandmotherly looking woman, bespectacled and wearing a long-sleeved, high-necked dress, her white hair knotted in a bun atop her head. The look on her face reveals both a twinkle in her eye and a sternness around the mouth, as if defying you to disbelieve her. There's a touch of the Granny Woman to her: older, wiser, and a force to be reckoned with.

Dougherty is in many ways the antithesis of Ruth Ann Musick. Whereas Musick was an academic and a career writer, Dougherty worked in the restaurant business and came late in life to professional ghost story telling. Musick gathered her folk tales as part of academic fieldwork, while Dougherty gathered her ghostlore from a lifetime of experience. Musick has a library named after her; Dougherty has only a sidebar on the home page of the Ghost Tours of Harpers Ferry website.

Yet there is a connection between the type of preservation work Dougherty did and the fieldwork of Musick. The two women are the keepers of these stories. While the better-known stories such as Zona Shue's have passed into national fame, some of the smaller local tales may have faded away without them. They are the Granny Women of ghosts, those who keep old tradition and knowledge alive for the next generation.

THE LADY OF THE HOUSE

Eliza Jumel

LEANNA

NEW YORK, NEW YORK

SHE'S ALWAYS THERE, WAITING. KEEPING A WATCHFUL EYE from one of the highest points on Manhattan Island.

The colonial-style Morris-Jumel Mansion has seen some of New York's most vibrant and potent histories, from the battles of the Revolutionary War to the dynamic and creative treasures birthed during the Harlem Renaissance. For all that the mansion has survived through the centuries, its longest-term resident seems committed to remaining a present force of nature.

A Rhode Island native born Betsy Bowen in 1775, beset by poverty and dubious circumstances, in her afterlife, Eliza Jumel reigns like the titled lady she yearned to be. Her presence lingers on as if she's never for a moment stopped living in Manhattan's oldest house, or was ever anything but New York's wealthiest woman.

Eliza moved into the mansion in the early nineteenth century, but it had a storied history before her arrival.

Completed as a summer home in 1765 for Colonel Morris of the British Army and his family, the view from "Mount Morris" was unparalleled, the whole of New York Harbor within its scope and one could see all the way to Connecticut.

In 1776, at the outbreak of the Revolutionary War, the Morris family abandoned their summer home. By autumn of that year, General Washington took over the mansion as his outpost. From that great vista, he watched as parts of Manhattan burned during the British invasion. The mansion's vantage point allowed for Washington's first successful victory in the Battle of Harlem Heights, though his army was forced to retreat on October 21. The house then headquartered both British and Hessian armies. After the war ended, the house, surviving it all, was seized by forfeiture law and was sold to cover war debts. For a time, the mansion was an unsuccessful tavern, until it was finally purchased by Stephen and Eliza Jumel, and they began several alterations on the house beginning in 1810.

In several books, I found versions of Eliza's early life containing wildly diverging details, from her being born on the high seas to her being born in a brothel. It seems the judgments levied against her in various accounts have simply parroted nineteenth-century high-society disdain without questioning or unpacking the inherent classism that viciously sought to keep her at heel.

In at least one account of her background in a collection of New York ghost stories, she was branded a prostitute with no mention of her theatrical career, a troubling but common conflation. Actors struggled throughout the nineteenth and early twentieth century for legitimacy and respect as artists. It's sometimes still an uphill battle my own theatrical career can attest to.

A wealthy French wine merchant, Stephen Jumel noticed Eliza Bowen on a New York stage and the two began a relationship. Self-educated and a voracious reader, Eliza charmed Stephen enough to demand he "make an honest woman out of her." Some accounts suggest a theatrical deathbed marriage and her dramatic, miraculous "recovery" soon after. The high New York society the self-taught Eliza yearned to be accepted by never let her forget her humble background and cast whispered aspersions at her at every turn.

After her marriage to Stephen Jumel, having taught herself French, she and her husband spent time in his native country, where she charmed the more amenable aristocracy, even Emperor Napoleon himself, and spent a fortune on lavish gowns and parties. Several gifts of exquisite furniture in her home she attributed to Napoleon. Fond correspondences with French aristocrats do still exist as a testament to Eliza's zealous efforts at living a grander life than she'd been born into.

Even ghost books that are ostensibly nonfiction do not seem immune from abject sensationalism when discussing Eliza. Several make pointed judgments about her character, painting her as haughty and unhinged, a quality that doesn't match the confirmed details of her successful and shrewd real estate ventures at a time when few women dared such a thing.

When Stephen Jumel's business began failing, Eliza used her acumen with books and numbers to make real estate investments, utilizing rental locations and turning over properties, efforts that were immensely successful at a time when women simply were not, as a societal rule, making such bold transactions. While her husband remained in France and she had returned to New York, she shifted finances into her name and thus shielded herself from his creditors—though many of the bills were of her making. This may seem somewhat mercenary, but there wasn't much a woman could do to protect herself materially or financially, and she refused to return to destitution.

Stephen Jumel eventually returned from France, but his luck

did not improve back in New York. He died from complications and injuries resulting from a carriage accident in 1832. (Some accounts claim his death was a haying accident, pitchfork and all.)

Hans Holzer, along with eminent medium Ethel Myers, driving forces behind myriad books on ghosts featuring séances held around the United States, are responsible for heightening suspicion about Stephen Jumel's death. Holzer and Myers insisted during two separate séances held at the mansion in the mid-twentieth century that Stephen Jumel's spirit came through in a trance and named Eliza as the cause of his death, claiming she had removed his bandages so he bled out. "Understandably, Jumel's spirit was furious at a murder that went not only unpunished but also rewarded. For now Eliza was probably the wealthiest woman in the city and again, at liberty."[1]

In another account that treats Eliza rather viciously, the same medium claimed Stephen's spirit went so far as to declare he'd been buried alive.

We know from Jan Bryant Bartell's displeasure at Holzer's accounting of her own haunted house, covered later in this book, that he may have had a tendency to embellish the results of a séance for personal effect, and historic details were often discarded if they didn't fit the narrative.

Many who have written about Eliza seem to fall prey to the same—sometimes drastic—assumptions, disregard, and rumor-mongering that New York's elite did during her lifetime, passing off accusation as fact and her resourcefulness as a vice. Strong-willed, confident women, especially if they tried to cast off their class or other constraints, were often labeled unlikable, suspect, or worse. Eliza certainly had a mind of her own, and she, above all, was a survivalist. Then and now. A life that began as hardscrabble as hers never allowed her to unclench her hands; the trauma of poverty is its own specter no matter how one's fortunes might change.

Eliza must have felt another marriage might afford her the societal acceptance that continually eluded her, and might shield her from further criticism. Perhaps a strategic alliance was in order.

About a year after Jumel's death, Eliza married Aaron Burr, who was more famous for killing Alexander Hamilton than he was for being a statesman. She thought her stature might finally be permanently elevated by becoming the wife of a former vice president, while he only thought about her money. Even though the duel ending in Hamilton's death had been thirty years prior, the shadow of it dogged him and remained the demon he could not exorcise.

They were an ill-suited pair. Burr didn't account for Eliza's keen grasp on *her* money, a fortune she was unwilling to let him squander. Accusing him of infidelity, she was granted a divorce, and the paperwork was finalized the day Burr died in rented rooms on Staten Island. She would live in the house she carefully and diligently never relinquished from her name until her death in 1865, aged ninety. In 1904, the City of New York purchased the house from descendants of the original Morris family, and the grand mansion became the museum it remains today.

The one thing every account regarding Eliza Jumel seems to agree upon is an event about a century after her death.

In 1964, a group of students from a nearby public school came to tour the mansion. They were frolicking loudly on the grounds outside before their tour when a gray-haired woman in a long dress came out on the mansion's upstairs balcony to sternly tell them to keep quiet. After her declaration, she swept back into the house. The chastened children asked about the woman when the museum curator finally opened up the house to the school. Baffled, the guide said there wasn't anyone in the house ahead of them. When the children who had been shushed saw the portrait of Eliza Jumel, they screamed that *she'd* been the one who'd admonished them.

The lady does like order in her home.

Eliza isn't the only ghost said to haunt the grounds, though she is the most commonly noted by visitors and staff.

A Revolutionary War–era Hessian soldier who died by falling on his own bayonet on the staircase is said to reenact his tragic death. Teachers have separately seen Revolutionary soldiers on the top floor. Aaron Burr's bedroom remains a repository of paranormal activity.

When the Travel Channel sent a small crew to the mansion to film a spot for their website years ago, I assisted the team by sharing historic details about New York and the house on camera. Vincent Carbone—mansion program director at the time, and leader of many paranormal investigations there—set out an electromagnetic field meter, a device meant to register electromagnetic energy, often thought to be an indicator of spectral activity. Upon entering Aaron Burr's bedroom, nearing his bed and chair, the meter began pinging wildly into the red, the maximum level of the device. Perhaps his and Eliza's tempestuous marriage left a bit of a psychic imprint. The reunion of Aaron and Eliza's portraits in the downstairs parlor kicked up additional paranormal unrest in recent years.

Years ago, I joined a dear friend for an overnight paranormal investigation at the mansion. I was game to attend, especially considering the overnights have been a significant source of funding for the ongoing maintenance and caretaking of the property.

The most memorable moments of the night fell near the witching hour, when the attendees sat on the floor in Eliza's chamber—a room that holds an eerie abundance of mirrors—and asked questions aimed at the lady of the house. A simple flashlight was set in the center of our seated circle, the lid unscrewed so the top only barely rested against the batteries and remained off. We posted questions to the room, the theory being that if a spirit in the house answered, it would cause the flashlight to flicker. The rules had been established: two flickers for yes, one flicker for no.

The investigation team wasn't having any luck with bold questions. The flashlight remained dark. Only when a fellow author and I pointed out that it was improper, from Eliza's perspective, to have mixed company in her rooms and strange men in her private chamber, did the flashlight flicker a definitive "yes," as if to prove the point. The men left and the women remained to ask questions, presumably of Eliza. Did she enjoy having company in her house, provided they were polite about it? The flashlight flickered a "yes." Forever entertaining in her fine home, a flicker of a bulb registered an affirmation. Even if she'd had to fight her whole life to be accepted as respectable, we'd come calling upon her as if she were a noblewoman. She deigned to answer us.

Much like the way the Winchester Mystery House guides have become fond and a bit protective of Sarah Winchester and her maligned reputation through the years, so has the Morris-Jumel Mansion's staff grown fond and protective of Eliza, and I think that energy made a real impression on me during my many visits.

I took part in *The Morris-Jumel Mansion Anthology of Fantasy and Paranormal Fiction*, a book that was published to benefit the mansion. My "Tea with the Lady" story opens the collection with a quiet little ode to visiting Eliza's ghost, her greeting manifesting in a flicker of lights and a cold chill. Yes, the anthology is fiction, but my offering has some truth to it. The lights have indeed flickered when I've said a quiet "Hello" at the threshold of the parlor, a room that holds a weight of spectral resonance.

I chose the mansion as the site for many of my book launch parties and receptions, where I'd always offer a theatrical reading from the front doors to the crowd on the lawn. The mansion's great porch, bordered by grand, two-story columns, makes for a lovely stage. Eliza seemed happy to share it with me, hearkening back to her own time near the footlights. Every time I've done readings, my left side has grown preternaturally cold in an isolation of drastic temperature, hairs raised in typical phantasmagorical frost. Friends who have sensitivities to spirits, before being told about the plummeting temperature difference I continually felt, noted a presence was with me, to my left: the lady of the house not missing an opportunity to be part of the show. One can never take the acting out of the actor, alive or dead.

I went back to *The Morris-Jumel Mansion Anthology of Fantasy and Paranormal Fiction* to glance through the reimagined tales of history and paranormal happenstance, and I'd forgotten that Andrea's own short story, "How Eliza Becomes a Ghost," fittingly follows mine. We wrote those tales *years* before we came together for this book. Andrea weaves real history into poetic speculation and, in a manner befitting Poe, Eliza throws an eternal soirée as parts of her disassembling body take up residence in various places in the house for all time.

I realize it might be ironic, or perhaps hypocritical, to discuss fictional stories in what we've noted as a true accounting, but my spectral experiences in that house have been my lived truth, and Andrea's fiction is an extrapolation from well-researched and proven historical events. We both work with an inherent respect for the subject and the site, and the truth is, the Morris-Jumel Mansion is a place where imagination runs wild and the past is extremely present. Eliza is felt and discussed by staff and visitors as though she's still alive, and certainly within earshot. Mansion guides mention other overnight examples of small motion-sensor lights set out during investigations going off one by one, flashing up each stair when no one *living* is on them.

As Andrea says in her story, "Nobody ever thinks it is Washington moving around up there in the empty rooms. He never loved those rooms. They never belonged to him."[2]

During one of the ongoing restoration projects within the house aimed to restore the entire mansion to Eliza's mid-nineteenth-century heyday, correspondence has been discovered that pinpointed a specific, beautiful French wallpaper, sky blue with bold, fluffy clouds. The bright day of a room is now exactly as Eliza had wanted it. Her wish to paper her home with the sky was honored, making the ballroom a liminal threshold; the distinction between air and wall becomes a trick of the eye as you are bid to examine the heavens as structure gives way to open space and endless possibility. Eliza is there waiting, a whisper among the clouds.

If you listen hard, she might come and murmur to you in the middle of the night. You might know her by a flicker of light and a passing shadow. But if you want her spectral company, you have to be polite and treat her as she always yearned to be treated. Defer to the lady of the house. There's no avoiding her.

Photo courtesy of Keith Corrigan, Alamy

PART 4

Bad Girls, Jezebels, and Killer Women

INTRODUCTION

ANDREA

One of the weirdest by-products of centuries of sexism in the English-speaking world is the expectation that girls are supposed to be "nice." I remember as a child wondering what flavor of spice I was, because when I heard the rhyme about "sugar and spice and everything nice," I knew at least two out of those three things didn't describe the way I felt about myself at all. Girls in nineteenth-century America—whence most of our ghost stories come—were uniformly expected to be good. Women were the moral guardians of men's souls: gentler, more pious, all that nonsense. Unless, of course, a woman was a Jezebel. A daughter of Eve. Virgin or whore, pick a side and stay there. It's the oldest story in the book, a trope so shopworn it's actually difficult to write about.

The instinct to rebel against this ridiculous dichotomy is so strong that many people have become deeply desirous of celebrating bad girls simply because they're refreshing. They slap, they clap back, they yell, they take up space. They won't sit down; they won't be told what to do. They embolden and provide gleeful, subversive delight. They cut through the treacle and add the spice. This section of the book might be the one a lot of people turn to first, looking for ladies with swagger, ones who drink and swear and fuck, maybe even smoke cigars. The whores and madams, the mistresses and Jezebels, the killers, the lawbreakers, the defiers of convention and the destroyers of conformity are often considered the *fun* ghosts.

But it should come as no surprise that nine times out of ten, these women were punished for daring to break with "acceptable" modes of behavior. Many of these stories have sad endings and lack uncomplicated resolutions. And without a willful gloss over reality, it's difficult to uncritically "celebrate" a lot of these bad girls.

So what is the benefit of using the trope of the "bad girl" to frame these stories? Well, let's start with the "Jezebels," the ones who defied prudish Victorian sexual mores; they usually had predictably tragic ends. By reexamining the tropes of the "fallen woman" and the "whore with the heart of gold," for example, we can try to open up new ways of framing these stories. Naturally, as usually happens any time you try this sort of thing, you end up with more questions than answers. But acknowledging the fact that these women are complicated and not two-dimensional stereotypes, you're at least beginning a more productive conversation.

Obviously, moral standards have changed greatly in the last 150 years, but one constant remains: sex work is a hotly contested topic, a flash point for all sorts of feelings and opinions from every possible camp. The representation of sex workers in American ghostlore is deeply complicated, reflecting a host of continued insecurities and fears about vice and order, agency and exploitation. Deepening this discussion is the matter of race, which layers other anxieties atop it, the specter of racism being one that continues to haunt this country.

As service workers in the tourism sector, the authors of this book also participate in an industry that often portrays these stories in highly problematic, sometimes exploitive ways. Ghost tours are reductive by nature; you cannot give a dissertation about the intersections of race, gender, sex work, and the spectral in the five or ten minutes allotted for a ghost story, which is pretty much the maximum time deemed acceptable by industry standards and guest expectations. Yet ghost tours provide a potentially wonderful opportunity for street-level history, and ghost tours that focus on forgotten, maligned, or problematic women offer an even better opportunity to discuss difficult subjects in an accessible way. Ultimately, a guide must acknowledge that none of these stories are easy to resolve, that they are only jumping-off points for further reflection and reexamination of the old tropes that have been handed down to us for far too long.

Perhaps our proximity to the ghost tour industry is what inspired us to look at the stories of spectral sex workers in more detail. A number of frontier narratives came to the surface when we started researching these stories, many of them stops on local ghost tours, and the iconic "Old West" prostitute seemed begging to be written about. Her portrayal in ghostlore defied easy answers, and we invite you to decide for yourself what significance you think she has in our history and folklore. We examine this iconic trope in our chapter on the "Soiled Doves of the American Frontier."

We've chosen two more bad girl narratives to examine in further detail in this book. When considering which stories to tell, we've selected the ones that are the most substantive, iconic, and prevalent in ghostlore, and the ones that speak to us the most.

No book of spectral bad girls would be complete without Lizzie Borden, infamous alleged committer of parricide whose former home is now ranked among one of the country's most haunted sites. On a personal level, her story is fascinating because of its unsolved nature and the profound mystery that surrounds Lizzie as a person; writing about her was irresistible.

We turned to Washington, DC, to find a really "nasty" woman. No, not that one: We're talking about Mary Surratt, John Wilkes Booth's copilot in the assassination of Abraham Lincoln. A Southern secessionist and pro-slavery sympathizer, and the first woman in American history to be executed by the federal government, Mary Surratt isn't a lovable figure, yet many representations of her ghost story portray her as an innocent woman. We were curious to examine why, and look more closely at what makes her ghost story in particular worth discussing in more detail. As usual, each answer led to new questions.

Because this book must have some boundaries, we weren't able to fit a myriad of other stories that were also compelling, but they're worthy of (dis)honorable mention.

Lavinia Fisher, for example, is known as "America's First Serial Killer," and her spirit allegedly haunts the Old Charleston Jail. Her story is a mix of fact and fiction, myth and history. According to legend, she and her husband John Fisher murdered scores of men while running the Six Mile Inn just outside Charleston, South Carolina. Lavinia apparently loved to serve male travelers poisoned cups of oleander tea while she surmised whether they had enough money to make them worth robbing. The Fishers were arrested after they tried but failed to murder a man named John Peeples, who escaped their clutches and promptly ratted them out. Both John and Lavinia were sentenced to death; John went meekly to the gallows, quietly praying as he accepted his fate. Lavinia, on the other hand, went kicking and screaming all the way and met her fate clad in her bedraggled wedding dress. Lavinia's last words are iconic: "If you have a message you want to send to Hell, give it to me; I'll carry it."

Her tempestuous and unrepentant ghost can still be seen in the old jailhouse if ghost tour guides are to be believed. Most historians agree that the Fishers were not executed for murder, but rather for highway robbery, and that "only a few" bodies were discovered buried beneath their inn.[1] Some go so far as to say that the entire story is poppycock from stem to stern. Either way, her story shows just how much Americans love the idea of a serial killing lady, particularly one who gives zero fucks and who subverts the whole ghost-bride-in-a-wedding-dress trope. Tellingly, her ironic nickname is "Lovely Lavinia."

As Clare McBride writes on Syfy.com, Lavinia's true story is vague enough that we can layer whatever we want over her: "The few details available about Lavinia herself, combined with her shocking final words to the crowd, proved to be an irresistible combination of unknown and lurid. [Ultimately] those Charleston ghost tour guides are right. Lovely Lavinia is a ghost—because she was never truly real to begin with."[2]

According to Bruce Orr, who wrote the definitive biography of Lavinia Fisher, *Six Miles to Charleston*, the myth originates with a Scottish writer named Peter Nielson, who wrote a "penny dreadful" style retelling of the execution in an 1830 memoir, *Six Years' Residence in America*. Neilson larded his book with sex and scandal to (surprise!) sell more copies. He created the "serial killer" myth, adding details like the oleander tea, the bodies in the basement, and the wedding dress at the gallows. Orr, a retired police detective, told the *Charleston City Paper* that 98 percent of the stories about John and Lavinia Fisher are untrue. "For 191 years, John and Lavinia Fisher have been a legend. Stories have been told about them and probably about 98 percent of them aren't true. If they had that trial today, there's no way they would be convicted."[3]

And the dozens of ghost-hunter TV shows that swear the jail is haunted? Or even the first-person accounts of something that felt a little "off" about the location? It's possible they're not entirely wrong, even if their facts are off. Who knows what other unquiet souls may rest there? And even if it is Lavinia, maybe she just wants someone to set the record straight.

If you're disappointed Lovely Lavinia maybe wasn't as bloodthirsty as advertised, perhaps Madame LaLaurie will satisfy you. A notorious murderer whose house is a mainstay of New Orleans ghost tours, Delphine LaLaurie was nothing short of a monster. Her crimes hardly need repetition here because she is so famous, but if you don't recognize the name, the story is basically this: Delphine LaLaurie was a wealthy, insane, beautiful Creole woman who tortured the enslaved people in her household in the French Quarter in the 1830s. She was caught when a woman she had chained to a stove set the house on fire in a desperate plea to draw attention to their suffering. When firefighters arrived, they found starving, dehydrated, mutilated enslaved persons in chains in LaLaurie's attic. An outraged mob stormed the house because she had overstepped the bounds of "decent" slaveholders. Unpunished, LaLaurie fled to Paris.

She sounds like the kind of person you wouldn't want to give free real estate in your mind, yet the constant thirst for the gory details of her story keeps the tours, TV shows, books, and movies grinding along. She is extremely well known: Nicholas Cage famously bought her house, she was featured on a season of *American Horror Story*, and she's a staple of virtually every New Orleans ghost tour. LaLaurie is popularly portrayed as such an aberration that she allows tourists to unleash their bloodlust in a socially acceptable space, while also distancing themselves—and other Louisianans—from this supposedly sociopathic outlier. In fact, historians have pointed out that, according to primary sources, while LaLaurie may have been more overtly sadistic and cruel than some other slave-owning women, in reality it was common for white women to physically abuse their bondspeople.[4] By presenting LaLaurie as an anomaly, the (mostly) white audiences on New Orleans ghost tours participate in the exploitation of Black pain for entertainment and profit, without reckoning with any of the realities of the legacy of slavery. Our advice for anyone wishing to satisfy their curiosity about Madame LaLaurie is to be mindful of their approach, and their sources, when reading about her or taking a tour that includes her story. We get into more detail about the intersection of race, gender, and ghost tourism in our chapter on the Sorrel-Weed House of Savannah, but as for Madame LaLaurie, we will leave her here. Harvard historian Tiya Miles has written the definitive book on the subject; if you are interested in learning about Madame LaLaurie in greater depth, we recommend you pick up a copy of Miles's *Tales from the Haunted South* for the most nuanced, thoughtful discussion of her story we have found to date.

LaLaurie is definitely at the extreme end of the bad girls spectrum and, quite honestly, someone we'd rather not spend much time with. If we're down in New Orleans, we'd rather spend that time getting to know Josie Arlington and her unforgettable "Flaming Tomb."

Josie Arlington was the madam of a celebrated brothel at the turn of the last century. She was wealthy enough to purchase an expensive cemetery plot in the respectable Metairie Cemetery. When she died in 1914, people hated the idea of a former prostitute resting in peace next to "worthier" members of society, and her remains were removed to an undisclosed location within the cemetery. By a strange coincidence, a red light shone on her former mausoleum, illuminating it so that it looked like it was on fire. The symbolic color red seemed just a little too on-the-nose, though, and the light was eventually removed. People still visit her abandoned tomb in the cemetery, though the mystery of her actual remains' location remains unsolved.

Less well-documented but no less fascinating than Arlington is Julie, the so-called octoroon mistress. She was a classic case of a woman punished for stepping outside societal bounds, but in reality, the boundaries presented to her were impossible to live within. In the 1850s in New Orleans, octoroons—women who were one-eighth Black—were usually groomed to become the mistresses of wealthy white men; their social status forbade them from actual marriage, so they were expected to be contented with being "kept women."

But Julie was in love with the Frenchman who kept her as his mistress, and repeatedly begged him to marry her. One night, growing tired of her repeated requests, he jokingly told her that he would marry her if she stripped naked and waited for him on the roof. He then promptly forgot all about it and went off to play a long game of cards downstairs. Meanwhile, Julie took it literally. She disrobed and waited for him on the roof. It was a cold, rainy December night, and by the time he came upstairs to bed, she had frozen to death.

Her ghost is said to haunt the house at 734 Royal Street to this day. Her story combines elements of the "fallen woman" and the "tragic mulatto" tropes, and continues to exert a haunting power.[5] The tragic mulatto trope originated in the antebellum literature of Lydia Maria Child and William Wells Brown. Child's novels, *The Quadroons* (1842) and *Slavery's Pleasant Homes* (1843), and Brown's *Clotel* (1853) introduced the idea of a mixed-race young woman whose heritage leads to her downfall.[6] In cinema, the most famous tragic mulatto is Sarah Jane in director Douglas Sirk's *Imitation of Life* (1959), who was famously described as "born to hurt." The idea that a mixed-race young woman was born to be hurt pervades the story of Julie the octoroon mistress, who goes passively to a death defined by unrequited love and sacrifice. Her status as a mistress also keeps her firmly within the bounds of the fallen woman trope, whereby her participation in a world of tacitly immoral behavior—sex outside of marriage—sets her up for a punishment that needs no justification in the eyes of Victorian moralizers. What's really interesting about Julie's story, though, is that even if she is technically inscribed within those tropes, she breaks out of those boundaries by virtue of being universally human: The romance and pathos of her story depends on the fundamental fact that almost everyone, if they have ever dared to love at all, has been hurt. It's hard to hear or read Julie's story and not identify with it on some level: Who among us *hasn't* misread a signal from a romantic partner? While Julie's story obviously takes this to an extreme, there is something powerfully universal in it, and although she would by virtue of her status as a mistress be considered a bad girl, to most readers she is sympathetic and relatable.

Her ghost is considered innocuous, friendly, even a wish-granting spirit of sorts, a patron saint of the lovelorn (some say you can leave her a note and she will grant your wish).[7] She has been described as the most popular ghost in New Orleans. Society at the time may have deemed her bad, but we have a great deal of affection for her. Julie's ghost story is the type that makes ghost tour guides like us feel as though we are doing a service of sorts; however she may have been mistreated and underestimated by the society of her day, Julie is remembered fondly by us now. We love her because she dared to love sincerely; it is fulfilling to think that on some level, if only in the afterlife, she is loved in return. Call us romantics if you will.

We'll leave you with one more potential bad girl to think about. In the 1920s, the sassiest Prohibition-era bad girl was the flapper. She was sexy, saucy, and cheeky; her spirits were as high as her hemlines. She drank, danced, and smoked, consequences be damned. Sometimes she worked as an actress or a showgirl. The flapper seems an innocent sort of bad girl to us, but at the time she was considered quite risqué. Americans' discomfort with this new, liberated sort of woman is reflected in the fact that the flapper/showgirl is second only to the prostitute in the frequency of her appearance in our nation's ghostlore (followed closely by ghost brides, mothers, and madwomen, who all have their own sections in this book). Seriously, try taking a ghost tour in any major American city without encountering at least one Prohibition-era showgirl floating through a former speakeasy. It can't be done.

One famous flapper ghost is Olive Thomas, whose glamorous lifestyle was made macabre by her unsettling death. Olive was a beautiful Ziegfeld Girl, flapper, and silent film actress who was married to Jack Pickford, the wild little brother of famed actress Mary Pickford. She has another special distinction, though: She is the ghost of the New Amsterdam Theatre.

Olive was born in Charleroi, Pennsylvania, on October 20, 1898. Around 1915, she moved to New York City and became a dancer in the famous Ziegfeld Follies. Lovely Olive soon caught the attention of the higher-ups at the International Film Company, and she landed a movie contract in 1916. She bid goodbye to Broadway and headed out to California, where she met and married Jack Pickford. Jack was never the consummate professional, unlike his sister. He was notoriously dissolute, but Olive couldn't resist his rakish charms.

It would be her undoing.

Various reports of her death tell the tale somewhat differently, but the facts of it are more or less these. In 1920, Jack and Olive went to Paris for a second honeymoon. They went out carousing one night, not returning to their hotel room until 3:00 a.m. They had been arguing all night, it seems, and apparently things ended up in a sodden, acrimonious fight. Jack stormed out of the hotel room and Olive, sobbing, grabbed a blue bottle of mercury bichloride that had been prescribed to Jack for his syphilis. The capsules inside were shaped like coffins, which should have been a sign that they were poisonous; it seems the mixture inside was meant to be applied topically. Nonetheless, Olive downed the whole bottle, with the inevitable results.

Evidently Olive found her way back to New York City. Her ghost has been seen flitting around the New Amsterdam Theatre, where she spent so much time in life. Her spirit wears a green beaded dress and clutches a blue bottle. Stagehands have spotted her on so many occasions that it is now customary, when leaving the theater, to say, "Good night, Olive!" on the way out. Olive's ghost prefers men to women, they say, which makes sense given her flirtatious personality in life.

The best-known contemporary sighting of Olive's ghost concerns a security guard who worked at the theater a few years ago. He made a frantic 2:30 a.m. phone call to Dana Amendola, VP of Disney Theatrical and current manager of the theater, saying he had seen a woman in a green beaded dress walking on the stage and carrying a blue bottle. He yelled at her, "Hey, you can't be here!" and she glided right through the wall and out onto Forty-First Street. To this day, the security guard maintains he saw the apparition of Olive Thomas. So the next time you catch a Broadway show at the New Amsterdam Theatre, don't forget to wave to her as you leave and say, "Good night, Olive!"

Whether it's a free-spirited flapper or a much darker sort of bad girl, all these ghosts exert an endless fascination. Keep reading to learn more about the spirits of the Soiled Doves of the Frontier, the specter of the enigmatic Mary Surratt, and the enduringly mysterious and iconic ghost of Lizzie Borden. To paraphrase flapper and original bobbed-hair icon Colleen Moore, with bad girls this interesting, why be good?

AMERICAN SUCCUBI

Soiled Doves of the Frontier

ANDREA

PROSTITUTE KITTY LEROY WAS THE STAR OF ONE OF THE OLD West's very first ghost stories. On December 6, 1877, poker dealer and "dancer" LeRoy was shot by her husband, Samuel Curley, who then turned his pistol on himself. *The Black Hills Daily Times* reported:

> *To tell our tale briefly and simply, is to repeat a story old and well known—the re-appearance, in spirit form, of departed humanity. In this case, it is the shadow of a woman, comely, if not beautiful, and always following her footsteps, the tread and form of the man who was the cause of their double death. In the still watches of the night, the double phantoms are seen to tread the stairs where once they reclined in the flesh and linger o'er places where once they reclined in loving embrace and finally to melt away in the shadows of the night.*

Kitty was a larger-than-life figure: she was a gambler, a card sharp, a performer, a possible prostitute or madam (the historic records are murky) and, apparently, an excellent shot. At one point she owned and operated a combination brothel and gambling den called The Mint. It was said that she left behind "five husbands, seven revolvers, a dozen Bowie knives, and was always armed to the teeth." Kitty the ghost was a great story; Kitty the woman was a legend.[1]

If American women have historically suffered from a lack of public visibility, the fun-loving, high-kicking Wild West whore hasn't had that problem: she's the preeminent female cultural cipher of Western legend, the most highly visible woman in the history of the American frontier. Madams like Kitty LeRoy and Big Nose Kate seized economic power for themselves in one of the only ways available to women at the time, running highly successful businesses and establishing themselves firmly and forcefully as presences to be reckoned with. They are documented, named, and photographed—unlike the sad, anonymous wisps of pioneer wives and mothers who are marked, only in passing, by bleak wooden crosses. Given the alternative ways to make a living—sewing, scrubbing, marriage to a man who could legally beat and rape you at his pleasure, teaching—you can't blame a gal for whoring.*

In their afterlives, these "girls," as they are invariably called, continue to be marquee names of Western ghostlore, the stars of ghost-bro paranormal TV shows, the highlights of vaguely racy ghost walks in tourist trap simulacra, patron sinners of ghost-themed bars. The ghosts of the so-called Soiled Doves of the Old West (which

* We've chosen to primarily use the term "prostitute" throughout this chapter; if we use "whore" or another term, we do so in a spirit of irony or critique. We have chosen not to apply the modern term "sex worker" retroactively to the women who worked primarily between 1860 and 1900, because the historic context in which they "chose" their professions was very different from the experience of a sex worker today. Therefore, the standard, more neutral designation "prostitute" is used throughout most of this chapter, except when referring to present-day sex workers.

sounds a bit as though they've had an unfortunate accident in their pantaloons) are in high demand. Their spirits are channeled into the service workers of late-stage capitalism, the tour guides and bartenders and waitstaff who make it all happen, while modest empires are built on their backs. The prostitutes themselves tend to be more anonymous than the madams, just as in life—as above, so below, if you will. Sometimes described as "colorful," and often ladies in red, our spectral scarlet women still rule the night, even if they no longer share in the profits.

The frontier was, at least for white settlers, a place where most goods had to be imported. This was no less true of human chattel, and women stagecoached their way into the hinterlands by the dozen. Then, as now, prostitution was primarily a means to an economic end. Though a small percentage of sex workers identifies their profession as a calling or avocation, the vast majority simply understand it to be the fastest, easiest route to the highest hourly rate they'll ever get in this life. And any late-nineteenth-century woman with a head for business and a bod for sin knew that a market filled with heaps of lonely, horny men guaranteed an excellent return on investment. Hence all that frothy, scandalous Old West vice was, at its heart, a business transaction (and any profitable business depends on an anonymous, replaceable army of underlings, which is why madams tend to have identities, while the working girls do not). But legend strips out the dry parts of history, which is why whores make for such excellent ghosts: by removing the transactional value of real-world work, you are left only with a sexy wraith eternally stuck on this earthly plane with nothing better to do than entertain you. This ghost will titillate you, if you want her to, and you don't even have to pay her. You do, however, have to tip your tour guide, you monster.

If the United States is defined, at least in part, by its devotion to the free market, then the Wild West, the Gold Rush, and all that mining and land-grabbing take that concept to its apotheosis. Even more uniquely American is the Old West prostitute's spirit counterpart: she is an American succubus. In traditional folklore, a succubus robs a man of his essence by draining him while he sleeps; by contrast, the whores of the Old West refreshed a man, leaving his vital essence intact so he could throw himself back into his work with renewed energy. A visit to a prostitute was a bracing tonic that restored the natural state of a man, leaving his mind clear for work (or gambling, killing, pissing, riding horses, or whatever he had on the docket for that night). These days, the mild thrill promised by a haunted bordello tour gives a tourist excursion added value, and everybody's happy, especially the tour operator who just took your fool's gold.

Thus do haunted hotels, brothels, tours, and television shows transmute old, dead, anonymous women into pure gold by smoothing over the rough edges of the reality of a frontier prostitute's life (we've all seen *Deadwood* and those onesie pj's with butt flaps dudes wore back then; we know it wasn't glamorous) and turning sad, drunk women into delightful entertainers. The Mizpah Hotel in Nevada does this with exquisite symbolism.

The Mizpah Hotel's resident Lady in Red is apparently the ghost of a prostitute who died there, though some sources characterize her as the "mistress" of the hotel's owner. According to sources, the woman, sometimes called Rose, was either murdered by her husband in a jealous rage after he caught her cheating on him, or she was beaten and murdered on the fifth floor of the hotel by her jealous ex-boyfriend, or maybe a john-turned-lover who wanted her to quit the biz. She now "reportedly makes her presence known by whispering in men's ears and leaving pearls from her broken necklace on guests' pillows."[2] The Mizpah Hotel offers a "Lady in Red" suite where you, too, can encounter the sexy ghost of this murdered, brutalized woman; it is one of their most popular rooms. This succubus is benign, defanged, commodified; her conflicting origin stories and lack of basis in reality leave her unmoored from any actual identity or subsequent guilt that may come thereby in the consuming of her. The sins of the past forgotten, she whispers seductively in her scarlet chamber and leaves pearlescent orbs reminiscent of drops of semen on the hotel's pillows.

In the language of ghostlore, a Red Lady ghost usually represents a fallen woman; a murdered prostitute killed in a crime of passion; a jilted lover; or a vain, jealous, highly sexualized, or objectified woman.* Robed in unsubtle symbolic crimson, she is usually attached to public spaces—in contrast to the angel in the house, she is the whore in the hotel. The Mizpah is a typical location; not only a public space (a hotel) but also a mining town riddled with brothels, an archetypical location for a Red Lady. Surprisingly, Red Lady ghosts are generally polite, friendly, and even seductive. This is somewhat baffling, because if I'd been brutally murdered, my ghost certainly wouldn't be leaving pearls on pillows.

Because red is also the color of anger.

The women of the night who haunt room 206 at the Hotel Monte Vista in Flagstaff, Arizona, seem at least a little angry. Two women who died at the hotel are said to try to asphyxiate men in their sleep. According to the hotel's website, in the 1940s two prostitutes were brought back from the city's Red Light District near the train tracks, just two blocks south of the hotel. "During their 'visit' they were killed and thrown from their hotel window to the cold street below." The hotel's euphemistic use of "visit" is interesting here; as is their contrasting image of the street below as being "cold," as opposed to the warm, inviting scene of the actual crime. Once again, the literal violence perpetrated on these women is held

---

* Traditionally, the phrase "red death" referred to death on the battlefield, awash with blood; in 1842 Edgar Allan Poe used it to evoke death by pestilence in "The Masque of the Red Death." For a "lady in red" ghost, the color red generally evokes sexual passion and, if her death is violent, blood, but the coloration almost always designates a prostitute, a lover, a "fallen woman," or a highly sexualized woman. The Red Lady of Huntingdon College (see the chapter "Dark Academia") doesn't strictly fit these criteria: she simply wore red and died a bloody death but, far from being sexualized, was characterized by her aloofness.

at a convenient remove, without which commodifying their deaths would be vulgar and ghoulish instead of enterprising. The hotel website continues: "Over the years, numerous guests have reported being awakened in the middle of the night and unable to return to sleep due to a feeling that they are being watched. The majority of the time, our male guests report the feeling of having a hands [*sic*] placed over their mouths and throats, and awakening unable to breathe." The violent women of the Monte Vista have done nothing to deter guests from requesting the Women of the Night Room; a five-star Tripadvisor review sighs with satisfaction: "Yes, it *is* haunted!"

Their violence is neatly counterbalanced by the ghost of a friendly bellboy who once allegedly knocked on the door of none other than John Wayne himself, who reported that the ghost seemed friendly and that he did not feel threatened by his presence. Less pleasant is "the Meat Man" of room 220, a 1980s-era lodger who was "known by his strange habit of hanging raw meat from the chandelier." Guests report "cold male hands" touching them in their sleep; one imagines asphyxiation by a couple of warm women of the night to be preferable to an encounter with the Meat Man.*

While we don't really know the identities of the Monte Vista's women of the night, or most of the phantom prostitutes who romp across the pages of American ghostlore, we do have a clue as to at least one of their identities: that of Maggie of the Fairmont Hotel in Deadwood, South Dakota. Maggie's primary emotion is sadness. A depressed alcoholic who was supposedly pregnant when she committed suicide, Margaret Broadwater was an "upstairs girl" at the Fairmont, whose obituary in the *Daily Deadwood Pioneer-Times* is maudlin to the point of being Dickensian. According to the August

* It's hard not to notice the sexual symbolism of the Monte Vista's Meat Man and Women of the Night. The women could certainly spice up any session of autoerotic asphyxiation. As for the Meat Man, he has darker connotations, evoking the imagery of snuff films and women on meat hooks; perhaps the ladies of the night in room 206 are the ghosts of Andrea Dworkin and Catharine MacKinnon.

31, 1907, edition of that paper, Margaret Broadwater jumped from the window of the third floor while "mentally deranged." She had been "terribly ruptured internally," a description that takes on new meaning in this context. She had no surviving father or mother but was survived by two brothers, a sister, and an uncle and aunt in Del Norte, Colorado. The coup de grace of pathos is delivered in the obit's final sentence: "The body was taken in charge by Undertaker B. S. Booth last evening and no arrangements have, up to this time been made for the funeral as it is the intention to await an answer to the message sent to relatives in Delnort [*sic*]."

The hotel is now a restaurant, the Oyster Bay, serving up fresh ghost tours and the famed fresh oysters of South Dakota daily. Suspicious bivalves aside, the Fairmont actually attempts to honor Maggie's memory. Haunted tours and events are described on their Facebook page as "celebrating the life of the Fairmont's most loved and most famous ghost," so unless they're being very tongue in cheek, they seem to have genuine affection for her. Somewhat disappointingly, most reports say Maggie does little more than simply pace the floor restlessly. She doesn't have much personality, perhaps the result of having been so despondent in life, meaning that despite the fact that she is one of the few ghost prostitutes with an actual name, history, and identity, she feels as much like a shadow as any of them. In addition to offering ghost tours, the Fairmont has fun with their ribald past, putting on cheeky drag shows and other assorted amusements.

The Red Onion Saloon in Skagway, Alaska, operates in a similar vein. The ownership leans into a "merry band of prostitutes" vibe, peppering their site with offbeat humor, offering drag shows, and indulging in a display of bedpans on the wall. They've also got a fun, if slightly creepy, display of dolls on the bar that harkens back to the saloon's brothel days: when a whore was busy, her doll lay supine on the counter; when she was ready again, a helpful bartender propped the poppet back up. An aptly named spectral madam, Diamond Lil, still circulates around her old joint, keeping an eye on the place; another girl named Lydia, described variously as a prostitute or a madam, depending on your source, unrepentantly flounces around . . . watering plants. Hey, it's all in a day's work. From time to time, Lydia can be "a bit rough on men," and it is believed she killed herself in her crib after contracting a venereal disease. Again, all in a day's work. Some stories say she was branded on her face after contracting syphilis, and the shame of it was what drove her to suicide. A bleak enough ending but, hey, judging by the happy faces of the tourists cavorting happily on the saloon's website, nobody's holding any grudges.

There are, of course, a few other ghostly prostitutes who don't seem eager to please.

Lucy of the Palmer House Hotel in Sauk Center, Minnesota, is a bit of a misandrist. Lucy was said to have plied her trade at the first Palmer House during the 1880s, until she was murdered by her pimp, Raymond (who apparently haunts room 22). She is known to physically attack men and will sometimes "react to male guests by slamming the room door so hard it rattles the pictures on the wall." At the same time, she lowers the temperature of the room to the point where it is "almost frigid."*

Bella Rawhide and Timber Kate of Nevada were partners in a live sex show in the Wild West, until a fight over a man tore them apart—literally; the man they fought over ended up disemboweling Timber Kate in a savage bar fight. Bella Rawhide eventually drank cleaning fluid and killed herself. In death, their spirits continue to stagger, moan, and brawl, and are not in the least bit sexy or allur-

---

* The old Palmer House Hotel burned down in 1900 and the current hotel wasn't built until 1901. It catered mostly to traveling salesmen. It's worth noting that prostitutes and escorts were in their own way a branch of the midcentury traveling salesman's industry. They were a crucial link in the chain of this other iconic, now-vanished American enterprise.

ing. Of course, like many of these anonymous and interchangeable women, Bella and Kate have no verifiable identities, and their stories spring from sources unknown.

And in Pennsylvania, far from the Old West, a nameless prostitute haunts the former Lincoln Hotel, now an antique shop, in a town somewhat aptly named Mann's Choice. The woman was murdered by her husband when she failed to bring in enough money, and her spirit is said to linger around a certain mirror near the closet where he hanged her body. It is said that women visiting the site feel an uncomfortable and even hostile presence, as though her spirit is at least disgruntled and not mere sexy window dressing.

But for the most part, these ghostly whores are happy to remain an entertaining part of local history. Whether Midwest or Southwest, almost all regions in this country have at least one or two prostitutes sprinkled into their local history, from the Storyville girls of New Orleans to the original "hookers" of Corlears Hook in New York City.* Depending on the locale and character of the people, these narratives may be embraced as colorful legend or swept under the rug. Many cities have dedicated tours exclusively of bordellos. This chapter is the merest tip of the iceberg; you can find myriad other stories online, in books, and on ghost tours. Internet roundups feature "10 Terrifying Ghost Stories of Dead Prostitutes," none of whom are particularly terrifying (unless you find mist, footsteps, or pearls terrifying). In many cases, these stories are, if not dreamed up out of whole cloth, at least lavishly embroidered for the simple, axiomatic reason that,

* Do ghostly prostitutes exist in any contemporary context, beyond the historicity of the Old West? Yes, in fact. In Nevada, the Mustang Ranch brothel is considered highly haunted, and is favorite fodder for macho ghost-hunting shows like *Ghost Adventures*. Ghosts still inhabit wing B of the labyrinthine building, sometimes attaching themselves to working girls; one ghost of a murdered man is said to hold women down; they later emerge with bruises. In this case, the sex workers are haunted by various entities, but the ghosts that haunt them are not themselves prostitutes.

well, it sells. Any actual rough edge is smoothed over in the commodified retelling of "scandalous" local history.

One unexpected effect of this approach is that it makes one realize that in a ghost story—perhaps more than in straight-ahead histories—prostitution is accepted without judgment as just another mode of being. Ghostly history is stuffed with so many unsavory characters, one realizes pretty quickly that having sex for money is fairly small beer in the grand scheme of sinning. So bring on the happy hookers, the whores with the hearts of gold, and never forget, ladies, to smile—even in death.

When it comes to our spectral prostitutes, the reasons behind our preferences for youth and beauty are self-evident: A whore who dies young never has to get ugly or wrinkled, pathetic or aged. The dead whore who perishes before she gets old lets us not think about the fate in store for flesh-and-blood women who trade on their beauty, once that beauty starts to fade. Our American succubi upend Old World traditions, energizing living folks and ghost towns in remote locations alike, with fresh influxes of fun and continued sources of revenue. Untethering these spirit prostitutes from their lived reality lets us sweep certain unpleasant circumstances under the rug: limited economic opportunities or the sexual violence experienced by all women, but especially sex workers and trans women. It even allows us to forget the trials facing aging women of *all* professions, not just the beauty and glamor professions.

The focus on Red Ladies and white pearls is also a neat bit of sleight of hand to distract from the lack of BIPOC women in this particular subset of frontier ghost stories, at least the ones we came across in our research. Though Old West brothels featured women from all backgrounds, sometimes marketed as "exotics," ghostlore shies away from asking difficult questions about, say, the lives of Chinese women imported en masse, enslaved, and treated like chattel, or the lives of Mexican and Native American women whose homes and lifeways had been disrupted and destroyed by Western expansion. In ghost world, the murder of a white woman is more palatable, and better entertainment fodder, than the historic experience of a disenfranchised woman of color.

In all our research we came across no ghost stories of Chinese women working in the sex trade, and only a single ghost story about a Native American prostitute—in Seattle, a city with a strong Native American presence in its ghostlore (the famed spirit of Pike Place Market is a Suquamish princess). This ghost haunts an old Victorian house in the once-blighted, now-gentrified suburb of Georgetown that used to be a bordello, gambling den, and boardinghouse known as "The Castle." When, in the twentieth century, an art dealer bought the crumbling mansion, he heard disembodied screams, loud crashes, and shouts of "Manny, no!" Later he learned a Native American prostitute was killed on that site in 1899, murdered by someone named . . . Manny. Seattle in the 1890s, like many frontier towns, had a disproportionate number of single white men, and so began to import white women to fix the "Indian problem"—that is, the problem of white men sleeping with Indigenous women. According to scholar Coll Thrush, the "ghost of an Indigenous prostitute . . . speaks to the ways in which class, gender and race—and conflicting ideas about 'vice' and urban order—have been inscribed into the urban landscape." These urban landscapes, Thrush writes, "continue to be haunted by the specters of encounter and exploitation."[3] The disproportionate numbers of Indigenous women who still remain victims of violence remains a blight on our national conscience to this day.

Is this where the endless fascination with brothels as haunted sites comes from? From a gut feeling that, despite best efforts to reduce dead women to window dressing, something in these seemingly entertaining places was, and is, difficult and unsettling? Sex work is and was complicated. Most of the people who visit these haunted sites understand that life in these places was emotionally intense, precarious, and sometimes violent, laced with crime and scandal and vice. We may also intuitively understand the difficult emotional work involved in situations of artificially created intimacy, known as emotional labor and shared by waitresses, flight attendants, and sex workers.

The work performed in brothels taxes one psychically, because one is performing the delicate dance of prostitution's not only physical but also emotional labor, the fluffing of egos and ids that all good sex workers must engage in to be really proficient at their jobs. Even though much ghostlore, with a few exceptions, strips these spectral women of any of *their* violent emotions, or creates historic erasure by downplaying the deeply complicated relationships between their personal identities and history as it actually happened (i.e., with all the racist violence of capitalist expansion), we know on some level that these ectoplasmic hookers are not as happy as they seem.

Most of us who grew up in the Western world have the trope of the "fallen woman" inscribed somewhere in our subconscious. From the Bible to *Carmen* to horror movies in which the first girl to have sex gets killed, the soiled doves are the first to go. There's an expectation that, yeah, of course this prostitute was murdered, of course she's a ghost. She showed ankle; what did she expect? This is an unconscious attitude we carry within us; it's the reason why sex workers have great difficulty finding justice if they bring charges of abuse or rape to a court of law. That same impulse is what makes us nod unquestioningly at most of the ghost stories outlined in this chapter. Live by the sword, die by the sword. Murder, madness, death; it's all part of the package. As outlined above, we get it. We understand why a brothel would be haunted. Taken that way, it's sad and fairly enraging.

What's really interesting about these ghostly prostitutes is the way they upend and even subvert the trope in surprising ways. These ghostly, comely (if not beautiful) prostitutes are ultimately less invisible than those wives, teachers, scrubwomen, and seamstresses who chose the other path. Autonomous in life and remembered in death—isn't that what we all want? It's hard to say.

As with anything related to sex, it's complicated.

Though it's easy to come down hard on a hotel that markets unproblematized versions of sexy ghost prostitutes, it's also important to have a sense of humor about it all. Like proctologists and tour guides, sex workers have to have a sense of humor about what they do. Is it really so awful that our red ladies are happily swanning around dripping pearls instead of rending their garments in penance? One of the most refreshing things about sex work is the way it deflates and undermines the hypocrisy of other societal institutions (marriage, say). I'd rather enjoy the lighthearted company at the Red Onion Saloon than engage in moralistic hand-wringing over the wretched souls of the soiled doves.

The thing is, these ghostly prostitutes—well, we have very little choice in the way we convey them. We can turn them into fallen women parables—though I don't think anyone seriously considers them to be cautionary tales—or we can keep it light and let them be remembered for the best parts of who they were. Empowered instead of cowed, dressed in their finest instead of clad in aprons and rags, actually earning and keeping their own money and property instead of dependent on the mercy of a husband, whatever his whims. Most of these women entered the profession because of a lack of choice. They're still bound by it, but they don't have to reinforce it. They can, by calling attention to the nonsense and hypocrisy of the fallen woman trope, subvert it. It is up to us to interpret their stories sensitively, to be aware of the omissions and elisions, to ask about the missing links in their narratives. We the living are charged with the remembrance of the overlooked women of color who have been written out of this narrative. We the living are charged with ensuring no female-identifying person has to face a world with so few choices, and that anyone entering sex work does so now by vocation and not desperation. That's our job. Their work is done.

CONSPIRATOR TO AN ASSASSINATION

The Ghost of Mary Surratt

ANDREA

WASHINGTON, DC

On July 7, 1865, Mary Surratt became the first woman to be executed by the US federal government, hanged for her role in the assassination of Abraham Lincoln. Three other coconspirators were executed that day: Lewis Powell, George Atzerodt, and David Herold. Four other coconspirators were also convicted for their role in the assassination: Dr. Samuel A. Mudd, Samuel Arnold, and Michael O'Laughlen were sentenced to life in prison; Edman Spangler got off with only a 6-year sentence.[1] Each one actively planned the unforgivable murder of the president. Together they plotted, they schemed, they brandished guns and knives, and they ran and hid when it was done. Mary let them use her boardinghouse and tavern as a home base for their plotting, and provided them ammunition, horses, and whiskey as they fled in the aftermath.

Throughout the trial, the press and public vilified Mary. They mocked her appearance, they reviled her, they caricatured her. On the night of her hanging, a mob stormed her boardinghouse on

H Street in Washington, DC, in a frantic hunt for macabre souvenirs. The American people thirsted for blood and justice, and they got it. The middle-aged widow was led to the gallows trembling and sobbing, begging for mercy. Her daughter, Anna, echoed her pleas, even at one point going so far as to bang on the White House door, screaming for clemency for her mother, to no avail. Her sons remained silent and absent, having fled to Europe. In the final moments of her life, Mrs. Surratt held the arm of her jailer as her knees buckled and she stumbled up the gallows steps. Her last words were, "Please don't let me fall."

Almost immediately after her hanging, the press and public did a sudden about-face. It was as if they couldn't believe she was actually executed. Suddenly there was an outpouring of remorse. People began to second-guess the trial, wondering if perhaps her sentence hadn't been a bit too harsh. As Surratt's biographer, Kate Clifford Larson, describes it, "Mary's wicked persona was recast into the sorrowful victim, a perfect Victorian mother murdered by immoral and unrestrained powerful men."[2] President Johnson was asked why he had ignored a last-minute plea for clemency cosigned by five of the nine sentencing judges; he claimed variously that he hadn't seen it or that he had decided her punishment was justified because she "kept the nest that hatched the egg," a highly feminized metaphor to describe a conspiracy. At the end of his life, Johnson confessed privately to a friend that if he had "interfered with the execution, it would have meant my death and a riot that probably would have ended with war."[3] As years passed and the details of her trial were further obscured by the haze of distant memory, it became easier and easier to recast Surratt as a sympathetic figure. In 1895, a judge from New York named David DeWitt wrote a book, *The Judicial Murder of Mary E. Surratt*, that further solidified the myth of her innocence.[4] The public's incredulity that the government had actually hanged a middle-aged woman, a widow and a mother no less, fed into this willingness to believe she had been unjustly treated. In fictionalized portrayals of Mary, the romantic, pathos-laden story with a tragic feminine trope at the heart of it has proved irresistible to any writer or director with a flair for the dramatic.[5] And in ghost-lore, the idea of an innocent spirit seeking retribution was a neat way to explain her spectral presence that fit comfortably within received ideas of what motivates a haunting.

Sightings of Mary's ghost began almost immediately after her execution. A little more than a year after her death, the Cleveland *Plain Dealer* unequivocally stated that Mary Surratt's house was haunted: "There can be no reasonable doubt upon the subject. She herself persists in treading its halls, and perambulating the premises in the dead of night, clad in those self-same robes of serge in which she suffered the penalty of the law."[6] By 1925, when the boarding-house was renovated and turned into a restaurant, her haunting was a firmly established legend in Washington, DC, lore. The Seward *Daily Gateway* declared, "Families moved in but soon moved out, and rumors spread that the ghost of Mrs. Surratt flitted through the corridors and tapped on the windows."[7] (It's interesting the paper is from Seward, Alaska; Secretary of State William Seward was another one of the conspiracy's targets on the night of Lincoln's assassination: Lewis Powell attacked him viciously, but he survived.) The house, incidentally, remains a restaurant to this day, the Wok and Roll. On the second floor, where Mary Surratt once had her bedroom, there is now a karaoke lounge. Landmarked in 2009, the building is now fairly quiet, if only in terms of ghostly reports.

Mary's spirit has also apparently been sighted in her old tavern in Clinton, Maryland, where she is spotted on the porch from time to time, and she is even mentioned in some guidebooks and ghost tours as visiting the US Supreme Court and Lafayette Square.[8] But the most vivid and disturbing spectral accounts are located around Fort McNair, which was the site of her execution.

As befits a Civil War–era ghost, Mary's specter cuts a classically terrifying figure. She is described as a "hooded figure in black, bound at the hands and feet." The ghost of this "lady in black" is reported to play with the children of soldiers stationed at the fort, which is an especially chilling thought.[9] When not playing with children, Mary wails and sobs freely. In Ohio, *The Clermont Sun* tells the story of an Army captain at Fort McNair who, in 1989, "reported hearing a woman crying for help. The cries then became loud screams."[10]

A surprisingly creepy account of Mary's ghost can be found in a 1991 *Washington Post* article that described the way the ghost weeps, paces, softly cries, "Help me, help me," and, somewhat oddly, melts snow in a spectral path—literally smoldering with rage. It's an image that stays with you, both inexplicable and somehow very sincere. Honest witness-based spectral accounts usually contain bizarre and unique details just such as this. Yet there is a sense that the witnesses and the author of this article rely heavily on the mythology that surrounds the story of Mary Surratt. The author goes out of their way to describe Mary as a "strapping" woman.[11] It's a revealing word, "strapping." Mary's appearance was often described by the nineteenth-century press as mannish, strapping, hulking, extremely tall; they even called her an "Amazon." Why her contemporaries described her in these terms is unclear, but it was probably because she defied other notions of feminine propriety, such as running a business and helping to murder presidents. Whatever the reason, it seems evident that whoever recorded the ghostly account for the *Washington Post* was taking their cues from the language of Mary's trial reports and not from reality, because Mary stood only about five feet four inches tall. Her ghost, then, takes more from legend than life.

Descriptions of her ghost remain coded in sexist language to this day: a blog for a Washington, DC, ghost tour company takes pains to describe Mary's appearance as an "austere looking woman" with "shiny hair in an abrupt part." They go on to say, "That hair became much less neat as she strangled by her own bodyweight [*sic*] pulling tight against a hangman's noose . . ."[12] Besides the fact that this description is baffling and sexist, it's also inaccurate: Mary was executed wearing a white cloth sack over her head, so nobody could possibly have seen her hair during the event. Creative license in nonfiction is one thing, but unnecessarily dwelling on the appearance of her hair during her death throes seems like a too-gleeful description of this woman's physical suffering.

The other salient thing about ghostly accounts of Mary is how often she is described as possibly innocent. A wronged figure whose specter searches for justice. Most of these accounts point out that her arrest, trial, and conviction were accomplished with astonishing rapidity—in just under three months from arrest to execution. They point out the fact that her trial was actually a military tribunal rather than a civilian case, that her lawyers were breathtakingly inept, and that her sentence was perhaps unduly harsh considering her relatively minor role in the plot to kill the president. "The trials were clearly unfair in terms of jurisprudence," says historian and DC tour guide Tim Krepp. "They clearly did not follow due process, so she becomes a wronged figure. Which is interesting in hindsight, because she *was* guilty." There is tension and ambiguity about the legal process and whether justice was properly served.

She also has a certain pathos that's hard to discount entirely, when considering why so many portrayals of her are sympathetic. Some of her story is genuinely sad. Her son, John Surratt Jr., was also a coconspirator, but fled to Europe to escape conviction, thereby abandoning his mother and *never reappearing to defend her even when she was sentenced to death.* After her execution, her only daughter suffered a mental collapse and never fully recovered from the trauma of her mother's death.

This is betrayal and heartbreak enough for one woman, but Mary Surratt also had a fairly hard row to hoe even before she became involved with assassins and conspirators. She lost her father when she was three years old; she married an alcoholic gambler ten years her senior at the age of seventeen; he squandered his inheritance and left her riddled with debt after his sudden death in 1862. Her widowhood was fraught with the stress of dealing with her husband's staggering arrears: She played whack-a-mole with the creditors coming out of the woodwork and almost miraculously managed to retain ownership of her modest real estate holdings, including the tavern in Surrattsville (now Clinton, MD), as well as the boardinghouse on H Street and other assets after his death.[13]

Mary had to really scramble after the death of her no-good husband. During the Civil War, creditors were especially aggressive, and it would have been no mean feat to fend them off. Give Mary due credit for being financially savvy enough to fight them with a combination of negotiation and shuffling around her assets. Mary refinanced her debts, leased her tavern, pulled her kids out of school, and ran a boardinghouse to keep her head above water. It was undoubtedly extremely stressful in a time when widows were especially vulnerable financially and hovered perilously close to the edge of penury, unless they chose to remarry right away.[14]

It's worth noting that Mary's ghost is dressed in her widow's weeds, the outfit she was hanged in. Author Chris Woodyard has pointed out that ghostly "women in black" were a common sight in the 1870s, and they were often characterized as widows. In the postwar era, these symbols of suffering and financial insecurity seemed a veritable craze throughout the country: "The Woman in Black [is] everything we fear: the darkness, poverty, pain, and loss."[15] No coincidence Mary was a widow, then; perhaps this is part of the reason why her ghost is almost always notably clad in shades of midnight and sable. You could also interpret it another way: Black is the darkest color in the spectrum and, in the language of ghosts in the Western world, it's a warning sign that you are not dealing with a particularly friendly spirit.

Yes, Mary did what she had to do to get by, and one wonders if her involvement in the conspiracy might have stemmed from her need to keep the wolf from her door. Perhaps part of the renegotiations of her debts involved staying on good terms with certain people, with the Southerners who surrounded her and made up her social milieu. At the heart of many stories of lawbreaking women, you'll often find a woman on the razor's edge of desperation, just doing whatever it takes to survive, and there's a kernel of that in Mary's story, however small. But, as Larson points out, the very fact that she cannily pulled herself out of the mire of widow's debts and potential poverty might be the very thing that points to her guilt. She was intelligent and savvy and managed to navigate a world that was inhospitable to widows without money or legal resources. This might be why it's a bit tricky to play the innocence card. Mary Surratt was not an ingenue. She was a capable woman who knew what she was doing. Knowing this makes it hard to believe she was innocent or ignorant of the assassination plot being hatched in her own boardinghouse. "There is no way that woman could have not known what was going on in that house," Larson said in a lecture for the National Archives Experience. "It's not that big of a house."[16]

It's less easy to have a ton of sympathy for her, then, when you think perhaps she did know exactly what she was doing. That she was this pro-slavery woman—and make no mistake, she really was. Krepp points out that "she was involved in a treasonous conspiracy against the government. She's not an innocent figure." But it is only in recent years that this narrative is beginning to shift: "Nowadays especially with the reevaluation of this 'lost cause' mythology, she's not as sympathetic a figure." In other words, it may have been acceptable to frame her as an innocent victim in the past, but it is less so in today's climate, with our knowledge and perception having evolved significantly.

Mary was indeed guilty of conspiring with John Wilkes Booth in the assassination of President Lincoln. She possessed strong Southern sympathies: She was a slaveholder; some of the enslaved people in her household were sold by her husband to pay his debts; one of her sons, Isaac, was in the Confederate army; and the other,

John Jr., was a spy and courier for the South. She was from southern Maryland and she was a staunch supporter of the Confederacy. She hung out with John Wilkes Booth, who once called slavery "one of the greatest blessings [that] God ever bestowed" on the American people,[17] and she aided and abetted him at every turn. Mary Surratt was a pro-slavery Southern secessionist, full stop. The author of the most recent and comprehensive biography of Mary Surratt to date states unequivocally that "Mary Surratt was not only guilty, but was far more involved in the plot than many historians give her credit for."[18]

Incidentally, Mary's biographer is the same woman who wrote a seminal history of the life of Harriet Tubman. One can't help but imagine Tubman leaning into this conversation, wide-eyed and dripping with sarcasm, as she says, "Oh please, Mary Surratt, tell me more about how *very hard your life* was. Please, I am all ears."

One might feel sorrier for Surratt's daughter, actually. By all accounts, Anna had a pretty massive crush on John Wilkes Booth. He was handsome and famous, a charming actor, and he spent time with her at the boardinghouse. She was more than a tad besotted with him, and one imagines there was a brief moment when Anna thought wildly that he might even be coming around to see her. But no, he was just there to hang with her Confederate courier brother and to plot murder with her mother. Tough break. (Booth, for what it's worth, had a secret fiancée at the time he murdered Lincoln; her photo was just one of five women's photos that were found in Booth's pockets after he was hunted down and shot by federal soldiers. As Sarah Vowell once said, it seems Booth was a lady-killer too.[19] Anna stood by her mother's side, visited her in prison, and had a total mental breakdown when it was all over. Her subsequent life was a muddle of anxiety, nightmares, and PTSD. She sold the boardinghouse for less than half its value. She had a moderately successful marriage, but emotionally she never really recovered. And she too, it seems, is a ghost. Every July 6, she continues to replay the eve of her mother's execution, knocking frantically on the White House door in a desperate final attempt for clemency.[20] While there's a great deal of ambiguity, reservation, and hesitation when it comes to Mary Surratt, it's easier to feel sympathy for Anna, who really did seem caught up in forces she neither controlled nor understood and events that would shadow her life forever.

SO, WHAT ARE WE TO MAKE OF MARY SURRATT? SHE'S NOT REALLY likable. You can't really cheer for her. What is the fascination with her? Why are the keys to her jail cell and the noose she was hanged with on display at The Lincoln Museum?[21] Why is her former tavern a museum now, an essential stop on the Booth reality tour, the "Vatican of the Lincoln assassination subculture?[22] Why does her black-clad figure float through our folklore, a mainstay of every book, article, and tour featuring DC ghosts, even as the real woman has been largely forgotten by the general public? And is this damned, cursed villainess even worth remembering? What significance does Mary Surratt's ghost ultimately have?

It's indisputable that Mary's ghost does possess some serious significance. She's mentioned everywhere: No account of DC ghosts is complete without her.[23] What's really interesting about the confluence of ghosts and the nation's capital is that even the most reputable, nuanced, and firmly historical sources will mention ghosts almost as a matter of course, from the *Washington Post* to the Library of Congress. That's what's so fascinating about Washington, DC—the great seat of American power is chockablock with ghosts, and everyone is so very willing to talk about them. In many social and intellectual circles, it's a bit taboo to talk about a ghost in anything approaching a sincere manner. Yet in Washington, DC, the spectral is taken surprisingly seriously.

You'll find musings on this topic from such reputable sources as the National Portrait Gallery and the White House History blog. These are outfits devoted to serious study of art and history, and their insights on the significance of ghosts are pretty solid. Ghosts serve a purpose; they "communicate culturally significant information" and enable "the anchoring of a chaotic past with the present."[24] We couldn't agree more. This country remains obsessed with Civil War–era ghosts; it's the great national wound that still hasn't healed. This goes at least part of the way toward explaining Mary's significant presence in national ghostlore; her specter still haunts us just "as the Civil War still haunts the United States."[25] Like history itself, Mary's story is unresolved and perhaps unresolvable.

It is tempting to dismiss Mary Surratt as purely terrible because of her pro-slavery stance, but at the same time it's also tempting to try to complicate her narrative, to frame her story in sympathetic terms because she was a human being, after all, a woman just trying to get by; because the terms of her execution were questionable, particularly if you don't believe in the death penalty; and because her treatment by the press during her trial was harsh indeed, just as her portrayal in contemporary ghostlore is sometimes problematic. There is a raft of literature discussing the "unresolved" nature of Surratt's involvement in the assassination that attests to this desire to, against all hope, clear her name. We want to believe, but at most all you can do is address the legality of the trial itself and not her actual guilt.[26] Ultimately, it is impossible to overlook what she did, no matter the circumstances of her life, the details of her trial, or the shocking finality of her execution. To do so would be to willfully rewrite history. The evidence against her is "overwhelming."[27] Mary Surratt was not innocent: She was a human being, deeply flawed, who committed a terrible act and paid the price for it with her life.

At the end of the day, all you can do is acknowledge her as the complex, unresolved specter she really is. "There's a utility in examining Mary Surratt for what she tells us about ourselves," says Tim Krepp. "Stories like hers are not neat and tidy; they're manifesting as ghost stories because we're still trying to wrestle with that legacy.

She's not easy and comfortable and she shouldn't be, and that's useful in its own right."

Mary's troubling ghost story embodies the moral gray areas that are not easily resolved, precisely because she is the specter of our own complicity, a handy repository for our collective discomfort. She is a symbol of dubious legal processes and rushed and shoddy justice, a *j'accuse* for every time the government ever overreached in its zeal to appear effective. She's like a mix of Lady Macbeth and Banquo's ghost all rolled up into one. And she is a very strong symbol of the kind of guilt that makes us most uncomfortable; not the dramatic, obvious guilt of the assassin, which is reserved for Booth himself, but the icky, awkward guilt of everyone who ever stood by when something morally reprehensible was going on and did little to stop it—in fact, may even have aided its course in some self-serving, material way, even as they knew it was wrong. Above all, she is a reminder of a terrible crime, something so unforgivable her spirit will never find rest.

Damned and doomed to wander the earth, she is a classic historical ghost if there ever was one.

THE HAUNTING OF LIZZIE BORDEN

ANDREA

FALL RIVER, MASSACHUSETTS

Lizzie Borden circa 1890. Courtesy of the Fall River Historical Society

ON A HOT AUGUST MORNING IN 1892, IN THE STAID NEW England mill town of Fall River, Massachusetts, Lizzie Borden said to her neighbor, "Do come over. Someone has killed Father." What followed would become one of the greatest unsolved crimes in American history, as Lizzie Borden was accused, then acquitted, of the murder of her father and stepmother.

Though the case lives rent-free in the collective consciousness of this country and hardly needs an introduction, it is worth noting at least a few facts for those of us who may need a brief refresher. Sixty-nine-year-old Andrew Jackson Borden and sixty-four-year-old Abby Durfee Borden were bludgeoned to death in their home with, presumably, a small hatchet. Abby received about eighteen blows and was killed in an upstairs bedroom. Andrew received about eleven to fifteen blows and was murdered on a sofa in the downstairs parlor. Abby is thought to have died around nine thirty in the morning, Andrew around eleven thirty or eleven forty-five.

There were no witnesses to either murder. An uncle, John V. Morse, was staying with the family at the time, but had gone out. His alibi was corroborated. Bridget Sullivan, the maid, was also home that Thursday, but her alibi also checked out: She was washing windows in the first part of the morning, then went upstairs to take a nap. Lizzie Borden's sister, Emma, was out of town. Only Lizzie was at home, with an alibi that could not be corroborated.

Lizzie notoriously disliked her stepmother. She had means, motive, and opportunity. Her testimony at the inquest was confused and inconsistent. She was eventually indicted and tried for the murder. A year later, unable to find sufficient evidence to convict her, the court declared her not guilty.[1]

Few criminal cases have inspired as much research, passion, argument, literary and dramatic adaptation, and full-blown obsession as the Lizzie Borden one. She is second perhaps only to Jack the Ripper in status, the undisputed queen of the unsolved murder. Popular opinion leans heavily toward her guilt, as evidenced by the notorious schoolyard quatrain ("Lizzie Borden took an axe"), and many nonobsessives (including this author) are surprised to discover she was actually acquitted. Once you do go down the rabbit hole of mondo Borden, it's jaw-dropping to discover how strange the case actually was, how each potential strand of certainty is almost immediately checked by a thread of doubt, weaving together tighter and more complicated knots the longer you immerse yourself in it. No wonder that one of the best-known Lizzie Borden fan blogs is called *Warps & Wefts*—besides being a tribute to the textiles of Fall River, the Massachusetts mill town where the Bordens resided, it deftly alludes to the many tangled threads of the case.

Let's start with the basics. Murder weapon? Not found. Yes, a short-handled hatchet that *fitted the holes* in the Bordens' skulls was found in the house, but its handle had been broken off and there was no blood or human hair on the blade. The Bordens' butchering produced buckets of blood that splattered the walls, but not a spot was found on Lizzie . . . well, one spot of blood was found on her, but only on the inside of her underskirt, and that was deemed to be menstrual blood. And yes, a pail of bloody rags was found in the basement, but, again, those were deemed Lizzie's menstrual napkins. And yes, Lizzie hated her stepmother, but by all accounts she loved her father. So why would she murder them *both?* And yes, a drugstore clerk testified that Lizzie had tried to buy prussic acid, a deadly poison, at his shop the day before the murder, but he couldn't positively prove it was Lizzie. Perhaps it had been some other woman who merely resembled her. And yes, the whole family had been violently ill that week, but it was only food poisoning—some bad mutton, or possibly swordfish. And, oh yes, there was the odd fact that Lizzie *burned an old "paint-stained" dress in her basement furnace* three nights after the murders . . . but what better time for a wardrobe refresh than right after your parents' bloody murder?

Finally, Lizzie's confused testimony about where she was that morning—she said, variously, that she was in the kitchen ironing handkerchiefs, or perhaps out in the stifling-hot barn looking for iron for a sinker for a fishing line, or maybe it was something to repair a window screen, she couldn't quite remember—was chalked up to the morphine her doctor gave her to calm her down after she found her father's body. Not that she'd been particularly excited. Lizzie was noted for her strangely calm, coldly stoical demeanor both at the crime scene and throughout the trial. Her testimony at the inquest was ultimately deemed inadmissible at her trial because she'd been speaking without her lawyer present. And what a lawyer he was! He was worth every penny. George Robinson cast doubt on every bit of testimony the prosecution produced. His client emerged from the courtroom at New Bedford in June 1893 a free woman . . . and a wealthy heiress.

Small wonder then that the tangled, twisted case of Lizzie Borden rivets the mind of every true crime fan in America. The case is literally a locked-door mystery; though there was always a slim possibility of an outside intruder committing the crimes, the Borden house was notoriously kept locked at all times, after they had suffered a burglary a year before.* And perhaps it's also no wonder it attracts fans of the paranormal in equal measure. Like the mystery of life after death, this one may be well and truly unsolvable, a puzzle that grows more complicated the longer you ponder it, an eternal conundrum we can never definitively know.

The ghosts of the Bordens appeared almost as soon as the blood was dry. The papers of Hosea Knowlton, the prosecuting attorney, contain several helpful letters from friendly mediums who came forward in 1892 and 1893, offering to solve the case.[2] Spiritualism had largely been discredited by 1892, particularly as the famed Fox sisters had, by 1888, disavowed the practice and essentially declared themselves frauds. But a large segment of the population still

* Some have hypothesized that this robbery was actually committed by Lizzie.

ardently believed in in communiqués from the other side, and Hosea Knowlton's papers contain "a multitude of crank communications." A letter dated August 10, 1892, declares:

> *I don't know as what I am about to say to you will be of any use to you as I am a spiritualist and believe in the communications of the dead. I get it there is a closet at the end of the sopha* [sic] *upon which Mr. Borden lay and in that closet was a man secreted at the time Mr. Borden lay down upon the sopha immediately upon Mrs. Borden going out he came out and committed the murderious* [sic] *act he went out by the end of the barn and cleaned the hachet* [sic] *and threw it into the celler* [sic] *the hachet was pretty broad blade claw hammer head.*[3]

A gentlemen named J. Burns Strand, a self-described trance and "business medium," offered his own services. "Should you Gentlemen think at any time that My presence in Fall River would aid you and the Officers I will come at once and do all that I possibly can for you as a Medium to unravel this great Mystery," and he notes in his postscript, "P. S. The Voice says to me now in closeing [*sic*] this Missive 'Arrest Morse Lizzie and the Man at West Port.'"[4]

But another medium speaking to the *Boston Globe* was less definitive, declaring that "there was a great diversity of opinion in the spirit world as to the identity of the person who murdered Mr. and Mrs. Borden. 'You see . . . spirits don't know everything, at least many spirits do not. And if they didn't happen to be looking just at the moment when the murder was committed they couldn't be expected to know about it . . . [T]he trouble is that when people go suddenly into the spirit world as Mr. and Mrs. Borden went, they are apt to be in a dazed or half-conscious state for a long while and unable to remember anything.' The medium," noted the *Globe* reporter, "said that spirits often find as great difficulty as mortals in solving mysteries and she wouldn't undertake the job of trying to discover the Fall River murderer."

Other mediums were less circumspect. On Aug. 24, 1892, the *Boston Daily Advertiser* wrote:

> *A woman, plainly dressed, with short dark hair, called at the police station this afternoon. . . . She told the marshal that she was peculiarly gifted from infancy, and went on to say that she saw a vision: Miss Lizzie Borden murdering her mother at 10:10 o'clock, Thursday, August 4. Later, she saw Miss Lizzie pass downstairs with a hatchet in her hand, go towards her father, putting a hatchet in a corner while she smoothed the sofa pillow for her father to rest on. Still later, she saw Lizzie standing at the head of the sofa hacking mercilessly at her father's skull. Marshal Hilliard says the woman appears to be sane.*

And an undated, typewritten transcript of a Ouija session found in the Knowlton Papers boldly asserts:

Q: Did she kill her mother and father?
A: Undoubtedly.

The transcript of the Ouija session is actually very interesting on one point in particular: the question of Lizzie's clothing. The subject of Lizzie's (mostly) blood-free clothes fascinated contemporary spectators of the case. Lizzie said she had been wearing a blue dress in the morning, a dress of cheap Bedford cord (a kind of cotton), and had replaced it with a pink wrapper in the afternoon. The police found several blue dresses in the Borden sisters' closet, but none were bloody. Later, it was the Bedford cord she claimed to have burned in the furnace, because it was stained with paint. The lack of blood on her clothes led some to speculate, shockingly, that Lizzie had perhaps performed the murder in the nude. Other, more modest theorizers, suggested she perhaps wore a raincoat. But the medium using this particular Ouija board had other ideas:

> Q: Did Lizzie wear a water-proof?
> A: No—pa's trousers and hat.

Some modern analysts also suggest Lizzie may have been wearing her father's clothes. Historian Lindsey Fitzharris points out that Andrew Borden's overcoat is clearly visible in the crime scene photographs, bundled up behind his dead body like a pillow. But Andrew Borden was not the type of man to bundle up his good coat and use it as a pillow. He was a fastidious and careful man, notoriously frugal, and absolutely the type to hang his coat, properly, on a hook when he returned home. Perhaps, Fitzharris suggests, Lizzie wore the coat during the murder as a butcher wears an apron, and wadded it up when she was done. It would explain the lack of blood on her clothes.[5]

The suggestion that Lizzie dressed in drag to kill her father is provocative. Throughout the many years of analysis devoted to the Borden murders, one theme has surfaced repeatedly: that of Lizzie's femininity. Or lack of it. Whether dressed in drag or not, Lizzie contains a constant tension between masculine and feminine, from her very name, Lizzie Andrew Borden, to the heaps of symbolism that permeate nearly every facet of her case. Lizzie has at times been variously described as a characteristic New England spinster, a "Protestant nun" who lived a quiet home life seething with repressed sexuality, a closeted lesbian, and a possible victim of incest at the hands of her father. Her contemporaries referred to her as a "girl," despite the fact that she was thirty-two years old. People were baffled at the idea that a woman could commit so violent a crime, not only due to woman's inherent gentle nature but because of her lack of physical strength.

Perhaps most tellingly, the bloody pail of rags hidden in the basement goes virtually unmentioned, because nobody—neither the defense nor the prosecution—can bring themselves to speak too much about the fact that Lizzie was menstruating at the time of the murders. "Despite the potential significance of the evidence, the men all let the matter drop; they averted their gaze from the contents of the pail as if it would require staring into the abyss."[6] Analyzing the undigested contents of the dead Bordens' bowels is one thing, but talking about periods? Gross. The idea that Lizzie may have gotten away with murder in part because men of authority were too squeamish to address a bloody pail of menstrual rags is almost . . . well, it almost makes you root for her.

Notably, many of the trial spectators who crushed and pressed their way into the courtroom were female, a "perpetual and swollen crowd of women idlers." The *Fall River Daily Globe* reassured their husbands: "The New Bedford man who comes home and finds it deserted . . . needn't be alarmed. There has been no elopement; the dear creature is probably in the crowd of morbid females who are storming the door of the county court house, trying to get admission to the Borden trial."

These "morbid females" may well have been on Lizzie's side. We all know women love true crime; it's a cliché by now. But as Megan Abbott writes, true crime serves "as the place women can go to read about the dark, messy stuff of their lives that they're not supposed to talk about—domestic abuse, serial predation, sexual assault, troubled family lives, conflicted feelings about motherhood, the weight of trauma, partner violence and the myriad ways the justice system can fail, and silence, women."[7] Attending Lizzie's murder trial may have been cathartic for some of "the wild-eyed, haggard-featured, thick-skinned women" in the audience; records of the time show that many spectators were in sympathy with her. It's easy to imagine that many nineteenth-century women had felt at some point at least an echo of Lizzie's anger, had secretly thought about murdering their whole families, perhaps during the hot months of August while ironing handkerchiefs, perhaps while bleeding silently.

There is a recurring theme in Lizzie's personal and family history: all things related to the female reproductive organs are fraught with peril. Her own mother died of "uterine congestion," and a distant relative a generation back, Eliza Darling Borden, suffered a mental collapse that was most likely postpartum depression and murdered two of her young children before she killed herself. And Lizzie's own "queer spells"—sullen moods, quiet rages, and depressive, almost trancelike moments of dissociation, well-known to all who were intimate with her—may have been the result of premenstrual dysmorphic disorder. It is known from the testimony of her friend Alice Russell that Lizzie declared feelings of foreboding in the days before her parents were killed, stating ominously, "Somebody will do something." Her dark moods seem to have come in cycles.

Lee-ann Wilber, the former manager of the Lizzie Borden Bed and Breakfast, once stated, "The house has mood swings." It was definitely haunted, she averred, but the hauntings would ebb and flow. Her word choice ("mood swings") feels significant in this context: "That's the only way to describe it. The strongest rooms for me are the basement and the third floor. I don't scare easily, but have been 'unglued' a few times when I'm alone in the basement."[8]

Wilber also described the things she heard at night, saying that she often slept in Lizzie's room when there were no guests at the bed and breakfast, occasionally waking to hear doors opening and closing, along with voices and footsteps in the hallways; she would lie in bed for an hour listening to an empty house alive in the dead of night, full of sound and movement.

In an eerie coincidence, Lee-ann Wilber passed away shortly after the Lizzie Borden house was sold and she retired from her long-running job as manager. Wilber had been a well-liked figure in the Lizzie Borden fan community, admired by true-crime devotees for her commitment to historical fact, and by paranormal enthusiasts for her willingness to "cultivate the occult aspects" of the house.[9] The amicable convergence of these two fan bases was an act of high-wire diplomacy on Wilber's part, as there is often tension between the two subcultures in the world of obsessive fandom (mostly stemming from the true crime side, which generally tends to disdain the paranormal fans). Until 2021, all factions seemed to get along, more or less. But in the spring of 2021, the Lizzie Borden Bed and Breakfast was sold to an entrepreneur named Lance Zaal, who operates a for-profit, multicity ghost tour outfit called US Ghost Adventures, worrying the subculture of obsessive amateur sleuths and hard-core Lizzie enthusiasts who have literally devoted decades of their lives to the details of the case.* Zaal is up-front about commercializing the paranormal aspects of the house, even offering the add-on of an EMF meter to the standard historic house tour, and intends to add more entertainment-related experiences, such as axe-throwing.[10] Some are concerned that this late-stage-capitalist version of the house will obliterate its value as a historic artifact and actual crime scene, and regard the new ownership as the end of an era.[11]

But the Bordens have always been about money. Andrew was a successful capitalist himself, first running a cabinet-making business whose wares included coffins and caskets, and later buying up "a brace of banks" and various properties around Fall River, including the plumb and upright A. J. Borden Building downtown. Most students of the Borden case ascribe Lizzie's murderous motives to money troubles, noting that she killed her stepmother *before* her

* The three totemic, larger-than-life experts in the field are female (Shirley Dziedzic, Stefani Koori, and Faye Musselman) and older, in their sixties or thereabouts, adding another layer of contrast with the young, male entrepreneur currently running the house.

father in order to eliminate any possible roadblocks to her inheritance. Borden's notorious tightfistedness prevented the "girls" from living the social life they'd always dreamed of, and kept them in a modest lifestyle they resented. Even Lizzie's legendary dislike of her stepmother was exacerbated by a scuffle over some property Andrew had purchased for Abby. Lizzie (and Emma) were affronted at this invasion of the Borden coffers. Lizzie, for all her cloistering in the feminine world of domesticity and charity work, hungered for money in a way no less manly than that of any Gilded Age titan of industry. As Lindsey Fitzharris opined, "She wanted more and she took it." The only way she knew how. Many people—psychics, staff, and guests at the Lizzie Borden House—believe they have seen or felt Andrew Borden's very disgruntled spirit at the Borden house. Maybe Lance Zaal's financially savvy presence will soothe Andrew's spirit somewhat.

But what of Lizzie's spirit? Is she there? Guests and visitors have claimed variously to sense her, Abby, Andrew, and ghostly children, often thought to be the murdered offspring of Eliza Darling Borden. Besides doors opening, footsteps, and voices, the house is also the realm of what witnesses have termed "the shadow people." A shadow of a woman has been spotted at the house, as well an "actual apparition that looks like Lizzie" who appears in the basement and has been witnessed by staff and a few guests.[12] Many think the female shadow figure in Victorian-era dress seen in the basement is Lizzie, still furtively trying to hide the evidence, as it calls to mind her act of burning the infamous dress. She was accompanied at the time by her friend Alice Russell, and many witnesses to spectral reenactments say they do indeed see two women there. Others have, of course, speculated that it is Bridget Sullivan helping her hide evidence. While going down to the basement to get supplies, tour guide Eleanor Thibault said she once heard the distinct sounds of footsteps behind her. Turning to look and finding no one was there, she fled.

Sightings also occur frequently in the downstairs parlor, where Andrew Borden was murdered. Thibault recalls sitting in the parlor one day when an "eerie feeling" came over her; looking up, she saw smoke begin to drift out of the kitchen, despite the fact that nobody was cooking at the time. The fog-like tendrils curled their way through the parlor, almost deliberately: "The way it traveled, very slow, until it got to the sofa—where Mr. Borden was hacked to death—and it just dissipated. I know I saw something that was out of this world. It wasn't from this world, that's for sure."[13]

There are reams of firsthand testimony to sift through in any analysis of the haunted Borden house. The guest book is a catalog of spectral visitations ("something choked me last night") and "messages of Hitchcockian suggestion" ("I won't say what happened, but I will never stay here again").[14] A cascade of testimony from guests and staff reveals experiences including the footsteps of a man's boots; disembodied voices; the shadow of a man walking on the back stairs; innumerable flickering lights; scratching noises at the door; the apparition of a tall, thin man; phantom sighs; an overwhelming atmosphere of sadness or a sense of presence; a gray lady floating across the cellar floor; scents of perfume; cold spots; feelings of hands or fingers on the body; impressions on the beds; covers lifting and pillows falling off beds, drawers, and doors; windows opening opening and closing; and orbs, fogs, lights, and mists.[15]

Many guests have reported hearing a spirit cat meowing in an upstairs bedroom; this is all the more unsettling because Abby Borden supposedly did once discover a decapitated feline in the basement, and nobody could ever explain how it got there.[16] Anyone who subscribes to the theory that Lizzie was a sociopath nods with recognition when they hear of the dead cats and dead pigeons that littered the Borden property, for this is precisely how one practices for murder.[17]

Two tour guides at the Lizzie Borden Bed and Breakfast, Kathie Goncalo and George Quigley, have said the spirits in the Borden home are "friendly spirits," presumably never having encountered Andrew at his angriest. Cameras have malfunctioned, or photographed "bizarre" clouds of mist, particularly near the couch where Andrew was murdered. Staffer Kerri Roderick once witnessed an imprint of a body in the bed where Abby Borden was murdered: "I arrived at work to start cleaning the house, and I was on my last room, and I had made the bed and cleaned, dusted, and everything. And then I turned around, and there was the perfect impression of somebody laying [*sic*] on the bed. . . . I looked at it for, like, a couple of seconds, and then I booked it out of the room."[18]

One former owner of the Borden house, Martha McGinn, described the house as "active." McGinn was one of the first to point out that the house was haunted. She lived most of her life there, and then turned it into a bed-and-breakfast when she inherited it. She said she has heard footsteps and doors that open and shut, and seen lights flicker on and off. McGinn is perhaps most responsible for embracing the legend of the haunted Borden house. She lived in the house from the age of seventeen, in 1968, when she moved in with her grandparents, the owners at the time, who had purchased the house forty-three years earlier. McGinn began to experience haunting activity almost right away. Once, when she was in her bedroom reading a book, she heard the distinct sounds of footsteps and rolling marbles on the floor above her, and what sounded like children's laughter floated down through the air.[19] Many others have felt or heard the ghostly presence of children, and attribute them to Eliza's murdered babies. It may also be possible, however, that they are place memories of young Lizzie and Emma.

One of McGinn's more famous anecdotes concerns a window: "I went up the stairway, and the window at the end of the second-floor corridor just began opening and slamming shut. It was just violently going up and down."[20] If she wasn't already convinced the house was haunted, a trip to the basement made her a believer: according to her memoir *Looking Back: My Life at 92 Second Street,* she witnessed what she described as a shadow floating in traditional spectral fashion about four inches off the basement floor. The shade wore Victorian-era clothes and was female. McGinn hightailed it up the stairs, frightened to the point that her hair literally stood on end.[21]

When McGinn inherited the Borden house in 1994 and decided to run it as a bed-and-breakfast, she embraced the ghostly aspects of the legend after "odd things" started happening to her staff.[22] "I think the apparitions and all the activity that has been happening in the house, it's a possibility that the spirits are trying to communicate through myself, my staff, or my guests of who really committed the murders so they can rest in peace, put the story to sleep once and for all."[23]

It is often thought that the ghost most desperate to communicate is Abby. Lizzie's relationship with her stepmother was notoriously strained; it is well-known that after the controversy about the property, Lizzie stopped calling her "Mother" and started calling her "Mrs. Borden." At the inquest, a police officer asked Lizzie, "When did you last see your mother?" Lizzie promptly snapped, "She is not my mother. She is my stepmother. My mother is dead."

Lizzie's hatred of Abby was an open secret around town; she once called her stepmother a "mean, good-for-nothing thing." Others had different opinions, and Abby was by no means universally reviled. Her own stepmother said of her that Abby was a "closed-mouth woman" who could "bear a great deal and say nothing."[24] Neighbors said Abby was a decent woman and Bridget Sullivan said she was kind to her, and good to work for. Bridget had on several occasions threatened to quit over the tension in the household, and Abby had repeatedly "coaxed her to stay and once raised her wages."[25] Hosea Knowlton called Abby a "faithful wife who has served [Andrew] thirty years for her board and clothes," which is rather faint praise and, as Cara Robertson points out, "reduced Abby to the status of servant in her own household."[26] It's hard not to have sympathy for Mrs. Borden. She is one of the most frequent apparitions at the Borden House, and no wonder.*

It hardly seems fair that the victim of a crime should be doomed to eternal restlessness, but according to psychics and paranormal investigators, she says she "cannot leave." Although, as some small measure of comfort, she did note that she was pleased with the way Lee-Ann Wilber kept the house.[27]

But, again, what of Lizzie's spirit?

Those seeking the ghost of Lizzie at the Borden house may be surprised that the basement shadows are pretty much the only manifestation attributed to Lizzie. Though the house is crammed with the phantoms of Abby, Andrew, Lizzie's uncle John V. Morse, Bridget, ghost cats, the dead children of Eliza Borden, and even, once, Southard Miller, an old friend and neighbor of Andrew Borden, Lizzie herself is probably the rarest appearance, even if her dark energy still permeates and suffuses the place.[28] Many believe she haunts her second home, Maplecroft, instead, because it was a place where she felt happy and safe. Unlike most killers, she does not seem too often compelled to revisit the scene of the crime. Instead, psychics have seen her smiling at Maplecroft in a purple dress, overseeing a children's Easter egg hunt. This certainly jibes with her later years, when she became "Aunt Lizzie" to her servants' children. She used to give them gifts: gold rings to the boys and Sunbonnet Babies dishware to the girls. Author Rebecca Pittman notes the ironic, subliminal choice in these gifts: Andrew Borden legendarily wore only one piece of jewelry: a "thin gold band" given to him by Lizzie. And

---

* Trance medium Maureen Wood declared that she could sense Abby's spirit in the house, and that Abby confirmed Lizzie was the one who killed her. Unfortunately, Wood's account of her practices at the Borden house, including table-tipping and glass-swirling, feels hokey; she also repeatedly refers to Abby as "Abigail," although that was not her name. Like Lizzie, she bore a truncated version of her Christian name. Andrew probably liked the thrift of it.

Sunbonnet Babies dishware shows different chores for each day of the week: the chore for Thursday is washing windows.[29]

Lizzie didn't die in the Borden house; she died at Maplecroft. After the trial, she became a pariah in Fall River. All her former friends avoided her, and she ended up hanging out at first with theater people from New York and then, finally, with the children of her own servants. Even her sister, Emma, left her by 1905, citing Lizzie's difficult personality as one of the reasons she left. Lizzie lived in an ostentatious home she named Maplecroft, when naming your home was considered a fairly pretentious thing to do in Fall River. She squabbled with the neighbors, erecting several "spite fences" around her property. She was once arrested for shoplifting in Providence, Rhode Island. And local children would egg her house and stick pins in her doorbell to make it ring ceaselessly. Lizzie could hear them laughing at her as they ran away. Like many of the female ghosts in this book, Lizzie ended her final years in reclusive eccentricity and isolation, becoming a "living ghost," as it were. This is a commonality between her and other ghosts in this book, namely Gertrude Tredwell, Eliza Jumel, and Sarah Winchester. Lonely women with money drift and die alone in their high towers, or so it seems.

But with Lizzie, the ghostlike quality of her later days echoes the aimlessness of her younger life, trapped at home with nowhere to direct her longing or ambition, if she ever had any. In his summarizing remarks at her trial, her defense attorney George Robinson "transformed Lizzie into the paradigmatic 'angel in the house,' her lack of alibi proof of her feminine normality. He argued,

> *They say she was in the house in the forenoon. Well, that may look to you like a very wrong place to be in. But it is her own home . . . I don't know where I would want my daughter to be . . . than to say she was at home, attending to the very ordinary vocations of life, as a dutiful member of the house-*

> *hold . . . Is there anything unnatural or improbable in her going to the barn for anything she wanted? Honest people are not particular about punctuation and prepositions all the time. Do you suppose that your wives and daughters can tell the number of times they went up and down stairs six months ago on a given day?*[30]

If your life was the same every day, with nothing to break the unremitting monotony, would you know the number of times you went up and down the stairs in a day? Did Lizzie ever think of these remarks as she went up and down the lonesome stairs at Maplecroft?

Lizzie Borden will forever remain an enigma at the tense center of opposing truths. She is a spinster, an eternal "girl." She is either a victim or a murderer. She may have been a sociopath, or she may have been a strong-willed person pushed beyond her limits by the confines of her stifled life. Looking at her photographs, it is no easier to pass judgment. She does look a bit crazed, but as Angela Carter writes, "Who among us doesn't possess photographs of ourselves that make us look like crazed assassins?"[31] She is at the center of larger forces, essential questions that radiate out from her in a taut web. There is the eternal fascination with the true crime case, a torch once held by the many women spectators at her trial, and now held by the keepers of "mondo Lizzie," the blogs and Facebook pages and meetups dedicated to her, and the tensions between them and the fans of her paranormal aspect, of the haunted house that forever bears her name. Time will tell how the house will be managed, and what the spirits will make of it. There is the tension between Lizzie's masculine and feminine selves, between her truths and her lies, between her life and afterlife, and, above all, the almost unbearable tension of the unsolvable mystery.

And yet what is so tantalizing is that the solution might be there, only just out of reach: In *The Trial of Lizzie Borden*, Cara Robertson writes: "On the 16th floor of an unremarkable office building, sits a file on Lizzie Borden, guarded by the law firm Governor George Robinson founded in 1866 . . . In Springfield MA, locked in a five-drawer filing cabinet, the file languishes."[32] Who knows what secret confessions may be revealed in that file? It is so theoretically easy to access, but so out of reach: the Lizzie Borden Defense File is protected by attorney-client privilege, and the current partners of the law firm refuse to breach that privilege. Whatever it contains will remain a secret, for now, and the threads woven around Lizzie Borden remain tight and silent.

Lucy Dutton as illustrated for Grace Greenwood's "A Night of Years—The Maniac," circa 1848. Image courtesy of the Cortland NY Historical Society

PART 5

"Madwomen"

INTRODUCTION

LEANNA

There's a long list that's been the subject of plenty of internet memes—the myriad behaviors and activities that could get a woman committed to an asylum in previous centuries. Whether it was reading too much, wanting to wear pants, wanting to vote or perhaps just having normal human emotions, institutionalization was a threat for many who veered outside cultural norms, depending on their background, status, race, class, identity, and environment.

A general discomfort with women's bodies, place, and sexuality crested to a near-fever pitch during the nineteenth century, amid radical industrial and global changes. This societal unease led to a profound disconnect. "Hysteria" became an increasingly frequent diagnosis for any number of things, from mere exhibition of opinions to the concept of sexual independence (let alone living it). The era made a concerted effort to divorce women from sexual agency and heightened the divisive idea of a frailer, weaker sex.

The idea that somehow women are inherently unstable has cast a long shadow through history. We're still battling the concept of a woman being "too emotional" to hold leadership positions here in the United States. Victoria Woodhull certainly faced that aspersion when she ran for president in 1872. Having come up from Spiritualist circles, she used the concept of talking with the dead entirely for her own purposes, galvanizing those circles as a tool to become a public figure with radical politics. Speaking with spirits allowed for passions and convictions, especially those challenging the status quo, to take a broader stage. Woodhull's candidacy, however, was not taken seriously nationally. Many people thought her quite mad indeed.

Having spent a career of more than twenty years studying, theatrically performing, and writing about nineteenth-century perceptions, I can tell you that we're not over the restrictive constraints that era placed on every marginalized person and on women as a whole. There are a great many civil liberties activists fought for then that we're still fighting for now, with only slight changes in the language.

It wasn't as though the era was without its passions and expressions. It's just that only some people were able to safely indulge their respective autonomies without comment, criticism, intervention of the law, or worse. Anything not heteronormative and gender binary–adherent was "aberrant." We're still clawing our way back from that repressive age, navigating the effects of narrow windows of expression, self-actualization, and opportunity. There are many aspects of sexuality, desire, and identity that weren't struck from either the FBI's lists of "deviant" behavior or the *Diagnostic and Statistical Manual of Mental Disorders* (the *DSM*) until the mid-twentieth century.

The science of mental health has fortunately progressed some through the years. In the 1892 *King's Handbook of New York City*, when discussing the Women's Ward of the New York City Asylum for the Insane on Blackwell's Island, a specific note warrants grim consideration: "The patients are kept without restraint, and every possible effort is made to ameliorate their condition, by allotting them some occupation to employ their minds."[1] At least they weren't chaining inmates up anymore. The handbook goes on to mention the recent founding and mission of an organization built to keep a necessary, watchful eye on a flawed system:

> *The Lunacy Law Reform and Anti-Kidnapping League at 10 East 14th Street was founded in 1890 to protect sane persons against unjust and unlawful imprisonment in insane asylums and hospitals, and to secure humane treatment and the protection of their legal and constitutional rights to those suffering from insanity. Legal and medical advice is freely given to all deserving applicants.*

Society still has a very hard time discussing, grappling with, and being honest about mental health. Calling someone "crazy" is a threat that often has consequences for the accused, whether a legitimate mental health condition is in play or not. People are all too eager to use that label on anyone or anything they don't like or agree with.

In the following chapters we'll meet three women from vastly different backgrounds and circumstances who challenge the status quo and confront the concept of "madness" in their own ways. Each woman experienced dramatic circumstances in which she was not always in control of her own story. Sometimes the concept of the "unreliable narrator" comes from the outside in, a dismissive designation forced upon the protagonist.

Jan Bryant Bartell was an actress and psychic who lived in one of the most haunted houses in New York City in the 1970s. She chronicled her strange, often harrowing experiences at 14 West 10th Street in a rambling, unfocused, at times poignant memoir called *Spindrift: Spray from a Psychic Sea*. Her memoir fits the unreliable narrator trope—a dramatic device often used in Gothic tales and haunted house stories—making us, the reader, wonder what may have been true at all. The unreliable narrator creates a necessary discomfort, forcing us to consider the unanswered questions all around us, and bids us examine our own stability and mental state. After chronicling the *deeply* disturbing number of deaths and tragedies in the house, Bartell died just after leaving those infamous premises, before she could even see her book published. The location wasn't dubbed the "Murder House" until 1987, well after Bartell's departure. She left us a warning we didn't know how to hear.

Sarah L. Winchester was intelligent, generous, and absolutely *sane*. She had her quirks and her preferences, and if a woman is rich enough and has her own mind, she might be graciously labeled an eccentric. But for the wealthy, reclusive widow and her incredible "Mystery House," even "eccentric" had its limits. The press and gossipmongers, whipping up wild suppositions about her throughout her lifetime, would continue to add invective to commonplace gossip. Vociferous opinions and rumors flourished about the heiress's endless house and the séances that *surely* must be taking place there. The Widow Winchester and her labyrinthine mansion became a repository for a nation's anxieties, ghosts making demands on behalf of a country whose relationship with guns has always been contentious.

The label of "madwoman" has often been ascribed to women who were simply bucking norms or ruffling feathers. That doesn't mean there aren't stories of legitimate mental health crises that pepper the ghost story landscape.

For all that there is cruelty, misunderstanding, and fear in the label of madness, there is also room to consider grace.

In a tale that showcases tolerance and charity, Lucy Dutton, the Wandering Woman, suffered a distinct, brokenhearted betrayal. The psychological trauma of her incident created a curious result: She spent the rest of her life in a disconnected, dreamlike state, adorning her hair with flowers.

As you'll see in these chapters, the idea of being "mad" is all a matter of perspective. Though none of these women had the ability to escape the label, their haunted histories would inevitably catch up with them.

AN UNRELIABLE NARRATOR

Jan Bryant Bartell

LEANNA

NEW YORK, NEW YORK

IT IS A CURSED HOUSE, AND IT HAS THE FINAL SAY.

In 1855 a redbrick town house was completed at 14 West 10th Street in Greenwich Village, around the block from the verdant, vibrant Washington Square Park. At first, 14 appears like any other fine residence on the block of utterly charming, beautiful town houses, all sharing walls with the next address. Window boxes teem with flowers and bay windows reveal interior treasures. Trees on the block live lush and full, and the basement-level patios are well-kept, full of potted plants and bordered by wrought-iron beauty. Emma Lazarus, author of "The New Colossus," which adorns the Statue of Liberty, boldly declaring hope and refuge, once lived just a few doors down.

Number 14 has fine brownstone detailing around black-painted sills. Its wide first-floor windows show darkness within. At a glance, passing by, nothing appears amiss. But if an observer pauses for closer examination, odd outliers reveal themselves. Its red bricks bear a discoloration that none of the other structures on the block does—a strange residue. Even after a recent renovation and cleaning of the building, it's still as if a dark mold, an inexplicable rot, has oozed out from mortar pores to mark the building with an eternal stain.

Unlike the town houses around 14 that have stoops that lift you up to beautiful glass doors with carved wooden details, the stairs to 14 go down. One must descend to enter. A brownstone arch shades the underworld approach.

There's a plaque on the side of the building, before that shadowed stairwell, stating that Mark Twain lived on the premises for a year, from 1900 to 1901. His departure, it was said, was due to the fact his wife couldn't keep up with the housework. Admittedly, an entire town house that had yet to be subdivided into apartments would be a great deal of upkeep without a full staff. But perhaps there was a darker reason.

During my first days in the city, having moved to New York in 2005, I vividly recall wandering the neighborhood of West 10th Street and the areas around Washington Square Park while researching the setting of a paranormal novel. I came across one building that made me short of breath and uneasy, but didn't think much of it, not until I procured *Ghosts of New York City* by Therese Lanigan-Schmidt and paused at the mention of 14 West 10th, noting a quoted line from Shirley Jackson's definitive haunted house tale, *The Haunting of Hill House*: "some houses are born bad." I correlated that address with the one that had made me queasy in passing and couldn't argue with that sentiment. Something was off. And it seems it had been for a very long time.

No stranger to elements of horror in my fiction, I deemed the address a perfect setting for a novel, so I began drafting a book that followed several spirits and generations dealing with the house.

The horror stories unfolded.

Spindrift: Spray from a Psychic Sea by Jan Bryant Bartell is an out-of-print, hard-to-find memoir published in 1974 about the author's time living both at 16 and 14 West 10th Street. An off-Broadway stage actress of note with certain psychic sensitivities, a lecturer and writer from Maryland who had settled in New York as an adult, Bartell was in her forties when writing *Spindrift*, but her health was fragile and kept deteriorating.

Spindrift was one of the first books I read during my early days as a New Yorker, and it is the only book to be written exclusively about the address, though the house had already made numerous newspapers for being haunted.

Hans Holzer, famed ghost seeker of the city, published several accounts of this address, one of which Bartell was directly involved with, and he utilized narratives from various mediums. Results varied, but there was always something unsettling in the house: consistent paranormal activity. Shadows that moved, items that moved too, the feeling of being watched, an oppressive air. When Holzer published *Ghosts I've Met*, which included the Bartells' séance, Jan didn't feel Holzer got things right. Having omitted her most palpable haunted detail—the presence of a ghostly gray cat—the distaste his account left in her mouth became the impetus for her writing her own book about her experiences.

Regardless of *who* tells the story of 14 West 10th, one through line remains unaltered: Whatever darkness took up root in the house, it did so early on and continues to cause trouble.

Both Andrea and I remember hearing something about a historic incident of child abuse as picked up in a séance or by sensitives at a point that predated the horrific events of 1980, but neither of us can pin down exactly where we heard it, and each of us remembers it as being said to have happened in a different era or decade. Perhaps the mind simply wants to grasp for purchase and understanding when trying to conceptualize something particularly terrible.

I felt deeply uncomfortable many times while reading *Spindrift*, working on my own fiction simultaneously. One of the earliest ideas I had for that book involved a morbid, past life trauma of a nineteenth-century character, one who miscarried a child due to violence at the address.

It was shocking, then, when I soon read an account of that same nature in *Spindrift*, a psychic picking up on that very malevolence. I felt as though I'd somehow stumbled on it like a mysterious radio transmission, a sense memory I couldn't have known and that wasn't even of my own creation, just a discomfiting recognition. Part of me felt even more compelled to continue my work; part of me felt warned to walk away. Quickly.

Things like that happened to Bartell too throughout her narrative; an odd passing thought, sight, or prompt would suddenly become strangely relevant the next day. Spray from a psychic sea.

While still enveloped in *Spindrift*, I traveled to Chicago to attend a doctoral thesis dissertation given by one of my best friends, after which our party went to get celebratory tattoos, and the only rule was that the image had to be something personally meaningful. When considering what to have inked, I felt called to choose an entwined alpha and omega. It wasn't a symbol I'd thought much about before, but I liked the idea of it: the beginning and the end, noting faith and also life cycles, the fullness of time, the past as prologue and the future within reach.

The next day I resumed my reading, picked up *Spindrift*, turned the page, and Bartell's next chapter began with an ode to the alpha and the omega.

I let the book drop from my hands as if I'd been scalded.

Whenever I explain this, it never fails to evoke a violent shudder from the listener, the desire to crawl out of one's skin. The utter, inexplicable strangeness of my choice of a meaningful but not top-of-mind symbol, then that symbol showing itself at the top of the next chapter I hadn't yet read, makes me feel like I'm only adding to the chorus of unreliable narrators who have clamored about this house for years.

I put the draft of fiction I'd been working on aside due to extreme unease about the psychic parallels, never to be picked back up again, deeming it a cursed manuscript about a cursed address. But I kept reading *Spindrift*, compelled. It isn't the most polished memoir, but I felt, being a bit energy-sensitive myself, the depth of Bartell's struggle on the page, watching in dread and empathy as the house depleted her and tried her senses. Despite the narrative running off into myriad tangents, her experiences remain believable. She's enough of a skeptic not to let her imagination rule. But it's clear she's suffering from depression in addition to increasingly frayed nerves resulting from truly inexplicable things: crashing noises when nothing was disturbed; a noxious smell of death that could overwhelm in one moment, something sickly sweet in another; the sound of rustling taffeta when no one is in the room; a looming black miasma that would disappear through the wall. Her descent is undeniably compelling, heartbreaking. Like the moments in a horror film when you keep shouting at the heroine to run. Or the times you can't help but turn your head to look at a car crash.

When Bartell moved from the top floor of number 16 to the top floor of 14, she had already lost her beloved dog, Penelope, whose fragile health had worsened as Bartell became more aware of her haunted surroundings. Tessa, the Bartells' next dog, was all too aware of spectral presences and reacted to them with similar unease. Canines in a proverbial coal mine.

Why Jan didn't vacate either 16 or 14 sooner seems to have been a mixture of not being believed by her amiable yet skeptical husband, her reluctance to leave the Greenwich Village area she adored, and the difficulties—as any New Yorker will tell you—of apartment hunting. When they left 16 for an apartment uptown, they were soon embroiled in a legal conflict with the upstairs neighbor. When an apartment became available in 14 West 10th, they returned to the neighborhood they dearly loved, Jan desperately needing peace and rest. But this address was no better than the one it shared a wall with. It was markedly worse.

Bartell begins to count the ill and dying at the address. Over twenty lives lost or irreparably changed during her fourteen-year tenure. A high number for an address that only houses a few apartments. She notes that out of ten families, five in the west and five in the east wings, respectively, three had been visited by death before the pace of misfortune increased in suicide and sickness.

During an ongoing litany of misery, her husband Fred's appendix burst while battling pneumonia, and Jan then describes further losses in quick succession: a tenant is attacked outside the apartment and dies of his injuries, another died by alcoholism, another of terminal cancer. The superintendent explained to Jan why he didn't live in the basement any longer: not with the boots. "Them walkin' boots. They goes up and down, up and down, and ain't nothing attached to 'em. Then they disappear right through the wall. . . . No, ma'am—if I'm next, I ain't goin' to be down there waitin'."

The inevitability of *Spindrift* is unbearable. An actress who once starred in the paranormal classic *Bell, Book and Candle,* Bartell was not unfamiliar with spectral language. But her exploration of psychic waters veers further toward the undiscovered country. The title of the book is apt; "spindrift" refers to the churning wake of a ship. The haunted premises of 10th Street cut the agitated waters of Bartell's sensitivities, and the spray in their wake grew increasingly dangerous. The reader knows Bartell's fate; it is stated on the dust jacket of her memoir. Reading the book is one elaborate, dread precognition. The house would take her in the end.

Just as Bartell had managed to escape 10th Street for New Rochelle, she died. The coroners listed her cause of death as a heart attack. Only a few weeks after she had completed the manuscript, the book she'd told friends was a kind of catharsis. The book was published posthumously. Transcribers working from her notes repeatedly fell ill, and the book nearly wasn't published at all. But *something* had to stand as a testament to her experiences.

In her last chapter, Bartell ominously states that while the book has been her own exorcism, she wonders if it is done haunting the reader:

> *The writing of this book has been an exercise in personal exorcism. I hope it is done haunting me, although for you, the haunting may just have begun. If it reads like a Gothic novel, it lived like one; being unprepared for truth, I found it strange, much stranger, than fiction.*

Her final line tolls like a funeral bell: "If the spindrift has not reached you yet, it will, it will . . ."[1]

As if this wasn't enough, the house wanted more.

Bartell's death came several years before Joel Steinberg moved into 14 West 10th, and the horrific murder that occurred in his apartment became a frenzied media spectacle.

In 1987, Steinberg, a then-disbarred criminal defense attorney, moved into the property with his partner, Hedda Nussbaum, and two adopted children, Lisa and Mitchell. His behavior became increasingly dark and violent. A real life *Shining* playing out in Greenwich Village. His former profession became the greatest irony.

On November 1, 1987, under the influence of crack cocaine, Steinberg struck six-year-old Lisa violently on the head inside their apartment. She lay unconscious and bleeding for ten hours, when the battered Nussbaum finally was able to call 911. The child died at nearby St. Vincent's Hospital. At the time doctors thought that if either adult had acted in a timelier manner, Lisa likely would have survived.

In court, friends mentioned that Steinberg changed when he moved into 14 West 10th. The trial was one of the first to be televised in its entirety. Nussbaum agreed to testify against Steinberg in exchange for exemption from conviction for negligence. Her face, showing obvious signs of physical trauma, shocked audiences. Steinberg was convicted of manslaughter and served his sentence until 2004, when he was released. Nussbaum underwent numerous reconstructive surgeries and began working with domestic violence victims, and retreated from public life until writing *Surviving Intimate Terrorism*. Mitchell was reunited with his birth mother.

The unconscionable events earned 14 West 10th a new nickname: The Murder House.

In Susan Blackhall's *Ghosts of New York*, she claims the caretakers admit the building is cursed. With all these accounts, it's easy to see why the address is dubbed the city's most haunted house. You won't find that on any of the real-estate listings. But the fact that it hasn't been fully occupied for years, in one of the most desirable and expensive neighborhoods in the country, is telling.

A *New York Times* article referenced in Lanigan-Schmidt's account brings us back to Mark Twain, referencing a 1930s tale in which a woman and her daughter discover an elderly man with bushy white hair who appeared suddenly in their living room to state, "My name is Clemens and I had a problem here I gotta settle." Bartell herself tells this story, as relayed to her by the superintendent of the property. It's likely *Spindrift* is the primary source.

Perhaps Twain's hasty exit had nothing to do with general housework after all, but an inherent paranormal mess in a structure "born bad."

I admit my own hesitancy to write all this. But I suppose it is inevitable. The house still haunts me, just as Bartell thought it would. There don't seem to be any reports of *Jan* haunting the house. I certainly wouldn't want that for her spirit, and I pray she's finally found the peace she yearned for. One certainly can't find it at that address.

I tell those I guide on my tours that the house and I have an uneasy understanding; it doesn't like me and I don't like it. It's still difficult for me to breathe when standing out front to quietly relay its dread tales. The house shortened the breath of so many through the years, snuffing the life right out. Hastening or prompting an unpleasant end.

When asked if I'd ever go inside its apartments, I adamantly respond that I won't, quite certain I'd fall ill or worse, like so many of the residents Bartell noted. I realize this makes me sound paranoid, my senses as precarious as Bartell's psyche, but if I must be seen as an unreliable narrator, I would prefer to act out of an abundance of caution and steer clear of a curse.

In séances mentioned in *Spindrift*, psychics note the appearance of a gray cat beside a woman clad in gray who reassures onlookers that "everything's just fine."

That's what the house would like you to think.

But it lies.

UNFINISHED BUSINESS

The Winchester Mystery House

LEANNA

SAN JOSE, CALIFORNIA

THE WINCHESTER MYSTERY HOUSE OF CALIFORNIA APTLY REmains an enigma. Even the precise origin of its "mystery house" title remains impossible to pin down. The phrase "house of mystery" was used in print when discussing the mansion as early as 1911, eleven years before its eponymous owner's death. The one unquestionable truth of the place so shrouded in myth is that it is absolutely, as the tagline on merchandise in the gift shop says, "beautiful and bizarre."* It most certainly is.

The seemingly unending edifice *is* haunted, if nothing else because the court of public opinion has always insisted it is. It cannot

---

* The tagline printed on the gift shop merchandise used to be "beautiful but bizarre," but the merchandise has changed in the past few years to "beautiful *and* bizarre." House historian Janan Boehme noted that the change happened without a company-wide discussion about it, but that it does have a different feel as a message.

escape its own mythmaking, and it may not entirely want to. The place does have its own mind.

I made the pilgrimage to the Mystery House solely for the purposes of this chapter and found the visit daunting and incredible; I left with an indiscernible feeling that took time to put into words. The house itself is an experience as much as anything, a force of nature, gargantuan and ponderous.

The 160-room mansion that was never entirely finished, and cost, at the time, some $5.5 million all told to build, is unlike anything else in the world. Not just because of its impressive numbers, but because of the persistent mythologies that keep it present in popular consciousness, as recently as Hollywood's rendition, *Winchester,* starring Helen Mirren as an enigmatic, guilt-ridden widow hounded by ghosts to keep building until she dies.

The idea that the house was built at the direction of spirits has remained with it for almost its entire life. Even the tour booklet in the gift shop bears the subtitle "the mansion designed by spirits." But if popular imagination hadn't seen fit to make this house even larger in life than its 160 rooms, would the impressive place still be standing at all? It wasn't listed as a historical landmark, and thus given a certain protected status, until 1974.

What is true about the real Sarah L. Winchester is that we'll never entirely know her, and she made it quite clear that's how she wanted it.

Helen Mirren is admittedly captivating and convincing as Sarah Winchester in the 2018 film, embodying the fiercely intelligent and interesting woman she was. Many scenes were filmed at the house itself. But once the film devolves into sheer horror-film excess, Winchester's character and the famous surroundings are placed into the frame the house has always been painted into: wild, dark flights of fancy. Because it's truly impossible to know the exact truth of why she made the choices she did regarding that house, entertainment has filled that void with creative supposition, armchair psychology, and the irresistible thrall of ghosts.

While it's tempting to lead with the wild myths of midnight séances conducted by an obsessive madwoman haunted by remorse over the deaths attributed to the Winchester rifle, such derisive notions plagued Winchester throughout her lifetime. Falsehoods expanded as if in proportion to the construction of her unique house and continued long after her death. It is only fair to begin with her actual history and from there untangle the knot of imaginative suppositions placed on her and her home.

Sarah Lockwood Pardee Winchester was born in 1839 and died in 1922. One of the wealthiest women of her time, she knew all too well that no amount of money could stave off death. The Pardee and Winchester families had known each other since Sarah and her future husband, William, were young, living next door to each other on Court Street in New Haven, Connecticut, in 1850. Their families each came from nothing and made something of themselves—Leonard Pardee became a skilled woodworker and Oliver Winchester a shrewd businessman who made money innovating men's shirt production long before he made a risky investment in a failing arms company on which he eventually put his name.

Sarah, one of six Pardee children, was well educated and showed interest and aptitude in many subjects. William was a dutiful son and was expected to take a position in his father's companies. They married in 1862, in the middle of the Civil War. Each family staunchly supported the abolition of slavery, President Abraham Lincoln, and the Union cause—regardless of the fact that their businesses would suffer economically. Both families deemed the moral cause of abolition superior to their bottom lines.

William and Sarah loved each other, and their families, deeply. After her wedding, Sarah moved into the increasingly crowded Court Street house with plans of her own ahead.

Death hit the family hard in quick succession beginning in the

1860s. William's nephew died and his sister followed not long after. The brutal loss continued when Sarah and William's firstborn and only child, Annie, died in 1866 from marasmus, an acute, harrowing condition that left the baby unable to digest. Without a cure, the infant starved to death within a month.

At this delicate time, the couple agreed to continue to live with the senior Winchesters, helping to direct and oversee construction of the family's grand new home on Prospect Street. The "house on the hill" would sit overlooking New Haven while Oliver Winchester spent all his time on his new Repeating Arms Company. The process of building allowed William and Sarah's mutual love of architecture and design to flourish, offering a respite from grief. In this, they were well-suited for the discipline, their collaboration an exemplary, trusted partnership.

From 1880 to 1881, Sarah suffered three more devastating losses. First, her own mother. Next, her indomitable father-in-law. Then, unbearably, her husband William succumbed to the tuberculosis he'd been fighting for years. She never stopped thinking of and hoping to honor him, as her own will would make clear decades later.

William left everything to, as his will stated, "my beloved wife Sarah." She was named executrix of his estate and was provided counsel by trusted advisers within the Winchester Repeating Arms Company. As she navigated her mother's estate and William's simultaneously, the inheritance from Oliver Winchester that had passed to William also became Sarah's to manage. Her husband's estate alone was valued at $8 million in today's dollars, and she would soon hold a third of the shares in the Winchester Repeating Arms Company. She couldn't immediately conceptualize the extent of the wealth she was inheriting. But for the rest of her life, she was both a shrewd and generous manager of the large sums and the dividends provided.

The grieving widow selected a plot in New Haven's Evergreen

Cemetery that was set near the senior Winchesters' but in its own distinct quarters. She honored William with a hulking, rough-hewn rock with WINCHESTER written across a large cross. Accented by carved foliage, the stone was dynamically different from the neoclassical structures around it. Their baby Annie was set under a marble cross with similar foliage near the base of the great stone. Winchester herself would be placed by her beloved's side some forty-one years later. A polished stone bench carved in loving memorial of Sarah, given by the workers of the Winchester Mystery House, sits to the side, offering a place for visitors to sit and contemplate the complex life of an inscrutable woman.

After William's death, and when the affairs of his estate were in order, Sarah removed herself from society on a European tour. The death of her sister Mary brought her back to New Haven in 1884, and there she began thinking of her next steps. She'd traveled to San Francisco with William years before, checking in on the West Coast offices of his father's company, and they'd found the Bay Area quite pleasant.

Many sources suggested, in newspaper articles and books—the notion repeated endlessly as cause for her upheaval to California and the resulting labyrinthine project there—that after William's death, seeking solace and guidance, Sarah had seen a Boston spiritualist who told her to go West and keep building to appease the spirits of those killed by Winchester rifles.

The Winchester Repeating Arms Company had innovated the design and production of repeating rifles by the 1860s. Oliver Winchester had tried to supply the Union Army with his rifle during the Civil War, but those Northern contracts never materialized. The Winchester "Gun that Won the West" became a symbol of westward expansion instead. Not only was it then associated with frontier lawlessness but also the forced removal of and increasing violence against Native Americans. Notably, however, the Battle of the Little Bighorn was won by Native Americans carrying Spencer and Winchester repeating rifles, as opposed to Custer's single-shot carbines. Tribes called the Winchester the "spirit gun" because it kept firing.

While it's possible Sarah Winchester discussed Spiritualism or consulted with a spiritualist medium in hopes of connecting with her lost loved ones, as was particularly common in the era and in high society, direct correlation between her and such a medium is impossible to prove, as are her own private thoughts about the guns themselves. If she had an opinion of the company one way or another, she didn't state one. But before the end of the century the concept of an addled, haunted woman using ongoing construction to stave off a ghostly reckoning of gun violence would be put in print by those who couldn't help but keep speculating about her actions.

A country that continues to have complicated, deadly, and obsessive relationships with guns began offshoring its guilt onto Sarah L. Winchester from the nineteenth century on.

A far more reserved, shy person than was suited for the demands of New Haven and East Coast high society, when her sister Nettie's husband, Homer Sprague, accepted a position at Mills College in Oakland, California, Winchester made plans for all her remaining sisters to move West together. Just past forty, she was already starting to feel the effects of rheumatoid arthritis. A warmer climate was often prescribed and supported by doctors.

Winchester was likely surprised that her social position, fortune, and name would end up drawing so much attention on the other side of the country.

Mary Jo Ignoffo, author of Sarah Winchester's most comprehensive and factual biography, *Captive of the Labyrinth*, offers additional context:

> *Winchester plotted her escape and imagined a self-contained enclave where she had only to rely upon her intellect and a bank book to retreat from the outside world. . . . Despite the*

> *fact that she continued to wear black mourning dresses and hats, the whole concept offered an unexpectedly positive outlook for a widow entering middle age.*[1]

Ned Rambo, the shrewd businessman who had made the San Francisco Winchester Arms office very profitable, suggested the Santa Clara Valley and took Winchester on a tour. Immediately captivated by the area, she soon purchased a farmhouse with forty-five acres, secured Rambo as her foreman, and would continue buying parcels of land in California. The Santa Clara Valley reminded her of the Basque country she'd seen on a trip with her husband ten years before—an open plain at the base of the Pyrenees. She named her new home Llanada Villa in honor of that journey to Llanada Alavesa.

What had been an eight-room farmhouse was transformed into a twenty-six-room mansion in a mere six months. And the building had only just begun. The idea that work was done around the clock grew from casual comments that she was always building. People just began taking that idea literally, that she was *always*, night and day, week in and week out, building.

Sensationalized accounts of the house grew up with it, in the moment, contemporaneous to its reportedly obsessive building. Sarah Winchester, like other widows and lone women featured in this book, had stories told about her long before her passing. Her fascinating, never-ending house, her reluctance to be seen (and if she was, never without mourning clothes and obscuring veil), her refusal to admit strangers coming to pay their respects, only increased gossip and curiosity. Everyone had thoughts about what was happening at the mysterious, expanding house.

One of the most distinctive rooms in the Mystery House is the ballroom, supposedly the inspiration for the ballroom in Disney's Haunted Mansion. The Mystery House ballroom contains a magnificent organ, an exquisitely detailed inlaid wooden floor, and two lovely stained-glass windows with quotes from Shakespeare. One side of the ballroom windows states:

"Wide unclasp the tables of their thoughts"

The window on the other side of the grand fireplace states:

"These same thoughts people this little world"

No one has ever managed to discern what Sarah Winchester meant, exactly, by these two quotes which, even if taken in context in their respective plays, *Richard III* and *Troilus and Cressida*, fail to offer further illumination. The windows have been a subject of, as has every choice regarding the house, fierce debate. Again, Sarah Winchester never explained herself or her choices. The two windows share the word "thoughts."

Everyone around her had *lots of thoughts*. About her, her choices, her tragedies, her properties, her inheritance, her sanity. It is clear that the retiring, contemplative, intelligent, introverted Sarah Winchester was always thinking, and often thinking of others in a generous capacity. But the thoughts of others *toward* her are what wrote her story and, in a way, are responsible for the house still standing today.

The house is an assortment of asymmetrical architectural styles that can be thrown under the eclectic umbrella of "American Queen Anne" and "Victorian." She and William had so enjoyed helping to bring the Prospect house to life in New Haven. But in California, Winchester sketched architectural plans for the house on her own. Having studied the process through books and records, noting ideas on whatever paper she had on hand, she instructed carpenters and skilled workmen to execute her designs, reworking them entirely if they didn't turn out as she'd hoped. The mansion has a nesting doll quality to it, as one can find parts of the shell of the previous exterior as part of the walls and interior of the expansions.

Aware there was far more fiction than fact surrounding the place, I tried not to have expectations of the house going in, even though I've been intrigued by it my whole life. I was surprised, however, that despite the house being dizzying to behold, enter, and venture through, I didn't feel as claustrophobic as many accounts made the place seem. Save for the narrow, low-rise, switchback staircase created so Sarah Winchester's arthritic knees could manage it, the house is surprisingly open. Clever uses of skylights and window angles offer a far lighter atmosphere than would have been thought possible. But the house absolutely confounds. There are ongoing sequences of hallways, rooms, and corners to turn before an entirely new wing splays out ahead, easily throwing off a sense of direction or easy understanding of the layout.

Sarah Winchester was an architect, something that only her race and wealth afforded her as a hobby. Society at the time would never have allowed her such a *profession*. Self-taught, she subscribed to journals like the *Architectural Record* and did her own rough drafting. Many of the things that don't add up in the house can be attributed to this workshopping nature. She was experimenting, and the house was her lab.

The many unfounded rumors about Sarah Winchester range from questioning the details of her house to her choices, her funding, and her staff.

Workers didn't mind building and rebuilding; she paid them twice the rate anyone else did. The idea that at the moment of her death, workers dropped their tools and left nails undriven is yet another fabrication. By the time of her passing, new work hadn't been done on the house in some time, save for the most basic repairs. The 1906 earthquake saw to that.

Sustainable in and of itself on the revenue from the vast fruit farm Winchester extended around her, the house was not, as gossip suggested, siphoning money away from the company that bore her husband's name. The houses on the land she bought she offered to her staff and their families. Apricots, plums, and walnuts were harvested, canned, dried, and sent worldwide.

The large bell at the center of her complex was rung for lunch and dinner, not, according to legend, for midnight séances to usher in the spirit world. In reality, nosy neighbors would never have tolerated bells ringing every midnight. Winchester wrote to her relatives regarding bouts of insomnia, and it's possible neighbors may have noticed lights on in the middle of the night, perhaps seeing a wandering figure through windows, and assumed, as the papers suggested, that she was conducting séances or any number of unusual practices.

The spiderweb, leaded-glass windows, a distinct feature around the house, aren't necessarily meant to be eerie; plenty of glass art of the nineteenth century featured spiderweb patterns, notably Clara Wolcott Driscoll's famous design for Louis Comfort Tiffany's stained-glass lamps and tea screens. Perhaps Winchester liked spiders because they, too, were always building. During her lifetime the house grew to an incredible seven stories with the completion of a great tower.

That her staff was more diverse than other business owners of her status and wealth additionally brought out racist notions that were disseminated in the press. "Beginning at this time, stories in the newspapers claimed that Sarah Winchester hosted unusual religious rituals in her home. . . . Winchester's appreciation for Japanese culture and willingness to hire Japanese workers added to her reputation as an oddball."[2]

Henrietta Sivera, the personal secretary and constant companion of Sarah Winchester, who was present at her death, denied the widow held spiritualist leanings. This is in direct conflict to the existence of what was dubbed her séance room—likely a gardener's bedroom—a plain, small, underwhelming, unadorned space that has an exit one can't get back into. The thirteen hooks for her supposed séance robes were added after her death, as confirmed by carpenter James Perkins.

The refrain of "13," popular as an "occult" number, is everywhere in the house, repeated in all kinds of iterations, from steps to candles in the ballroom chandelier. The obsession with the number didn't appear in print until after 1929—another added embellishment.

And, of course, adding to the various external discomforts surrounding this sprawling manor was that there was no lord of this great castle. A lone woman ruled this empire.

Colin Dickey pulls no punches in his "Endless House" chapter in *Ghostland*, stating that Winchester's legend illuminates several cultural discomforts: "An uneasiness about women living alone, withdrawn from society, for one. An uneasiness about wealth and the way the superrich live among us. And perhaps, largest of all, an uneasiness about the gun that won the West and the violence white Americans carried out in the name of civilization."[3]

A nation displaced baggage, unresolved guilt, and crises of identity onto one woman, her wealth, and her choices. But Winchester wasn't paying attention to any of that; she was trying to take care of the remaining people she loved after having already lost so many.

Several female relatives took shelter under her expanding roof for different spans of time. Her sister Estelle, in failing health, nursed the wounds of a troubled marriage and divorce, taking time with Winchester at Llanada Villa. Estelle died in that house, due to complications arising from cirrhosis of the liver.

Winchester's favorite niece was Marion "Daisy" Merriman, who lived with her for fifteen years. The Victorian "language of flowers," a popular, widely used way to converse in bouquets or add messaging to gardens, posits that a daisy means attachment. Daisies were often used in mourning jewelry of the time, held in a graceful hand, or carved onto tombstones. In the Winchester Mystery House, the Daisy Bedroom features beautiful motifs of the flower in stained-glass windows where the blossoms climb around clear ovals displaying the grounds below. Many of the choices Winchester made in her later years were to provide for Daisy or to have residences nearer to her after her marriage.

Only parts of the Mystery House were ever fully finished and inhabited. She didn't end up housing her whole family, as she may have once dreamed. At some point the construction may have been, in part, an excuse.

> *Letters to Jennie Bennett hint that perhaps she kept building not to accommodate more houseguests but to avoid having them. . . . "Although I am sufficiently settled to allow a small family to live quite comfortably, I am not so situated yet, as to feel I can make invited guests as comfortable as to justify me in giving pressing invitations." What must her sister-in-law have thought, that after twelve years, the California home was still not ready for visitors.*[4]

Winchester expanded her acreage in proportion to the house, buying up nearby plots, reaching nearly 160 acres. She was a particular woman, fond of close family, generous to her staff and, anonymously, to charity. But her reclusiveness became the basis for all the rumors about her. And like all rumors, they expanded and metamorphosed.

The 1906 earthquake along the San Andreas fault, measuring 7.8 on the Richter scale, one of the largest in California history, changed everything. The house still bears the scars of that day in cracked plaster, broken tile and brick. While debris was cleared out, the quake left many parts of the house skeletal, lending all the more to the concept of an unsettled nature.

Guides at the house say Winchester was trapped in the Daisy

Bedroom when it happened, the house rocking and shifting around her, debris blocking the door and taking workmen significant time to get her out. Whatever she thought about the earthquake or how she managed the terrifying experience, no letters or comments survive. But the house suffered catastrophic damage; the tower became a leaning danger. Sarah had the top stories of the house torn down for safety; her retreat and castle had suddenly become a perilous trap. What didn't make architectural sense before the earthquake may have been a quirk of design and experimentation gone wrong; after the earthquake, doors led to nowhere because of its damage.

> *California was defiant in the face of loss and devastation and vowed to rebuild, swiftly. The fact that she did not do so flew in the face of the bravado of the time, which deemed her pessimistic at best, a madwoman at worst. Articles about her after the earthquake proposed that only someone who was insane would refuse to rebuild, and since she did just that, the wealthy widow Winchester had to be certifiable.*[5]

Again, society projected their own emotional needs and justifications onto her own very personal decisions.

Winchester spent a great deal of time after the earthquake on her houseboat in Burlingame, off the San Francisco Bay, and in one of her properties nearer to Daisy. Back at Llanada Villa, "Mrs. W." would stop in periodically, as would be noted in the caretakers' notebooks. Once the widow's already fragile health began to fail further, at the age of eighty-two, she returned to Llanada Villa to be closer to her trusted doctor, Dr. Wayland.

Sarah Winchester died of heart failure on September 5, 1922, in her elegant bedroom at her mystery house. Entering into that space offers a curious sensation, almost as if the room is remembering the moment as the tour guide announces it. Time lengthens, allowing for more poignancy than in other places in the house.

In Sarah Winchester's will, her wealth was divided up between her relatives, significant sums were paid to her staff, and an enormous sum—several payments totaling millions—endowed the William Wirt Winchester tuberculosis hospital in New Haven, in honor of her great love.

The Mystery House itself was not mentioned in Sarah's will. Its contents were cleared by Daisy Merriman and Henrietta Sivera before the mansion went up for auction. Sarah's trusted attorney, Frank Lieb, noted that the house itself was assessed and deemed "of no value."

As shocking and perhaps heartbreaking as that may seem to those who have enjoyed this house through the decades, in this respect the wild rumors about Sarah Winchester proved helpful. *They* were of value, in the moment. Someone saw an opportunity in the rambling house in need of repair. When the auction of the house itself garnered no bids, John Brown leased the house with the plan to buy it eventually. Within nine months, the home was open to tourists, courtesy of Brown's new Winchester Amusement Company.

Having invented one of the earliest roller coasters at the Crystal Beach Resort near Niagara Falls, Brown knew what captivated theme park attendees. The "house of mystery" at Crystal Beach was one of its most popular attractions. The mysterious and unknowable had proved to be profitable, and the already infamous Winchester mansion was a ready-made "fun house." Brown offered tours to local press and celebrities, among them Harry Houdini. Legends of a fearful, haunted widow driven by vengeful ghosts became codified. Houdini deemed the house a curious, magnificent wonder.

This house, like so many historical buildings around the world, has to make its peace with ghosts. To stay alive, one has to keep courting the dead.

"I have to walk a fine line," Janan Boehme said, when generously guiding me around to places on the grounds that were not a part of the formal tour. Janan is the house's first designated house historian, a recently created position. "Everyone comes here with different expectations and I have to manage that."

Janan is a friendly, warm presence; her love for the Winchester house is absolutely palpable, casting an ebullient light over everyone's experience there. A justified protectiveness about Sarah Winchester's besmirched reputation is also clear in any discussion. Thanks to Janan's work, a representation of the crumbled tower lives again on an open upstairs floor, where molding and gingerbreading is laid out around the former windows that hang from rafters. Winchester saved and stored everything, and pieces of her home have been returning to their rightful places.

Winchester House View from Central Courtyard prior to 1907. Photo courtesy of Winchester Mystery House

A new renovation of the dining room has revived its original splendor. Janan meticulously oversaw the details and used as many of the house's existing puzzle pieces as possible. In a curious synergy, while attempting to ascertain the manufacturer of the room's stained-glass windows, a letter addressed to Sarah Winchester from the company thought to have made the windows was found behind the walls, confirming the provenance. Now and then the house might give up one of its secrets, but only if you're looking in the right place.

Under Janan's guidance, tour guides have gently amended sensationalist scripts to begin with "Legend has it . . ." to create the best of both worlds. Winchester likely wouldn't appreciate the arcade-style shooting range set up outside near the axe-throwing stalls—an attraction Lizzie Borden has to contend with at her infamous house as well—but the widow may have enjoyed the clever addition of a finely appointed new "escape room," replete with a secret passageway. In terms of income, the house has to innovate; the fruit orchards are long gone and the grounds aren't cheap to maintain.

My tour guides for my extended visit were Star and Jett, talented professionals who shared a clear love of the house and a sincere fondness for Sarah. Star took her audience through the house at an impressive clip in order to see all the rooms promised, a pace that only adds to the dizzying effect of the place. Star made particular note of details upstairs that would have likely gone unnoticed otherwise: how many additions Winchester made for the sake of her staff, from specific electrical features to huge washing sinks with hot and cold running water taps and built-in washboards that would have been state of the art at the time, to expansions of staff quarters and break rooms in order to make their jobs easier and more comfortable. Decorative details in staff areas showcased a level of consideration generally not afforded workspaces in other fine mansions. Those sheltered under the burgeoning roof were considered family. Fiercely loyal throughout her time there, Sarah's employees said not one bad word about her after her passing.

Jett, at the beginning of her "Explore More" tour, bid her audience remember that this was Sarah Winchester's *home* and we were lucky to get to see it. It was a welcome reminder that we were going through something intimate, something that the reclusive Sarah had only shared with a select few (and the occasional set of neighborhood children). And that is a truth of the house: It has an unmistakable thrall. It's full of those who care for it, those who work there now and all the energies of those who came before.

Considering the current general manager of the Winchester also came from an amusement park background—Disney, to be specific—that fine line between fact and selling point is clearly being walked all over the grounds. In addition to the gaming spaces, lavish Halloween decorations outside—and disturbingly creepy ones inside—demonstrate the popularity of their after-dark haunted house tours. Numbers are significantly down for the historic daytime tours once fall begins; everyone is in the mood to be scared instead of instructed.

Again, though, the labyrinthine house *is* haunted. Not just by expectation, rumor, and legend. Spirits still take care of the house, an entity living in past and present.

The most persistent and plausible ghost stories are those regarding Sarah's staff going about their routines. One of the old workmen, "Clyde," appears often around the grounds in a distinct pair of overalls and Victorian boater hat, checking the ballroom fireplace or attending to other duties, some visitors thinking he's a modern staffperson in costume. When staff correct that assumption and point out Clyde in a framed picture of early twentieth-century staff, the workman's amiable expression offsets the chill of having seen a ghost. Clyde has also been seen coursing the basement boiler room with a wheelbarrow.

The cellar is admittedly the creepiest part of the entire complex. It's an enormous space lying in wait below; stairs descend sharply to a landing with an impossibly long hallway lit by one eerie light. The smooth, dark corridor seems positively endless, with further hallways for the deposit of ash and soot at its other end. No one can blame tour guides who refuse to enter the cellar. One guide saw a figure looking back from the end of that interminable hallway and wouldn't go downstairs ever again.

On the other side of the cavernous basement sits a monster of a coal boiler resembling a stage set from *Sweeney Todd*. A mountain of coal ash, a remnant from Sarah's era, right up until her death, still sits piled high behind a wooden wall.

Exiting out around one of the elevators Sarah had installed whenever her crippling arthritis required a wheelchair, Jett told the story of another guide who, when alone and closing up for the night, heard disconcerting, disembodied singing coming from the bottom of the elevator shaft. Someone managed to upload a recording onto the Winchester Facebook page.

Thom Truelove, artist, author, and cocreator of my *Time Immemorial* psychic fiction series, explained what he saw when he toured the Winchester: several spirits who flitted in and out of frame, going about their business as tourists coursed the rooms, only vaguely interested in the company, pausing only if someone took note of them—as if in mutual recognition of a clairvoyant moment. Thom credits his epilepsy as the reason for his ability to see luminous spectral forms—some neurodivergent mystery that expands his senses. Everyone will have their own distinct, deeply personal experience in this place, and each experience, like each room, will be different.

Stories are still being told; legends are still unfurling. All a matter of perspective, the house in and of itself remains a *spiritual* enigma, an incomplete structure full of twists, turns, cracks, scars, and unfinished business. The house is an uncanny reminder of everything inside us that remains undone and unresolved.

Herself a house of mystery, a legend long before her death, speculation and local lore surrounding her becoming an international fascination, Sarah Winchester didn't dispute things said about her; she simply ignored them. But in her lack of rebuttal people assumed a truth. She never denied being a spiritualist, so people thought Spiritualism and spirits had to be involved in the ongoing construction of the house. The house doesn't really mind the speculation; it does seem glad for the company. It has an absolute, vibrant sense of being alive. Winchester's ingenuity and creativity made manifest. Per the Winchester website, medium James van Praagh claimed that during a séance dinner Sarah seemed happy that so many visitors were enjoying her home.

A lesson from Sarah Winchester may be helpful: Be confident in your own decisions. Act boldly without care of gossips. Be unique. Own the mystery for yourself. Interpret as you will, because Sarah Winchester never said one way or another, but she acted according to her interests, as "mad" or unfathomable to us as they may be.

You'll never know all the answers to the house, and in that divine mystery, rejoice.

A CORRECT HISTORY OF THE LIFE AND ADVENTURES OF THE WANDERING WOMAN

LEANNA

CENTRAL NEW YORK

CENTRAL NEW YORK IS BREATHTAKING, WITH OPEN, DRAMATIC, sweeping vistas, green peaks, and remarkable gorges. More than 200 miles northwest of the chaos of New York City, it is through the lush, verdant landscapes of several Central New York counties that Lucy Dutton wandered in life. Her spirit continues to do so after death.

Born circa 1795, Lucy lived near Cazenovia Lake in Madison County, New York, a peaceful, small body of water surrounded by rolling hills, picturesque countryside, and lovely old homes that bear a pride of place. With Cazenovia Lake as an epicenter, Lucy Dutton's meandering path grew as wide and large as the tales told of her.

Cortland County, southeast of Madison County, one of the places "Crazy Luce" was said to have wandered in a curious delirium, was one of the first towns responsible for putting her lore in print. The Cortland Historical Society is a charming, welcoming, saffron-yellow nineteenth-century building whose archives hold varying accounts of this unique, wandering woman.

While the names of the ancillary characters change depending on the authors of her tale, Luce remains the central focus of any narrative concerning her life, and her general through line remains the same: A sweet, charming, intelligent but unassuming young woman, Lucy is preparing for her marriage to a man she loves passionately when she is jilted by the groom—who marries her sister instead. Her madness is instant upon learning of this betrayal. As reason flees, detached restlessness takes logic's place. Her memory vanishes and she begins wandering.

"Crazy Luce, or a Correct History of the Life and Adventures of the Wandering Woman" was first published in the *Cortland Republican* newspaper and was given its own printed pamphlet edition in 1836.

In this disjointed account, Luce is a lovely orphan who lives in the woods surrounding Cazenovia Lake, where she wanders to gather food and flowers. She is singing with a robin when the bird is shot by Eugene Mervyn, a man who enters her clearing and is immediately cast as a rake by the author. That this story opens with violence done to an innocent bird sets the foreboding tone and allegory quite plainly. Eugene manages to convince the startled and sorrowful Luce that he wasn't trying to be terrible. With charm and guile, he manages to win her attention, naïve as she is.

Upon returning to his companion, Harry Martin, Eugene is chastised by his friend: "You never see a pretty girl but you must fall directly in love with her."

Eugene visits Luce regularly and tries to make advances, but Luce pushes back, asking when they'll be wed. The rake vanishes instead and goes out West. Luce waits for him, unaware his attention was fleeting, and when he returns to town for another reason, with his new wife in tow, Luce is thunderstruck to see his bride is her own sister, who had gone out West when their parents died.

Her madness is swift and thorough and she takes to wandering immediately.

Her account is taken up and told by the rake's former friend, Harry Martin, who finds Luce some thirty years later, dressed in layers of rags. He fends off a group of urchins who are taunting her. His heart goes out to her, but he notes her persistence, her determination to live, as well as the community that helps ensure her nomadic survival: "Still on she wandered, finding a home in every hamlet and pity in every breast."

This narrative ends with the notion that her state was actually a blessing: "The arrows of disappointment were blunted by the prostration of her reason, effected through the wise purposes of Him 'who tempers the winds, to the shorn lamb'; and she had not suffered in reality for she had been wandering in a dream."* That Luce's delirium was a *preferred* state to being rejected by a man, preferable to such disappointment, is a loaded supposition. As neurology and mental illness was its own scientific wilderness in the nineteenth century, it's likely that the storytellers who collected tales of this wandering woman were trying to find a reason *why* she rambled, restless and alone for the rest of her life.

The full subtitle of Luce's first published account, *or a Correct History of the Life and Adventures of the Wandering Woman,* offers a kindlier nuance to her tale than simply her derogatory nickname, humanizing her as a wandering adventurer, a quirky explorer managing the world in her own way.

Grace Greenwood's account of Luce, published in *The Ladies' Garland and Dollar Magazine* in 1848, is titled "A Night of Years—The Maniac," and this more incendiary title promises a narrative that waxes dramatically rhapsodic and melancholic.

An illustration is included opposite the title page, where Luce

* From "Crazy Luce, or a Correct History of the Life and Adventures of the Wandering Woman," Cortland Village, NY: Printed for the Pedlars, 1836.

is depicted with flowers around her head, a detail that factors into her story directly but can't help put the reader in immediate mind of Shakespeare's Ophelia, who similarly went mad after tragedy and adorned herself with blossoms. But Luce, unlike Ophelia, never commits suicide in a river. Luce's spirit decided to be associated with a lake instead.

According to Grace Greenwood, Luce was "winningly rather than strikingly beautiful. Under a manner observable for its seriousness and a nunlike serenity were concealed an impassioned nature and a heart of the deepest capacity for loving. She was remarkable from her earliest childhood for a voice of thrilling and haunting sweetness."[1]

Each account discusses beauty as a feature of why Luce was well-liked in her youth, though she was plainer than the rival woman involved, and this proves an important factor in the deception or the change of heart. Considering society's consistent emphasis on the importance of feminine beauty, this would serve the purpose of making her more sympathetic—certainly all the more tragic. In every account, Luce is designed to be pitied.

Grace Greenwood's account posits that the man Luce falls for, in this case named Edwin, fell for her sister Ellen—the spoiled and more beautiful sister—who lured Edwin away from Luce deliberately. Luce is readying herself to be married when Edwin arrives having already married Ellen, saying to the girls' parents that he hadn't known real love until Ellen. Luce approaches them slowly, cries out in anguish, collapses, and when she awakes, reason has fled. Edwin and Ellen leave together, haunted and chastened by the turn of events.

In this account Luce begins wandering once her parents die. The town and surrounding environs take care of her as she roams for the rest of her life, adorning her unbound, long, unbraided hair with flowers she plucks from the wayside along her journeys.

In an overdramatic ending, Luce "comes to" just before her

death at the side of a childhood friend, acknowledging the Lord and passing to "the morn of an eternal day."

Mrs. Luna Hammond wrote an extensive, fully researched, and meticulous *History of Madison County* in 1872. There are a few biographies of important local characters mentioned in her work, one of them being Lucy Dutton. Hammond pulls extensively from Grace Greenwood's account, noting: "She had a great repugnance to the society of men, and would climb fences in the most tedious wintry weather to avoid meeting them. Her friends, knowing this peculiarity, humored her—the men by never appearing to notice her, when in her presence."[2]

There is a certain fondness and care, an indulgence of her eccentricities that weaves its way through each of these narratives, and the avoidance of men is mentioned in each one. Luce still has friends, as noted above, and she is taken in and taken care of by a community far and wide. But ghostly attributes haunt her living state. Grace Greenwood wrote, "she also seemed possessed by the spirit of unrest. She could not, she would not be confined, but was continually escaping from her friends and going they knew not wither [*sic*]."

Placed in the Cortland County archives alongside the full journal in which Greenwood's account appears, a yellowing card catalog card with a carefully typewritten account offered by the donor of the journal notes: "Mrs. G. H. Grennell of Berkshire, donor of this magazine says that her grandmother, Orelia Susannah Crandall Hubbell told her about this demented girl, Lucy Dutton, stopping at the Crandall home at East River and being cared for there until she became restless again and wandered on to some other place."

These tales told to the Cortland Historical Society (also all notably written by women and presented to Cortland's archives by women) do suggest that Luce was a real person who had indeed suffered a tragedy and wandered the area as a consequence. Her precise circumstances continued to depend on her storyteller.

The Madison County Historical Society, located in a gorgeous Victorian home, features similarly helpful staff. Their archives hold myriad newspaper articles and old typewritten accounts detailing Luce as a local legend. One *Utica Daily Press* article, published in 1951, details the 150-year-old Edgarton House in Bouckville, where "Crazy Lucy" stayed many a night. William Edgarton describes stories passed down to him of a haggard woman in patched, ragged clothes with a small bundle of belongings that included her well-worn Bible. "There was a fireplace in the living room and grandmother would allow her to sleep by it. Lucy never came in the house until all the men-folks had retired."[3] The article shares more details about Lucy, but quotes Grace Greenwood's account directly to do so. Greenwood, herself a local figure from Pompey, New York, is the most consistently quoted source regarding Lucy.

Lucy isn't the unreliable narrator of her own story; it is the varying accounts of others remembering Lucy that utilize her as a metaphor, shifting her tale into one that has a distinct moral of Christian suffering and the tragedy of a too-gentle and too-fragile spirit.

Luce's tale combines many loaded feminine tropes of maiden, spinster, madwoman, and crone, but she herself seems to have glided through these archetypes unfazed. Luce's madness effectively functions as a relief from sadness, her state preferable to a life of pain, and the rejection of one man meant she rejected the presence of men for the rest of her life.

On one hand, Luce is never victim-blamed for her condition and situation; but, on the other hand, a certain degree of "womanly weakness" is taken as fact. What is important to note, however, is that her condition is not met with fear, revulsion, or even committal to an institution, an all-too-easy nineteenth-century option for a family or husband to get an inconvenient woman out of the way.

It is surprising, for a society that has dealt so poorly through the centuries with mental illness, that in Luce's accounts, her situation is presented simply as a tragedy of time and lost love, as if everything is entirely understandable, rather than the so-often alienating or fear-mongering accounts of mental illness. The term "alienist" was the first term for modern psychologists, the title coming from the idea of a person being alienated from themselves and society by their mental state. Lucy may be sort of sleepwalking, but she is not ostracized.

The phrase "would not be confined" directly pushes back against the nineteenth-century "angel in the house" and the pervasive idea that a woman should be kept in a domestic sphere. The fact that Luce was not punished societally for breaking from what was expected of her makes her somewhat of a radical figure. Hair scandalously unbound, adorned with flowers like a fey creature, she would accept hospitality but then vanish unpredictably, a figure between worlds with a time line all her own. Luce is accounted for by women authors, and she is taken in and taken care of by fellow women. She may have been an object of pity, but she didn't seem to pity herself. She just kept moving.

It is noteworthy that words attributable to ghosts, like Luce's "haunting" voice, were given her during her life and the accounting of it. She was a "restless spirit" long before she became a literal one.

Luce has captivated local legend, inspiring photo blogs and even going so far as to have been given a historic roadside "Legend and Lore" marker by the New York Folklore Society. Photos of the marker can be pulled up easily, the text reading:

> *"Crazy Luce" Lucy Dutton, lived ca. 1795 near Cazenovia Lake, jilted by man who wed her sister. Went mad and wandered Madison County for 30 years.*

When I tried finding this sign by its geolocation tags, no marker could be found. Perhaps it too has gone wandering.

As might be expected, Lucy Dutton's tale of wandering in life shifted into that of a traveling ghost, with the lake as her spirit's focal point.

In the HauntedPlaces.Org directory, Cazenovia Lake has a few noted hauntings, Luce at the forefront: "Yet another ghost sometimes seen walking around here is a sad woman whose beau ran off to marry her sister."[4]

It is telling that *sadness* is what's mentioned in her ghost stories when Luce's condition in life seemed to have suspended that sorrow. We often discuss ghosts or haunted spaces as being frozen in points of intense emotions that psychically imprint themselves. It is a harrowing concept in this case, that her ghost might remember the sorrow and pain that her mental suspension in life alleviated for so long. Insisting that Luce's wispy, eerie, luminous form along the lakeside is a *sad* figure forces her back into a limited box that her mental state and wandering life broke her free from.

Perhaps the sadness is only projection. Perhaps it is just the trope of the jilted, heartsick woman that urban legend clings to: a romanticized, melancholic impression focusing on loss and betrayal, reinforcing the idea of a woman needing a lover to be fulfilled in life, rather than an accurate account of who this woman really was and what forces motivated her to wander in "nunlike serenity."

Perhaps it's just the circling imprint of a woman alone that unsettles us, a phantom form reflected on the lake, an extension of the glimmering water itself, lighting surrounding trees with an eerie glow, a ghost continuing to explore in her own little world, lost in a state we can't possibly know. A spectral lighthouse beside still waters, lost to endless delirium. She is the undiscovered country.

In life, Lucy would have frozen to death in hard Upstate winters had she not been given shelter by residents who spanned several counties, taking her in for at least thirty years. Modern society would rather not see the homeless, rendering them invisible, ghosts among us, even though unhoused populations are only growing across the country. Those with mental illness are especially displaced and forced even further into the margins. Would Lucy find pity, welcome, or a place by the fire today? A ghostly form eternally meandering along a beautiful lakeside calls to mind images of international myth and legend, evoking the "woman in white" or "by the wayside" ghosts, prevalent along roadsides and paths traveled worldwide.

In the 1951 *Utica Daily Press* feature about her, a bold-type paragraph states, "For 30 years or more she traveled the highways." It seems Luce's legend may have merged with some of these wayside women in white whose stories abound around Upstate New York's many sharp and dangerous turns, an inexplicable, luminous form appearing and disappearing just beyond your headlights. The collective, enduring presence of the "women in white" bids us remember something: to take care, perhaps to watch the road, or, in Luce's case, perhaps to watch your heart in this cruel, unpredictable world. Perhaps she's telling us that a soul can reject what happens in life and instead become an unburdened creature of eternal, if not unfathomable, momentum.

May her spirit forever wander, adorned with flowers, stopping to rest when she needs, blocking out pain, entirely free.

The Merchant's House Front Hall. Photo by Leanna Renee Hieber

PART 6

Spinsters and Widows

INTRODUCTION

LEANNA AND ANDREA

A WOMAN ALONE HAS REMAINED SUSPECT THROUGHOUT TIME. Encouraged and socialized toward the gender roles of wife, mother, and domestic caretaker, the spinster defies her "place" in societal structure. The widow, depending on her race and class, could also be seen as a societal liability.

And yet many women vastly preferred spinsterhood to a life with an ill-suited partner of mere necessity. Or, for those so inclined, perhaps a "Boston Marriage" instead—as was the nineteenth-century term for women romantic partners living together.

With employment options for women very limited, spinsters would only be able to live as such if they were blessed with financial stability or provided for themselves by their own resourceful employment in one of the few fields available to women. Widows had some measure of acceptability in society, having fulfilled at least one of their prescribed roles for a certain time, and sometimes with that status came the ability to own property or control their own accounts.

But for working women and the lower classes, there was no resting on inheritance. In the 1880s and '90s, Clara Wolcott Driscoll, manager of the Women's Glass Cutting Department of Tiffany Studios, designer of Tiffany's most famed and iconic stained-glass lamps, cycled in and out of Tiffany's employ three times, depending on her marital status. Single when she was hired, she had to leave when engaged, as was company policy. Once widowed, she returned to become designer and manager, eventually commanding as much pay as the manager in the Men's Department, but had to leave again when she remarried. Her name has only now become associated with the art that made Tiffany so famous, thanks to historians in the twenty-first century, who found a treasure trove of letters that detail the cycles of her married life versus working life. Boarding-houses in cities were havens for working women like Driscoll, where they would stay, often with strict rules about fraternization with men, until they made a match and were expected, if they had any means, to get out of the workforce and become a housewife.

Many spinsters relished their lot in life. Some into their afterlife, such as the joyous ghosts of the Van der Voort sisters of Manhattan. Rosetta and Janet Van der Voort owned a brownstone mansion. These Victorian sisters' favorite winter pastime was ice-skating on the frozen waters of the nearby Central Park. Ice-skating was a popular sport for women; as women's physical activities were always policed and limited, ice-skating was considered socially acceptable. The sisters loved doing figure eights across the frozen ponds. In 1880, the two passed away within months of each other. Their spirits were later seen doing what they loved best, two luminous, ghostly figures skating on the ice in their Victorian finery, well into the twentieth century.

But generally, as we'll see in this chapter, tales will be told of a spinster or a widow long before her death; especially, the longer she lives, the taller her tales. She'll be deemed a crone, a witch presiding over a haunted house.

This house is inseparable from the woman. Most spectral spinsters and ghostly widows cling persistently to the material spaces which at once defined and entrapped them. Here, the local ghost story begins to entwine itself with the tropes of gothic literature.

From *Jane Eyre* to *The Haunting of Hill House*, "the theme of women driven mad by isolation or entrapment in a house is a mainstay of Gothic literature and ghost stories," writes Corinne May Botz in the introduction to her book *Haunted Houses*. "Historically, the home has been a site of female oppression. Female ghosts entrapped within domestic space reflect the ambivalent relationship between the desire for protection in the home and the potential for suffocation and isolation."[1]

The conflating of woman and house is a long-standing Gothic tradition. When a woman is troubled, the house she inhabits must also be uncanny, in the Freudian sense and vice versa. In *The Haunting of Hill House*, Shirley Jackson created the character of Eleanor Vance, a repressed, virginal old maid dominated by her overbearing mother and sister. Eleanor's troubled and fragmented psyche is a central component of the novel—she is as haunted as the house. "The house is the haunting," Jackson wrote in her notes to the novel. "The house is Eleanor."[2]

Unfortunately, as we've seen in the case of the Salem witch trials, becoming a widow only heightened the chance of being accused as a witch. A great deal of the goings-on of the witch trials had to do with land grabs, taking advantage of laws designed to disenfranchise girls, single women, and widows from property that might be granted them.

Sarah L. Winchester rightly belongs in this section as a widow: a misunderstood, reclusive woman who remained devoted to her beloved husband William Winchester's memory for the rest of her life. However, the utter societal insistence that she was a "madwoman" places her under the heading we then soundly refuted.

Much like Winchester, tales were told of Gertrude Tredwell long before her death. Having kept her nineteenth-century town house on 4th Street in Manhattan as a carefully curated time capsule from the 1870s, the last resident of the now Merchant's House Museum is still very active there. A vibrant and participatory spirit, having spent all ninety-three years of her life in its rooms, she watches over her home to this day.

We'll also examine the effect of Mother Ann Lee, leader of the Shakers, who effectively created communities of spinsters and bachelors in her celibate followers, who eschewed oaths and sacraments. The Shaker belief system laid the groundwork for Spiritualism in the 1840s, and Lily Dale, New York, Spiritualist capital of the world, became a haven of a town where a single woman could work as a medium or healer without pressure of marriage or censure.

Similarly, spinster spiritualist Sybil Phelps, who lived in the Burned-Over District of Palmyra in Upstate New York, is one of the few spinsters who is celebrated rather than pitied or reviled. An eccentric figure in her community in her day, she lived as a near-recluse from the mid-1930s until her death in 1976, communicating with fellow spiritualists in a voluminous correspondence, and emerging in town mainly to go to the movies. Now her home is a museum, and townspeople and spiritualists from near and far gather to throw her a birthday bash every October 10, and Sybil often obliges them with a spectral appearance.

Widowed women who lose a spouse or life partner may experience periods of devastating loneliness. Some may go searching for answers and some may take drastic steps in their grief, creating a range of spectral stories that may follow.

In Cincinnati, Ohio, at the grand Hilton Netherland Plaza Hotel, an elegant, mysterious "lady in green" is said to haunt the building where her husband, a painter who worked on the grand Art Deco murals in the Palm Court lobby, fell to his death. After checking into the hotel during its grand opening in 1931, the painter's widow was said to have flung herself from a window. Described as a Black woman in a lovely green ball gown in a period style, she's been seen many times throughout the hotel. "One day an employee entered an elevator with a woman in a green dress. The two talked about how beautiful the Hall of Mirrors was. The man turned just for a second, and when he looked back, she had vanished."[3]

Her sudden disappearance after being noticed wandering along the painted mezzanine murals or chatting for a moment in the elevators before vanishing has left guests startled and reeling. The hotel's Hall of Mirrors offers glittering reflections from all angles and in some, the woman in the distinctive green dress can be glimpsed, wandering the hall with a curious air.

She may be searching for answers as to why the safety of her artist husband wasn't better assured to avoid the tragedy that befell him. Perhaps she wanders in hope his spectral presence may join her for a dance through eternity in a mirrored ballroom.

In the complex and very personal moments of grief and loss, it's possible a door between worlds might be just a bit easier to access: a bridge between the living and something otherworldly.

We'll detail a wild, humorous—and likely artfully embellished—ghost story from absolute legend Joan Rivers, involving a "demon meter," a questionable priestess, and the manifestation of a lively paranormal entity in the Upper East Side New York City apartment she bought and renovated after the loss of her husband. Featuring in an episode of *Celebrity Ghost Stories,* Rivers credits "Mrs. Spencer" for helping her through one of the most difficult periods in her life.

So too did pioneering news correspondent Emily Briggs, a new widow in the late nineteenth century, find an unlikely friend in a ghost. Overcoming the sad fact of the specter's tragic and extremely violent end, there can be something oddly fond and healing in Emily's commiseration from "across the veil." We end on sisterly, companionable notes of unique comfort in preternatural company.

Whether spinster or widow, societal pressures have remained, tongues have wagged, and myths have been woven into community folklore. The collective power, the mere defiant act of a woman alone, haunts us still, here to remind us that they are still their *own* person with complex histories, many of which have continued into the beyond with stories still to be written.

MISS TREDWELL IS AT HOME

ANDREA AND LEANNA

NEW YORK, NEW YORK

THE MERCHANT'S HOUSE MUSEUM AT 29 EAST 4TH STREET IN Manhattan is a perfect haunted house. When you first see the elegant, nineteenth-century, redbrick town house with white marble detailing rising into view, it feels like you've unearthed an artifact of a long-vanished New York that you alone have stumbled upon. A lonesome survivor of a bygone era, the house seems to sigh with age and weariness, and yet holds itself as upright as a corset. Its welcoming white-marble stoop, a lavish expense that speaks of the social climbing its inhabitants did daily in the bustling, industrializing city, bids you to rise to ring the bell. When you cross that threshold, you enter into the mid-nineteenth century, and you are now in the company of the dead.

Inside you are met with the history of a single family, the Tredwells, whose aura-rich belongings still furnish the rooms. The Tredwells purchased the house, built in 1821, from its original owner, Joseph Brewster, in 1835, and inhabited the home for almost a century. An 1855–65 time capsule, with red silk settees, gilded mirrors, and ornate chandeliers in the parlor and dining room kept grand for company while the rest of the home maintains a stately modesty, there's very little modern adaptation in the Merchant's House; even the electricity is wired into the old gas lamp fixtures.

During her days as a museum volunteer, Andrea joined one of the regularly scheduled ghost tours, avidly taking notes. Though it was a bright June evening—the summer solstice, in fact—the windows were shuttered to create a suitable dimness, and the atmosphere was close and warm. No breeze or draft moved through the house, which does not have central air conditioning.

As the group moved into the front parlor, Andrea felt a strange and sudden shift in her mood, an abrupt and inexplicable weightiness, even sadness. Standing by the pocket doors between the front and rear parlors, she felt something caress her arm. It wasn't a breeze or a draft. It was more akin to the feeling you get when someone brushes by you in a crowded subway. Whatever *it* was brushed by her and then palpably moved past her and disappeared beyond the pocket doors. Later, when she mentioned it to the docents, they nodded and said, "When you came into the house earlier tonight, we heard footsteps in Seabury Tredwell's [empty] bedroom." The portrait of the family patriarch hangs in the front parlor, on the wall near the pocket doors leading to the rear parlor—exactly where Andrea had been standing.

Gertrude Tredwell seems destined to have been a ready-made ghost story. She was the family's youngest daughter, born in the rear bedroom of the house in 1840 and living there her whole life; she died a reclusive spinster a month before her ninety-third birthday in the front bedroom. It was a womb-to-tomb scenario for Gertrude, whose story is brimming with all the elements of a great Gothic romance, oddly replete with ready-made symbolism.

It was said Gertrude fell desperately in love with a medical student who later became a famous doctor, Luis Walton, who at one time worked at the Northern Dispensary in Greenwich Village, a location that allegedly treated Edgar Allan Poe for a cold in 1837.

But an impossible, uncrossable gulf was soon discovered. The good doctor was Catholic. *And* Irish. Such a match would *not* be tolerated. Prejudice against "papists" and Irish immigrants ran high in the city's WASP crowd, and the Tredwell family were well-to-do, stalwart Episcopalians. Gertrude may not have defied her father and run off to marry her love, but she is said to have maintained a correspondence with Luis or members of his family for the rest of their lives. His photograph was identified in the museum's collection. Neither of them ever married. Perhaps a telling detail about a "one true love."

It is understandable that the ghost stories surrounding the house usually surround Gertrude, the love tragically denied her an irresistible component. Add in a domineering father wary of any man who might look to marry for his own financial gain, and it's almost too perfect. Over time the story has been honed and polished until everything else about Gertrude and her family has been worn away, and we are left with an ideal, archetypal spectral spinster.

Gertrude's spinsterhood seems to have given the house an aura of having been haunted even as she lived. Local legend apparently has it that children were already referring to the house as "the haunted house" as early as 1934, a mere year after her death.[1] This is especially interesting, as it indicates the house already had an eerie reputation coterminous with its inhabitation by Gertrude in her later years. The Tredwells themselves had also been the subject of speculation and gossip about their eccentricities as early as 1906.

A *New York Times* human interest story from that year asserts that Gertrude and her sisters, "in spite of their great wealth, were seldom seen, led reclusive lives, and were eccentric."[2] The article claims the Tredwell sisters were related to the Vanderbilts and owned $6 million worth of real estate. Its anonymous author then goes on to state: "The house had always been a noon-day subject among the shopgirls of the neighborhood. They told one another how three women had lived there for more than seventy years, *yet no one had ever seen a man enter the old house*." Gertrude penned a dignified letter to the editor, responding, "Suffice it to say, despite assertions to the contrary, [the Tredwells] are only in comfortable circumstances and are practical, thoroughly loyal citizens of the substantial old type of character handed down from generations back."[3] Gertrude's response hardly seems like that of an unhinged Miss Havisham, rattling around her house like a living ghost, and yet the tendency to force a woman like Gertrude into a Dickensian trope prevailed.

While local ghost stories started swirling immediately after Gertrude's death, some of the first documented written accounts we've been able to find date from the early 1950s. *New York Times* reporter Meyer Berger wrote an entry in his "About New York" column in 1953 called "There's Still a Ghost of a Chance Old Merchant's House Near the Bowery May Be Haunted." Perhaps he was inspired by journalist Helen Worden Erskine (famed for her coverage of notorious Harlem hoarders the Collyer brothers) who published a book that same year called *Out of this World*, in which she singled out Gertrude Tredwell among her selection of newsworthy New York City hermits and recluses.

George Chapman, Gertrude's second cousin, who bought the house and turned it into a museum, seemed more than willing to embrace Gertrude's "lost romance" narrative, mentioning her lost Luis and the existence of a secret passageway and hidden trapdoors in the house that facilitated clandestine affairs. According to Chapman, the passageway was discovered at the bottom of a closet between the second-floor front and back bedrooms. "Nobody could have been more surprised than I. Underneath that bottom was a trap door. When I raised it, I found a ladder extending down to a small secret chamber on the first floor, between the drawing room and what is now the dining room."[4] Chapman said he found a man's jacket there, in circa 1860s style.

This, then, is the vision of Gertrude that was handed down to the public. Not a substantial woman of the old type of character, but rather a brokenhearted victim of her domineering father, and perhaps her own stubborn pride. It is an irresistible story, to be sure, and one that fits neatly into our conception of what a lone female ghost *should* be.

The other unmarried Tredwell sisters don't get much press because they were not real-life Gothic tropes, as Gertrude was. Sarah, Phebe, and Julia all died spinsters—Phebe quite dramatically in a fall down the stairs—but they are rarely, if at all, mentioned in the same breath as Gertrude in Merchant's House ghost stories. In the face of an archetypal narrative like this, it almost feels too messy to include other facts about the Tredwell sisters. Like the fact that four of the six of them never married. All but one remained in the house until their deaths. In some iterations of her ghost stories, Gertrude's sisters Sarah, Phebe, and Julia do make an appearance, but their identities are often merged, as though by a film director adapting a novel, attempting to simplify a complex narrative. Sometimes she lives with Sarah, sometimes Phebe, sometimes Julia, and from time to time a combination thereof. In reality, she lived with all of them at different points, remaining the one constant in the house as her siblings filed in and out, according to the needs of their lives. Sarah was the only unmarried sister to move out, and she lived at the Hotel Cadillac at Broadway and 43rd Street. (Sarah returned to the town house and died a year later in 1901, though not in the house.)[5]

In one of the few accounts to cast another Tredwell sister as a ghost, Hans Holzer's rendition in *Ghosts: True Encounters of the World Beyond* verges on the absurd, claiming Sarah gave birth to an illegitimate baby who was murdered by a servant at Seabury's behest. Holzer sensationalizes the notion of the secret passageway, claiming it ran from the house all the way to the East River as the means toward lovers' rendezvous. Holzer's conclusions from a psychic reading on the house cast Sarah in a vein of frailty and madness, while introducing fantastical architectural extremities. Today's museum staff and board members believe the caretakers of the house during Holzer's investigations were purposely leading him on.

After reading a few Merchant's House ghost stories, one could be forgiven for being unclear as to the exact number of Tredwell children. Like their house, which is variously listed as having four, five, and up to seven floors (it has five), the number of offspring changes from one account to the next (there were eight).

Hans Holzer seems to have been among the first to literally entwine Gertrude with fiction, asserting she was the inspiration for Henry James's famous spinster, Catherine Sloper, in his novel *Washington Square*, notably adapted into the famous play and film *The Heiress*; this claim was picked up and repeated often enough to seem true.* The tropes and the stories informed each other until they solidified and ossified into lore. Because it was so easy to picture, the archetypal ghost of Gertrude became a rich, lonely old spinster, even though she probably may not have been so lonely (or so rich) as has been suggested—and even her spinsterhood may have been thought of differently in her own lifetime.

Ghosts are supposed to "flock to women left alone."[6] But it is a myth that Gertrude was entirely alone. Though Phebe died in 1907 and Julia died in 1909, Gertrude had a nephew for companionship in her later years. Her sister Elizabeth's son, John T. Richards, also known as "Tred," lived with Gertrude near the end of her life. Tred was a divorcé, a refined, dapper gentleman-lawyer of "the old school," who moved into the commodious front third-floor bed-

* It isn't true. The story was very likely started by the marketing department at Paramount Pictures at the time of the movie's release.

room, which he outfitted with luxe ebony furnishings. He spent the next several years accompanying his elegant elderly aunt to chic vacation spots such as Saratoga Springs.[7] Tred lived until 1930.

Nobody thinks of Gertrude gallivanting around Saratoga Springs with Tred in a *Travels with My Aunt*–type scenario. Because the ghost stories of Gertrude confirm societal expectations of how we think an unmarried ghost should behave, all supporting characters such as Tred have been eliminated in her story.

Yet the whole Tredwell household, fighting the ongoing tendency to erase them for Gertrude, has a way of inserting themselves into the hauntings at the Merchant's House. Ask anyone familiar with the museum's spirits and they will be quick to tell you: Gertrude apparently does not haunt alone. Staffers, volunteers, docents, and visitors offer innumerable accounts, so many that the house has compiled them into a booklet, *Some Say They Never Left*.

One docent tells of coming face-to-face with a specter when she opened a door on the fourth floor of the house, the servants' quarters. The docent averred the face was "clearly not of this time and place."[8] Father Seabury and brother Samuel Tredwell have both been heard and spotted by various witnesses. As has Elizabeth, the firstborn.

Board member Anthony Bellov had an apparitional experience on the stairs one evening. He was seated on the bottom stair, heard rustling up above, looked up, and saw a woman leaning on the curve of the railing, looking down at him with curiosity. He later identified her through family photos as Elizabeth.[9] Emotionally, the Merchant's House ghosts range in tone from sad to joyous, though they are very seldom, if ever, actually frightening—most witnesses describe them as merely unsettling.

On a cold December day in 2012, a volunteer named Marguerite was closing up the house following a special "open house" exhibit designed to evoke the nineteenth-century custom of going house-to-house among neighbors during the holiday season. Throughout the day the house had been filled with lively music and laughter, and she had a slight headache as she closed and locked the front door after the last guest left. She was glad of a little silence as she worked in the dim, quiet "tea room" the staff uses for ticket-taking and accounting, now bathed in the early evening darkness of winter. She had little more on her mind than toting up the day's receipts and heading home for a hot bath and a Tylenol. Suddenly, Marguerite heard bells:

> *I thought it was the front door, but then [I heard] different bells with different sounds. . . . It was loud and very fast . . . like a church carillon, the beauty and the upward sound, loud and louder, and even louder, in their harmonious mixing of tones. . . . They kept ringing ceaselessly.*
>
> *I thought it might be in the street so I opened the door and looked out. Fourth Street was all dark and quiet, deserted, with the pools of light of the streetlights on the block. . . .*
>
> *I closed the door, puzzled more than afraid. The bells were still ringing but quieting down. I passed the back staircase and I saw the little bell at the bottom of the stairs still shaking and moving. Then I got really freaked out and ran downstairs to look at the servant bells in the kitchen but the sound had stopped by the time I turned on lights. The bells looked like always: very still—dormant.*
>
> *I looked in the kitchen, I looked in the garden, I reopened the rooms one by one leaving the lights on and all doors open. I went from top to bottom. There was no one in the House except myself.*[10]

Whatever was ringing that bell could not have been any earthly entity anywhere in the house, for the servants' bells are no longer functional, and none of their wires is currently attached to anything.

After a moment that felt like an hour, Marguerite ran up the stairs and "finished the accounting very very very fast (Basically throwing everything into the box and that's it!) . . . and left the House scared out of my wits and shaken. I am still shaken thinking of it."[11]

Whether it's ringing bells or showing up spontaneously at a Christmas concert, the spirits of the house have been known to join in socially from time to time. However, they have also been known to turn the occasional visitor away.

Susan Blackhall's *Ghosts of New York* describes the story of a museum visitor who had been received at the front door by a woman dressed in a brown silk Victorian dress who sadly shook her head and denied that the house was open, urging him to return at a different time. When he did so and told the staff what had happened, no one could make any sense of it. The staff do not wear period costumes. When he saw a portrait of Gertrude Tredwell within the museum, he stopped cold, insisting *she* was the woman who greeted him. This could have easily been dismissed as a prank or hoax, except . . .

> *In this case, however, the visitor described the dress that "Gertrude" wore very clearly. Although it was not on display at the time, a dress exactly matching his description does exist in the museum's collection and at one time belonged to one of the Tredwell sisters. How this visitor to the museum could have known or guessed about it remains unexplained.*[12]

Gertrude, then, remains a hybrid of myth and fact; the lone ghost of her looms larger than the long life of her. She has, folklorically, become larger than life. Once out from under the shadow of Seabury Tredwell, instead of radically changing her life, for Gertrude—and sisters Phebe and Julia, and possibly Sarah, when she wasn't at the Hotel Cadillac—perhaps the house and her place within it became even more of a focal point of consistency. Change was not in the picture. The museum allows time travel into Gertrude's prime of life, a time when the house was full of life, family, and visitors, the fullest it would be over the course of Gertrude's ninety-three years.

The unchanged nature of a house left "just like Papa would have wanted,"[13] wears deeper the psychic groove, creating a spiritual permanence. Ghosts love nothing more than a building that hasn't changed. We treat the Merchant's House with fondness and respect, and often thank Gertrude for her permission as we stand outside on the stoop and share a bit of her life with our visitors, saying hello and goodbye, as is only polite. Her presence looms, but we respect her need for privacy.

Everyone should have that respect.

That the house still stands is a miracle in itself, a close shave that would move any preservationist—alive or dead. Leanna had a particular spectral experience in the fine front parlor that was reserved for the family's more lavish entertaining, said to be the "fullest" location of spectral energies. She stood alone with only one of the beautiful parlor settees to her right. The docent was discussing George Chapman's last-minute intervention to save this treasure; on the very day the house and everything in it was planned to be auctioned off, Chapman swooped in to save the house, with plans for it to be turned into a museum immediately. The closeness of that call so affected Leanna that she blurted out in the midst of the docent's lecture, "Thank God it was saved!"

An unmistakable gesture of commiseration met Leanna's emotional outburst. There was no one standing to her right. And yet, as if to say, *We're so glad you feel about it as we do*, an ice-cold hand grasped her elbow and gave a friendly, comforting squeeze, despite the touch being some thirty degrees different from the surrounding air. It was an unmistakable, tactile sensation of sentiment. When she told the docent about it, the staff smiled and noted that she *had*, after all, been standing in the most spectrally active area.

This haunted moment was subtle, sweet, and profound. Perhaps a "welcome back" to a parlor that felt familiar, as Leanna has always been drawn to such architecture and has written many novels featuring the museum as a template for characters' homes. A familial gesture from a spirit celebrating this house as every tour and visitor does when they step inside, and out of time, to appreciate Gertrude's life choices and all the elements that led to our being able to visit her house today. The moment was not unlike Andrea's experience; a spirit reaching out for contact in that grand parlor where so many were entertained.

Gertrude's story remains complex, a woman bound by the demands and permissions of her time. She was denied her agency, her heart; there is a certain tragedy to it. But at some point Gertrude owned her choices. Long after her father died, she remained and chose to do so, on her own, the last vestige of an era. What one person might deem a lonely life, another might find comforting and well-lived.

There is a freedom and personal ownership in spinsterhood, and that may be what some people find truly unnerving about it.

She still waits and watches, on her own terms, in the one place that was unquestionably *hers*.

FROM MOTHER ANN TO SYBIL

The Spirits of the Great Burned-Over

LEANNA AND ANDREA

UPSTATE NEW YORK

THE DYNAMIC SWATH OF NEW YORK'S "BURNED-OVER DISTRICT," where the "fires of the holy spirit had scorched the land," gave birth to myriad offshoots of new religious sects and denominations. From Mormonism to Seventh-Day Adventism to Shaker communities to Spiritualism, all groups were asking the eternal questions of life, death, and the spirit, and how the ineffable soul may be accessed, understood, or saved by the living.

Born on Toad Lane in Manchester, England, in 1736, Ann Lee was involved in the religious sect known as the "Shaking Quakers" for two decades before she was beaten and jailed on charges of sorcery and public disruption. An offshoot of protestant Christian Quaker tradition, Shakers were known for their ecstatic dances and shaking in spirit trances. Their religious practices appalled local English authorities with their otherworldly focus. "Mother Ann" escaped persecution by fleeing for New York in 1776 with eight followers—one of them being her reluctant husband, who later separated from Ann and her flock after she began adamantly espousing celibacy.

Mother Ann and her disciples formed a tiny colony of the United Society of Believers in Christ's Second Appearing near Albany in New York's Hudson Valley. They declared the place "Wisdom's Valley." Still, the sect could not escape further suspicion and derision. In New York their pacifist principles, which forbade them from taking a side in the Revolutionary War, painted them as supremely suspect. Ann Lee was briefly jailed in Albany on charges of sedition. She weathered all with an eerie calm. Her followers referred to her as Christ returned in female form.

Like Quakers, Shakers followed the Bible in a liberal approach. They performed neither baptism nor communion nor other sacraments, would not take oaths or participate in government, believed in total pacifism and abolition of slavery, used the more archaic language of "thee" and "thou," and passionately believed in the free workings of the spirit world and their own ability to communicate with it. Due to harassment no matter where they went, the Shakers ended up living communally for their own protection, and continued to maintain celibacy as a core tenet and salve for the world's carnal wickedness. That Mother Ann did not believe women should be forced to "be fruitful and multiply" branded her as a witch.

> *Following a brutal upstate New York winter in 1780, two men from across the Hudson River in the farming community of New Lebanon took advantage of an early spring thaw to visit the Shaker settlement . . . They began asking Mother Ann about her mystical teachings and rumors of the sect's practices, in which members spoke in prophecies, saw visions of the dead, danced, jumped and shouted in the thrall of the Holy Spirit. "We are the people who turn the world upside down," Mother Ann enigmatically told them.*[1]

Returning to New Lebanon, the men spread word of the people in the woods and, after a mysterious "Dark Day" when the daytime skies mysteriously blackened, the ideas of Armageddon that Mother Ann had predicted due to mankind's wicked ways seemed plausible, and new converts came to her, as she also had predicted.

Mother Ann died in 1784 but continued to loom large, her influence extending further in death.

On August 16, 1837, a group of young girls at Watervliet began to shake, fall to the ground, and sing songs in unknown languages. Claiming to have seen Mother Ann, the girls described journeys to heavenly places where they had been guided by angels. "The phenomena spread, and spiritual manifestations lasted for about ten years, a period known in Shaker literature as the New Era, Mother Ann's Second Appearing or Mother's Work. During that time Believers in all the communities became 'instruments' for the spirits, exhibiting classic possession phenomena: stiffening bodies, agonizing distortions, screeching, preternatural strength, and the smell of sulfur."[2]

In the early years messages came primarily from Mother Ann and other deceased leaders, but the list grew to include Jesus, Mary Magdalene, St. Paul, George Washington, Queen Isabella and Queen Elizabeth I, martyred saints, William Penn, Native American guides, and the Prophet Muhammad.

By the 1830s, Shaker activity was influential and widespread, and "Mother's Work" had spread as far south as Kentucky. Directing supernatural activity and a wide range of instruction, her followers created many works of beauty in her name. In the thrall of ghostly visions, Shakers took down haunting melodies; created strange, wondrous, mystical paintings; and composed stirring hymns that exist, beloved, to this day. *How Can I Keep from Singing?* is a personal favorite. Expert craftsmen, the Shakers were neither interested in nor preoccupied with the material world, and yet they produced furniture, art, and music that live on and are highly valued to this day, even though their sect dwindled and faded away.

Mother Ann had become the matriarch of spinsters, bachelors, and single people. Providing an option for adult life that was not focused solely on a traditional patriarchal family unit attracted many people who did not wish to adhere to said family model but also appealed to those whose hearts lay far beyond this mortal coil and incarnate life, who placed their hopes and dreams entirely on the spirit world and the afterlife.

The Shakers predated the Spiritualist movement, which would pick up directly on the foundations the Shakers laid for them.

In Lily Dale, New York, along the shores of idyllic Cassadaga Lake, Amelia Colby founded the capital of Spiritualism as the Cassadaga Lake Free Association in 1879. (In 1903 the name of the community was changed to City of Light, in part because of it having one of the earliest uses of electricity in the region.) Women could come to Lily Dale and practice as psychics, mediums, spiritual conduits, intuitives—however they wished to define themselves, and not be troubled by the scorn of others by existing as single women. The aspersion of "spinster" was rendered null here, and the town hosted many famed speakers and activists, from Emma Goldman to prominent reformers and suffragists like Susan B. Anthony. Women in Lily Dale were considered talented, equal members of society. It's important to note that due to communities like this and the people who populated them, interest in ghosts and spirits is entwined with a greater understanding of women's rights and empowerment.

Palmyra, New York, is a village that lies within the Burned-Over District, just east of Rochester and north of the Finger Lakes. The region rolls with gentle, fertile hills and valleys, glittering lakes and lush vineyards, before dropping off into the dramatic cliffs, waterfalls, and gorges of Ithaca to the east. Palmyra is the birthplace of Mormonism; to its south lies a landmark called "The Sacred Grove," a holy site for adherents to Joseph Smith's religion. (There's also a Best Western.) Palmyra itself does a thriving business in haunted history. The Historic Palmyra nonprofit corporation runs five museums in town, including the William Phelps General Store. According to their website, the building has served as a boardinghouse, a tavern, a bakery, and a general store since its construction in 1826.[3]

Proprietor William Phelps completed renovations to the store by 1875, subsequently left untouched by his son Julius, who locked the doors in 1940, leaving a curious retail time capsule for us to explore. Upstairs you'll visit the elegant Phelps family home. with post–Civil War furnishings and Victorian splendor, unspoiled by electricity or indoor plumbing, where Sibyl Phelps resided until her passing in 1976! The haunting presence of the Phelps's 108-year legacy remains to this day. Sybil Phelps is one of the rare spinster ghosts who is celebrated rather than pitied or reviled.

Born on October 10, 1895, Sybil Eugenia Phelps was the only child of Julius and Mary Phelps. She was a unique child: intense, solitary, and talented; as a teenager, she convinced her parents to let her attend the Eastman School of Music in Rochester. She never graduated, but somehow again ended up convincing her parents to let her dash off to drama school, this time in New York City, where she was now determined to become an actress. She attended theater school there briefly, but fate intervened. The school she was attending shut down, citing money difficulties caused by the onset of the first World War. Sybil herself had also run out of funds, and so she returned to Palmyra, dejected, and lived above her father's store. Her dreams of stardom dashed, she would remain there for the rest of her life.

Sybil earned a modest living giving piano lessons to local children. Sometime around 1926, she discovered Spiritualism. She became profoundly interested in numerology and astrology, and delved deeper and deeper into her mystical interests. Sybil maintained a wide-ranging correspondence throughout her life, and cultivated a circle of friends with like interests. She would remain a spiritualist until her death in 1976.[4] Sybil never married, and lived alone after her father died in 1964, continuing to live in a residence "unspoiled" by electricity, running water, or indoor plumbing. (There are shades of Gertrude Tredwell here: the fraught, intense relationship with her father and the time-capsule nature of her home.) One imagines the effect of candlelight on her living quarters, creating a perennially ethereal atmosphere for this woman of otherworldly habits and interests.

The eccentric Miss Phelps was fairly well-known in Palmyra in her day, though she rarely went outside. When she did emerge from her chambers she was often found at the movies and, apparently, styled herself with flair; some locals said she "looked like she had just walked out of a Jean Harlow picture," a look she undoubtedly retained well after it passed from cutting edge to charmingly vintage.[5]

Nowadays, she continues to be something of a local celebrity. To this day, her birthday is celebrated in the museum that was once her home. Every October 10, the museum throws a party, complete with refreshments and psychic readings by spiritualists from the Angel Heart Chapel of Newark, for those in attendance—and naturally, Sybil herself is in attendance. It must be quite a show. Readings given that night are said to be extraordinarily accurate, and Sybil's spirit is an uncommonly cooperative one, making frequent appearances, much to the eternal delight of all present.[6] Frankly, it sounds like the best birthday party ever. Of course, Sybil remains at home throughout the year, sometimes appearing in her kitchen or sitting at her piano (soft notes are often heard wafting in the air as she plays). She is sometimes seen in her third-floor bedroom, where an impression often appears on the bed she once slept in. But most of all she loves the parties, which give her the attention her theatrical soul craved so strongly in life.

By being absolutely true to herself, this spinster piano teacher has earned a place in the hearts in the people of Palmyra. It's a wonderfully comforting thought, to imagine that this woman—who must have been somewhat disappointed by her failure to take the world by storm in a dazzling stage career—finds what she so longed for in these afterlife soirees. The spinster is often considered a woman manqué, passed over, left behind. (One cliché about Sybil as spinster that is true? She had a lot of cats. And apparently you can still hear their spirits meow!) In Sybil's case, as with so many people, life simply "got in the way," and she never did what she dreamed of doing. This is hardly unique. The percentage of people who actually achieve their dreams is very small indeed. But despite this fact, spinsters are often disproportionately pitied. What's fascinating and heartwarming about Sybil is that she seems not only fulfilled but also loved. Her circle of spiritualist friends continues to surround her, and she continues to join them, unfettered by the lack of an earthly body. She has "posthumously become the 'star of her own story,'" in the words of Bonnie Hays, executive director of Historic Palmyra.[7]

Sybil's story shows us that the traditional yardsticks for measuring success in life don't really matter all that much. Money, marriage, children, and fame never came to Sybil Phelps in life. But something else was visited upon her. Something that transcends these mundane material milestones. Friendship, a circle of like-minded people, community, and spirit—these are the things that truly matter, and these are the things that Sybil Phelps enjoys. We salute you, Sybil. And we sincerely hope that, next October 10, we'll be able to make it to Palmyra and raise a glass of Champagne in your honor at your birthday party.

THE WIDOW AND MRS. SPENCER

ANDREA

NEW YORK, NEW YORK

IN 2018, A BAR OWNER ON THE UPPER EAST SIDE OFFERED ME A generous sum of money to tell ghost stories there the night before Halloween. I live in Brooklyn and it's a slog to get up there, especially to First Avenue, but it was a good paycheck for two hours' work. I took the gig and rolled up my sleeves, looking for some good local ghost stories to share.

Most of the Upper East Side ghost stories were, like the neighborhood, pretty quiet. But one story of a Saudi prince, a talk show host, and a voodoo priestess caught my eye. Best of all, it involved one of the most fabulously tacky apartments I've ever had the pleasure of ogling online, giving me the exquisite joy of scrolling through photo after photo of sublimely kitschy faux-Versailles décor. The apartment's late owner? Why, the only woman in the world with the balls to decorate a place like that: the legendary former host of *Fashion Police* and other less consequential shows, the grande dame of filth, the glorious incarnate being who taught me the word *schmeckel,* a woman so nutty she actually voluntarily served on her building's condo board for twelve years: Brooklyn's finest, Joan Rivers. Get paid to drink for free and tell a bunch of Upper East Side denizens about the demons in Joan Rivers's subbasement? Sometimes I truly love my job. Obviously, I also love Joan Rivers. The fact that she's entangled in one of the most gloriously bananas ghost stories I've ever heard is just a fun bonus.

Here's how it happened.

Joan Rivers was having a bad year. It was 1986, and her husband, Edgar, had just committed suicide. She had lost her job and been banned from the Johnny Carson show (his loss). After making a series of bad investments, she was so broke she could only afford one little penthouse on East Sixty-Second Street. The penthouse was located in an eight-unit condo, a former Gilded Age mansion that had been converted into apartments in the 1930s. Apparently nobody ever wanted to buy it, so she got it cheap. It was in total disrepair, but she loved it. It was an enormous, top-floor ballroom with a small addition on top, a bedroom described as surprisingly small (though with a private terrace). She used to wander there late at night after the workmen had left, surveying her new home, imagining a new life unfurling for herself there; she invested everything into the apartment, literally and financially, spiritually and emotionally. Joan undertook lengthy and extensive renovations to bring it up to her liking and make her new home perfect. There was just one problem. Her dog didn't like it. Also, it was haunted.

One hot August night, Labor Day weekend, she decided to stop by the apartment to check in on the ongoing renovations. As she walked in, she noticed it was freezing cold. Her dog, a Yorkie, refused to go in. Joan left him on the threshold, walked inside, and was aghast to see that the place seemed to have been vandalized. There was "pornographic writing" and images scrawled on the walls, and the whole place was filled with a dark, negative energy. Suddenly her new home had turned into a set piece from *The Exorcist*, and Joan hightailed it out of there. She breathlessly told all this to the elevator operator, and he said, "Oh, I guess Mrs. Spencer is back."

Initially, Joan was terrified. *This can't be happening,* she thought. *I've put all my money into this apartment and it's fucking haunted.* The first thing she decided to do was figure out who Mrs. Spencer was, and give her a good pedigree. Mrs. Spencer, Joan declared, was the niece of legendarily wealthy financier J. P. Morgan; she had supposedly lived in the house back when it was a mansion and had apparently died seven years before Joan bought the apartment.

The next thing Joan Rivers did was pick up the phone and call NYU's parapsychology department and ask for a ghostbuster. "We don't do that," they said. "But . . . well, we really shouldn't tell you this, but we do know of a voodoo priestess down in New Orleans who can help you." Joan flew the priestess up from New Orleans, and what happened next was like "something out of a bad movie." After ninety minutes of chanting, drumming, speaking in tongues, and the like, the bad energy spontaneously cleared out of the apartment. The ghost was gone.

By this time it was two thirty in the morning, and Joan and the priestess decided to knock on every door in the building to offer to clear their demon energy. "Not one person slammed the door on us," Joan recalls proudly. "Everyone had a story." Joan and the priestess cleaned the whole house and restored good energy and peace to the building once more.

The only problem was the ghost returned. Pretty much as soon as the renovations were completed and Joan moved in, it was back. She had the same problems as before. The house was cold, none of the electrical appliances worked, and her Yorkie kept running for the door. Finally, Joan cried out in despair, "Mrs. Spencer, I am a widow, all my money's in this apartment, you cannot do this to me, you must, must, must, MUST leave me in peace!" And then one day Joan was in the basement, working alongside a handyman, when she discovered a dusty portrait lying among the various bits of regular basement detritus, a portrait of an imperious grande dame of a woman. And the doorman said, when she showed him the portrait, "That's Mrs. Spencer." Joan dusted off the portrait and hung it in the lobby.

One night Joan got a phone call from the voodoo priestess. "I've had a visit from Mrs. Spencer," she said. "She's happy with what you've done with the place. She likes how you've decorated it. She likes her portrait in the lobby. And she loves how you always keep fresh flowers." From that day on, Joan always kept fresh flowers in her home. And from that day on, Mrs. Spencer would visit her. The ghost made peace with Joan; her nightly visits, which usually occurred between three and four in the morning, were simply the ghost swinging by, passing through Joan's bedroom to check on her to see how she was doing.

It is a presence Joan described on an episode of *Celebrity Ghost Stories* as, "More than friendly. Protective. It's a comfort. It's like she's checking on me. We're friends. And I know that Mrs. Spencer"—Joan choked up when she related this part—"I get very emotional about this, I know she's there, and she's there to help me. My whole life turned in that apartment. It turned in a wonderful way. It gave me a real home and a real sense of belonging. And I think what I did for her is I restored her home. So we both gave each other something that we both love."

I very quickly became obsessed with this story. There was something so beautiful about it. I would get misty-eyed watching clips of *Celebrity Ghost Stories* on YouTube. Here was this woman, this widow, at the lowest point in her life, nearly about to succumb to despair, when suddenly she strikes up this unlikely and vastly comforting friendship with a ghost. A friendship so comforting, Joan didn't even mind repeatedly getting woken up at three in the morning, which for me would be a deal breaker, honestly, no matter how lonely I was. The only entity in the universe who could ever get away with waking me up repeatedly at three in the morning was my exquisitely beautiful newborn daughter, and even then she was treading on thin ice. The tender friendship between the widow and Mrs. Spencer lodged itself in my mind and I was determined to find out more. I knew immediately there were many problems with the story, but I also knew, even as I set out to fact-check them, that I didn't really care.

First off, and I don't even have to look this up to tell you this: NYU does not have nor has it ever had, a parapsychology department. If it had one, I would not only know about it, I would be camped outside its office in a sleeping bag. Second, why send all the way to New Orleans for a voodoo priestess? You could probably find one in the Bronx. Who was this voodoo priestess anyway? Even though in the *Celebrity Ghost Stories* re-creation she is portrayed as a Black woman, in real life she is a white Jewish woman from Maine named Sallie Ann Glassman.[1] And finally, Mrs. Spencer herself is a problem. According to every Morgan family tree I have access to, she does not exist. J. P. Morgan does have Spencers in the family—his father was Junius Spencer Morgan—but no niece of that name, and none who died in the late 1970s or early 1980s, which is when Joan's timeline ("she died seven years before" Joan bought the apartment in the late '80s, or so she says) would put it. Also, no Morgans or Spencers ever lived in the building that I know of.

The building was actually built in 1904 for a millionaire named John Drexel, and the only grande dame in the place was his wife, Alice. Their daughter, also named Alice, eloped with a penniless nobody, and the Drexels left New York in disgrace. The building passed into the hands of another millionaire, James Blanchard Clews, who died in 1934 after living there for only four years. The place was then converted into luxe apartments, and in 1959 Hemingway lived there briefly, wrote *A Moveable Feast*, then moved to Ketchum, Idaho, before blowing his brains out.

So, no Mrs. Spencer.

Other discrepancies emerge when you read Sallie Ann's version of events. The priestess, who is apparently actually pretty well-respected in her circles, describes the subbasement of the building, where a former superintendent used to live, as "deeply demonic." Why would a super live in a subbasement? A basement is bad enough, but even in New York we don't make people live in subbasements (or the "pre-garden" level, as the Realtors say). The priestess recounts that she and Joan visited the subbasement with a "metaphysical scientist" who had some sort of "demon meter" that was apparently pinging like crazy. There are other divergences in the stories of Joan and the priestess, including the amount of time the house cleansing took them, and the location of the cleansing (Sallie Ann says they did it in the lobby and it took three days).[2]

Neither Sallie Ann nor the Morgan Library has responded to my inquiries regarding the identity of Mrs. Spencer, so I will say that, as of this writing, I believe she does not exist. (Also as of this writing, Joan's penthouse, which was sold for $28 million to a member of the Saudi royal family in 2015, is back on the market. His Highness currently has it listed for $38 million.) Despite the lack of evidence linking any Mrs. Spencer to 1 East Sixty-Second Street, the building blithely refers to itself as "the Spencer Condominium." It is possible the portrait Joan found was that of Alice Drexel, who would indeed be very pleased with having her face in the lobby, fresh flowers daily, and Joan's extensive use of plush Louis Quatorze dining chairs.

It really doesn't matter to me if Mrs. Spencer exists or not, or if Sallie Ann Glassman is from Maine, or even if Joan herself tweaked her story from time to time, like so many tiny narrative face-lifts. I believe Joan. I believe she found something, and felt something, in her apartment. I believe something spiritual and healing happened to her there. "I don't know if it was a coincidence," Joan said, "that I found this broken-down apartment at the same time that my life was also broken down." Her story resonates with many tropes of classic ghost stories: the mourning widow, the fierce protectiveness of her living space, the overidentification of the woman with the house in classic Gothic style. The *New York Times* even reported that Joan was absolutely "humorless" about the building, ruling over the condo board with an iron fist and going by the moniker, "the scary lady upstairs." A madwoman in the attic—Gothic indeed.

I also love that a spontaneous friendship broke out between Joan and Sallie Ann Glassman, and that they became lifelong friends after the house cleansing. Sallie Ann opined that Joan liked her because she was the only one who never charged her for anything. Joan repaid Sallie Ann by performing comedy at benefits for Glassman's charity. Sallie Ann would make Joan gris-gris bags to carry with her. It was a nutty, beautiful friendship, and I dearly would have loved to have a cup of tea and a long, gossipy yet metaphysical chat with them.

People often ask me if I think ghosts are frightening. I think they can be, which is why I stuck my kid in the haunted bedroom. (This is true: The man who used to live in the apartment next door killed himself after his wife left him and took the kids. I used to feel the presence of someone watching me while I put my own daughter to bed, and I sometimes wondered if it was him. She later nicknamed him "Mr. Ghosty.") But ghosts can also be a source of comfort.

One other amazing thing about this already perfect story is that Joan Rivers wasn't even the first widow in American history to make friends with a ghost. In one of those wonderful moments of research serendipity, I was flipping through a book about the ghosts of Washington, DC, when I came across this hot item: At the turn of the last century, a woman named Emily Briggs lived in the historic house known as The Maples, in what is now the Capitol Hill neighborhood. Back then, The Maples was known as "a fine brick house in the woods," and it was purchased by Mr. and Mrs. Briggs in 1872. John Briggs died shortly thereafter, and Emily lived alone in the house until her death in 1910. Emily was a true original: an unconventional, gender-role-defying, society-loving writer and journalist who threw fun parties and worked as a news correspondent for the *Washington Post*. She was, in fact, this country's first female news correspondent, a career she started after writing a letter to the editor one day. The editor apparently liked her writing, and she soon began an exciting career writing under the pen name "Olive."

After her husband's death, the large house seemed lonely . . . for a while. Before long, Emily started to notice what sounded like soft weeping coming from one of the bedrooms. She eventually discerned its source was "a most genteel and benign female ghost."[3] Emily was no coward; she approached this specter with the same open-minded curiosity that had stood her in such good stead as a journalist. She observed the ghost without judgment, and the spirit responded by becoming a friendly, benevolent presence, providing Emily with good, if ethereal company. The two women settled into a companionable routine. After several years had passed in this way, Emily awoke one day to find the energy in the house had shifted. She found herself drawn to one bedroom in the house in particular. When she got there, it looked as though a bed had been slept on—the sheets were rumpled and there was a distinct impression on the pillow. A single pearl lay atop the pillow, as though for a goodbye gift, and Emily knew her ghostly friend had departed.

Author Tim Krepp has a theory about the ghost's identity, by the way. He surmises it may have been Helen Nicholson, who once lived in The Maples with her husband, Augustus. At some point Helen became unhinged, possibly due to her husband's infidelity or possibly due to postpartum depression. A month after the birth of her eleventh child, Helen went to a friend's house, "shooed the friend's child out of the room and cut her own throat with a dinner knife." That's rather a sad note to end on, but we can find a bit of comfort in the fact that "Helen Nicholson found a better friend in death with [Emily] Briggs than she had in life with her husband."[4]

This comforting, rather beautiful story has echoes of Joan's tale. In both cases, widows found solace in the ghostly companionship of other women. (Another similarity worth noting: both women were unconventional, trailblazing media personalities in their own times.) It's such a refreshing antidote to the usual tropes about the widow, who is generally portrayed either as a cartoonish "merry widow" enjoying her late husband's fortune or a sad, possibly frightening, usually destitute woman. The widow, as we have seen in previous chapters (see "Conspirator to an Assassination") has traditionally been seen as a figure of fear, desperation, poverty. It's nice to see her instead enjoying her own home and finding genuine friendship in a most unconventional way—a way that, incidentally, is probably also a method for processing her grief (or the unresolved feelings of dissatisfaction with a less-than-ideal spouse who died prematurely). The friendship between the widows and their phantom roommates is a sweet, lovely idea, like a ghostly *Golden Girls* of sorts.

It comforts me to know that Joan found this kind of companionship in her Mrs. Spencer, precisely when she needed it. "How nice," Joan said, "to know that I have Mrs. Spencer to say good evening to every night." How nice indeed. Rest in peace, Joan.

A mannequin at the Merchant's House poses in a ghostly manner in period clothing.
Photo by Leanna Renee Hieber

Actor Pauline Frederick as Potiphar's Wife. Courtesy of the George Grantham Bain Collection, Library of Congress, LC-DIG-ggbain-12499

PART 7

Frauds, Fakes, and Mythmaking

INTRODUCTION

ANDREA

HOW CAN ANYONE SAY WITH ANY CERTAINTY THAT ANYTHING in ghostlore is "true"? It's a question that comes up on our ghost tours a lot. "Is this story *really* true?" Well, it depends. Beyond basic facts—names, dates, locations—almost everything in a ghost story is open to question and interpretation. When you're dealing with ghosts, determining what is true is a near impossibility. Ghosts are a question of belief: One person's lived truth of seeing a ghost may not be accepted by another, more "rational" person. Ghost stories are often rooted in a seed of truth, but are so malleable and migratory that they shape-shift over time.

British author Susan Owens acknowledges the way ghosts change and shift over the ages in her thorough study of 500 years of English ghosts, *The Ghost: A Cultural History:* "Ghosts are mirrors of the times. They reflect our preoccupations, moving with the tide of cultural trends and matching the mood of each age." She notes that the wispy, floating ghost we think of today was not always so. In the Middle Ages, ghosts were substantial, violent, embodied entities, "more likely to break the door down and beat you to death with broken planks" than "drift gently towards a door and disperse." In various epochs, by various interpreters, ghosts have been described and depicted as "walking corpses, as unruly demons and as see-through wraiths." The story, as always, depends largely on who is doing the telling.

And whether we think ghosts are real is, if you'll forgive the pun, immaterial. Most aficionados of the spectral tale are unconcerned with such matters; we prefer, like Owens and others who have tackled the topic of spirits, to remain "fascinated by ghosts while not being quite sure what they are." One writer of this book counts herself in that camp—as open-minded, curious, humble, inquisitive skeptics. The other writer genuinely believes that that spirits are a verifiable presence and exist among us. We'll leave it to you to guess who is who, and just leave it to you to draw your own conclusions. We cannot say, and wiser minds than ours have tried and failed. No ghost book is complete without the legendary quote from Samuel Johnson:

> *It is wonderful that five thousand years have now elapsed since the creation of the world, and still it is undecided whether or not there has ever been an instance of the spirit of any person appearing after death. All argument is against it; but all belief is for it.*

Yet despite the fact that it does very well to let the mysteries of the spirits lie where they may, many great minds and great people have devoted themselves to the pursuit of ghost-hunting as a scientific inquiry, searching vainly for some principle of truth or proof. Some have seemed the victims of a near-irrational obsession, such as Harry Houdini, who was possessed with the idea of uncovering fraud and fakery among practicing mediums; others genuinely curious about the mysteries of the universe (William James, for instance).

There is a decided gender divide between skeptic and believer, shored up by centuries of ingrained gender norms, as well as the gendered nature of ghost stories and Spiritualism and mediumship, the latter skewing heavily female. Victorian-era concepts of women as spiritual and irrational fed into these notions, yet these same women also understood that modern Spiritualism was a potentially feminist enterprise and was, in fact, one of the few avenues that allowed women to speak in public, gather in groups, raise their voices, and take center stage. They adapted the concepts and tenets of Spiritualism to bolster social causes from abolition to women's suffrage.

Other women grasped that modern Spiritualism was a potentially very profitable enterprise and could provide a woman with a steady income in an era when the only other means of providing for her own support consisted of menial drudgery, marriage, or prostitution. At times, the temptation of easy cash outweighed genuine spiritual impulses. Some "mediums" indeed resorted to deception in order to provide a steady flow of good material for their séances (as Houdini loved to point out). Medium Florence Cook claimed to have materialized an apparition whom she named Katie King, in one of the most intriguing cases of fraud in Spiritualist history. We've looked at this story in more detail here, exploring its fascinating and profound implications for the myriad ways true belief intersects, sometimes awkwardly, with trickery and desire.

Edgar Allan Poe understood this impulse a decade before Spiritualism. He knew that the line between truth and fiction was mutable. And Poe often ripped from the headlines when looking for inspiration for his stories; one such tale, "The Mystery of Marie Rogêt," which we've examined in more detail, draws directly from the real-life murder of Mary Rogers in 1841. In Mary Rogers's story, reality is nearly impossible to pin down, and her phantom presence haunts the eternal unanswered question of this puzzling and still unsolved cold case.

Modern skeptics often enjoy laughing at the Victorians' apparent gullibility when it comes to the obvious fakery of manifestations like Katie King, or the spirit photography of William Mumler, but it's important to remember that universal credence wasn't the norm. There were skeptics back then too, and many of them would laugh right back at us if they saw an episode of *Ghost Adventures*. The uncritical or complicit acceptance of falsified or dubious ghost stories is the foundational myth that undergirds both the paranormal reality TV and ghost tour industries, and we all participate in it whenever we partake of it.

We examine one current example of this in our chapter on the Sorrel Weed House in Savannah, Georgia. The house, supposedly one of the most haunted houses in that very haunted city, is featured on numerous ghost tours and television shows. Its ghost story relies heavily on the problematic romanticization of the antebellum South, and features sex, slavery, and suicide, seductively packaged for the tourist trade. But the most rudimentary historic research reveals troubling plot holes in the Sorrel Weed House's version of history, and the story unravels at the slightest touch. So what value does it have for us today to examine this questionable story and the way it functions within the ghostlore of the American South? And why does it continue to be one of Savannah's premier haunted destinations?

Maybe because people simply don't expect truth on a ghost tour. There is an unwritten compact that ghost stories are exaggerated, falsified, and sensationalized, and that because ghosts are by definition unprovable, there is no burden on anyone—not your friendly neighborhood tour guide or celebrity ghost hunter Zak Bagans—to provide anything close to a true story. Folklore, of which ghostlore is a subset, is all about mythmaking. Saying "legend has it," or "according to local lore," or the infamous "they say," immediately places a story in this context. That's not to say it's acceptable to uncritically repeat "fakelore" or problematic ghost stories such as those presented at Sorrel Weed. But there is a social contract that acknowledges the mythmaking aspect to ghosts and must, on some level, be okay with that, lest one risk becoming an embittered, obsessive pedant.

In our early days of giving ghost tours, we were obsessed with "truth," until we finally completed our fool's journey and ended up a little wiser. These days we're more interested in how and why certain stories are told in certain ways, how point of view elicits or elides crucial pieces of information, and what the telling of these stories says about the people who present them. We've come to understand that perspectives are not fixed, and we're not here to prove or force you to believe anything. As women who write about ghosts, it's endlessly interesting to us to notice how everything is constructed: gender, history, and, yes, ghostlore. None of these are objective essential truths, and all of them change depending on the perspective of the participant. As for ghosts themselves, well, they're part of the great, unsolvable mystery of life after death, a vast puzzle that is all the more tantalizing for its unknowability. And we're okay with that. When it comes to ghosts, truth is as elusive as the spirits themselves.

THE PRESTIGE OF KATIE KING

LEANNA

PHILADELPHIA, PENNSYLVANIA

IN 1874, THE SPIRIT MANIFESTATION OF KATIE KING, GHOSTLY daughter of infamous pirate Henry Morgan, held sway over the hearts and minds of Philadelphia society and beyond, garnering newspaper attention across the nation. She became a larger-than-life entity unto herself, a sort of Frankenstein's monster of Spiritualist creation. The kind of Spiritualism that was putting on elaborate shows is a fraught history of deception, the domain of actors and magicians.

But one thing cannot be denied: Spiritualism was an extraordinary vehicle placing women in the spotlight in matters of spiritual authority, leadership, and public presence that had been entirely denied them before. It also, often, was responsible for one hell of a show. And a show that took place in Philadelphia would be one that would get people talking.

The Spiritualist movement began in 1848, when the young Fox sisters of Hydesville, New York, near Rochester, claimed to be communicating with spirits via a sequence of raps on a table. What began as a prank, and was later denounced and debunked through the whole of the sisters' fraught lives, caught on as a new realm of possibility.

Quaker communities in particular embraced Spiritualism. The Quaker tradition of Protestant Christian faith has always been a more progressive and open one—one that vehemently denounced the horrors of slavery and fought for abolition, as well as supported the equal education and treatment of women. They allowed women to speak openly regarding spiritual matters, and that specific detail accounts for Spiritualism's rise as an empowerment tool for women.

The greatest mystery of all, proof of life after death, wasn't something just one faith sought. It has remained a constant human question. The rise of Spiritualism was somewhat inevitable at a time of great change and speculation.

Women were quick to take to the stage of Spiritualism as a means to an end, a way to gain a platform at a time when women speaking in public was still taboo. If one went into a trance state and spoke ardently about a new way of thinking, living, and being, about equal rights and women's suffrage, and if the audience didn't like it, one could just blame it on the spirits, after all; one was just a channel, a messenger. Victoria Woodhull used Spiritualism as a way to gain the audience and employment of Cornelius Vanderbilt and later make her 1872 run for president, with Frederick Douglass as her running mate.

Spiritualism as a concept was an extraordinary comfort at a time of high death rates from what are now largely preventable or treatable diseases; infant mortality rates and deaths in childbirth were very high. More than 600,000 soldiers died in the Civil War, and during a time when most funerals and wakes were held in homes, soldiers' bodies generally could not be returned for those rites. Many people feared that a spirit could not pass peacefully on to the "undiscovered country" if their body wasn't whole; thousands of limbless, broken Civil War corpses lay in vast swaths across a mourning country. The idea of communing with a whole and unbroken spirit, saying a last goodbye, regardless of the state of the corpse, was a huge comfort. That yearning hasn't left; it's a ghost that still haunts us.

There was also a distinct, simple allure to Spiritualism. "Unlike Christianity, which demanded unquestioning servitude, Spiritualism demanded only that followers suspend disbelief."[1] The suspension of disbelief is a cardinal rule for any performer. With that in mind, a spiritualist looking to create a spectacle already had the upper hand in this general rule. Sitting circles were curated and self-selecting. Philadelphia, the "Quaker City" famous in its own right, was generally amenable to Spiritualism, and the community was very well established by the 1870s.

Philadelphia has a unique, bold, unmistakable character. The city loves a good story; whether it's true or not is hardly as important as if it's entertaining. Philadelphia also takes great pride in something of theirs garnering national attention. Katie most certainly did. It's not surprising that one of the nineteenth century's most-talked-about spirit "manifestations" came out of Philly: the celebrated daughter of a centuries-dead pirate.

Katie King first began appearing as a full-body manifestation in England via Florence Cook. Cook "retired" Katie after her act had been debunked too often, and an American couple named Jennie and Nelson Holmes took up the mantle. After having seen Cook perform at the height of her popularity, Katie King began "appearing" in Philadelphia, courtesy of the Holmeses, by 1874. While presenting a few similarities to Cooke's version of King, the basic narratives that this new couple presented of the patriarchal dread pirate and his lovely daughter were different, and *certainly* didn't corroborate the actual history of the self-serving, oft-treacherous Henry Morgan or his family, though he was said to have remained childless.

That the facts didn't match up never stopped Jennie and Nelson Holmes. There are no official records for these two and their origins; it is as if they simply appeared, ready to make a scene. Nelson was described as slight and sometimes effeminate, and Jennie as "mannish," so they were couple already subverting societal expectations of gender. That they appeared uneducated, possibly even illiterate, didn't detract from their zealous talent for spectacle.

Katie King would appear out of a device commonly utilized by Spiritualist performers: a spirit cabinet. Many trance mediums using spirit cabinets—literally wardrobe-like cabinets within the room—would go into a performative catatonic state outside the cabinet as a precursor to "materializing" a spirit within it. By using the energy of the medium, a sound, dim movement, or image would be seen from within or come out from the cabinet. Faces or limbs might appear at openings or apertures. Eerie forms, veiled and unsettling to behold, made use of simple, dim lighting, black curtains, false doors, and panels to extensive effect. But most shows maintained a boundary between the mortal sitters and the spectral realm, mediums, and managers, insisting that the manifestations would flee if they were disturbed.

But Katie King did something entirely new.

A slight, ethereal form with gray eyes and deathly pallor, and dark ringlets beneath a gauzy veil, King broke the fourth wall between spirit and audience. Even more shocking, she could be touched. She interacted with her guests, but only the true believers—a practice that heightened the ardor within the sitters of the circle. It gave Spiritualism a feverish new threshold of what was possible.

The Holmeses' sitting room at 50 North Ninth Street was filled twice a night. Admission was a dollar per person. The audience was curated; only those introduced by friends or who could produce a testimonial—an impassioned flock—were allowed in. The audience was shown about the space, allowing them to see for themselves that there were no props on the Holmeses' persons, nor any obvious false floors, walls, or doors in the spirit cabinet setup. The Holmeses' first cabinet was a simple convention; merely by opening two adjacent doors at the corner of the sitting room into a triangle and preparing openings in the doorways, covered over by dark curtains and a board atop the open doors, the spirit stage was set. Once the lights were dimmed Jennie went into her trance; various faces might appear at the spirit cabinet apertures as a bit of a warm-up, but it was the lovely and compelling Katie King everyone waited to see.

She was first introduced as the same manifestation that had been so talked about in London, giving Philadelphia an exclusivity and high regard. The excitement in the room was always palpable. Whether believable or not, it seemed people truly got caught up in the show as King explained her family history and untimely death at the age of nineteen before interacting with the audience. At first the interactions were in conversation, but as confidence grew in proportion to her infamy, she took more liberties with her biggest fans.

Many people commented on how lifelike she was, or that the lock of her hair she gave a most ardent supporter was astonishingly real—and how incredible that it hadn't faded into the ether after a week. It's hard to imagine that no one recognized the truth of it: that she was an actress hired to play the part, and utilized stagecraft, trapdoors, boards, white makeup, and eerie lighting to make her case. But many people truly wanted to believe in the power the living might have over the dead, the control that might be possible over something that terrified them. What people thought they *knew* about life and death was being tested every day.

Science was still a wild card in those days. Darwin had shaken up everything people thought they knew about God and humankind. Technology was making what seemed like magic happen, whether in radio waves, telegraphs carrying invisible messages around the globe, or in man-made light, harnessing the heavens. People believed the supernatural was just something we hadn't found the science for yet. While that may yet prove true, what was true *then* was that Katie King was played by Eliza White, hired by Jennie and Nelson

Holmes after having seen Florence Cook produce the act in London, and knowing they needed something new for their own stale act. Placing rubber masks in the apertures of their spirit cabinet was no longer exciting (or convincing) anyone. Katie King provided a burst of fresh life, notoriety, and attraction.

A magician's craft is called their *prestige*. The prestige of Katie King owed more to a nineteeth-century obsession with spirits and the idealized concept of a beautiful young woman than any actual stagecraft or performer's talent.

Eliza White's early history is as murky and unknown as the Holmeses', and her personal account given to newspapers was likely embellished, but the trio clearly created a mutually beneficial partnership that had a really good run for a great deal of 1874, until too many people started asking too many questions and too many others disrupted the act and caught glimpses behind the scenes. For all that there were believers, there certainly were detractors and skeptics. Many Philadelphians viewed Spiritualism as harmless entertainment. Others made it their mission to debunk spiritualists as simply magicians taking advantage of the grieving or deluded.

But consider for a moment the idea of Katie King, the invention at the center of the scandal.

Katie was an entity who was entirely objectified. Her beauty was extolled, but as a commodity. She was divvied up into an assemblage of pretty, dainty parts. Sometimes just a hand, a part of an arm, a glimpse of her face would be all that would materialize from the cabinet. A tease. Transactional. She was called forth, she was ogled, not always sexualized, but often. And she was evoked in constant service and labor to her mediums. She epitomized the Victorian ideal of a historic beauty cut down in her prime, and wasn't that romantic?

One would think that those of a spiritualist mindset might once have asked her why she was not at peace; why she chose to haunt this place? For many circle sitters, their thoughts were about their own experiences, not the ghost's. Titillation, the thrill of the show, and the chance of touching the beyond were all the motivations necessary. But King had no character arc. And when she was no longer titillating, when the debunkings couldn't be ignored, she was discarded, the women who called her forth and performed her derided.

The woman who played her was effectively a prisoner in her job. It would not do for someone to recognize Katie King taking a daytime stroll. That was one of the reasons Eliza White and the Holmeses fell out. That, and the money, of course. After a separation in the fall of 1874, when it was clear their act needed King on their marquee, Nelson Holmes tried to make this right in a pleading letter, saying they would all go to Chicago and Eliza would have free rein to come and go as she pleased.

When Eliza had quite enough of the business, she explained everything to two well-respected men who had once been Katie King's most ardent admirers, who, with heavy hearts but a duty of responsibility, took the exposé to the press, and the story was widely circulated in nationwide papers. She discussed the particulars of the spirit cabinet and the ways in which she came and went. In each case, while sitters were indeed encouraged to examine the cabinet, materials, and surrounding rooms, and the Holmeses themselves, no matter where they performed, there was always an entrance or exit unseen by general inspection that Eliza would utilize. After her appearance as Katie King, while Jennie led the audience in a song meant to bring back the spirit, the noise was used as cover so Eliza could retreat and either hide in a special wooden cage under a bedroom mattress to remain unseen, or to escape to an adjoining apartment.

The Eddy and Davenport Brothers, famed contemporary performers, had sat tied inside their spirit cabinets. The audience was made fully aware they were in restraints before the cabinet doors closed. And yet once the séance began, music burst forth from the cabinet—bells, guitars, and other instruments. Only when they were debunked were their easily loosened restraints made clear. All these methods were basic but reliable magician's tricks that people like Harry Houdini would swiftly denounce and reveal well into the twentieth century. Houdini would only reveal a prestige if the performer lied about its provenance. If performers simply called themselves illusionists or magicians, they didn't violate his code. Spiritualist tricks like this, he thought, made a profane mockery of faith and magic alike.

There's often a lack of nuance in texts about Spiritualism; a reductive all-or-nothing. You either believed in the truth of science or in the "wonderful delusion."[2] But it is important to note that not all people who identified as spiritualists or believed in the faith were out to con others like the Holmeses were. Many folks worked quietly with clairvoyant gifts, often just for a modest donation, receiving spiritual messages and reassuring the grieving of the possibility of a continuation of spirit without physical manifestations or theatrics. People still look for answers via psychics to this day, and then, as now, some psychics are absolute frauds, while some have an inexplicable skill. The names of talented, truthful spiritualists of the era didn't get national debunkings; they weren't the subject of the same kinds of rightful skepticism as those who were looking to fleece the unwitting. Spiritualists around the world, like Hilma af Klint, used Spiritualism as a way to innovate. Hilma af Klint became the first surrealist artist long before Kandinsky seized that title as his own.

The basic tenet of Spiritualism acknowledged the unbroken existence of the spirit beyond death. This resonated in the time of its creation; it resonated again in Britain after the senselessness of World War I; it resonates amid any global pandemic or large-scale crisis, and always will. One cannot argue with the comfort of the basic premise, even though we *should* argue with how spiritualist performers took advantage, how magicians and stage technicians and early photographers used every trick of their art and trade to perpetuate illusions passed off as real.

If we reject the first, simple rule of spiritualist thought—that some sort of energy or echo of a person continues after death—the premise of this book is already in question. Are the thousands of ghost stories across the nation, the millions around the world, just one delusion after another? There has to be nuance in a discussion of what constitutes communication with the dead. There has to be room to wonder.

The women involved, whether Eliza White or Jennie Holmes, who was the face and more-showcased "talent" of the team, bore the lion's share of the derision and the backlash. Nelson would barricade himself in the spirit cabinet if a particular circle got out of hand. Often debunked male performers either rebranded or just went about their merry way. Debunking didn't necessarily stop the show; it all depended. Some spiritualist women never recovered. The once-famed Fox sisters died in poverty.

Jennie Holmes was called before the Society of Spiritualists to prove herself, but after several days of failed trials, she quite literally ran away, and the society had no choice but to deem her an impostor. By 1875, Florence Cook had resurrected her original Katie King act in England, only to be caught in her spirit cabinet as herself. A Parisian Katie King act was sentenced to jail for fraud. There was no further recourse for the lovely daughter of the pirate to continue to materialize. But for a year Katie King was the world's most famous ghost, believed by countless people to be a very real specter. Her story still lingers on, her creation and fall from international grace a cautionary tale just as fully realized as many other "real" ghost stories.

Just as there are no official records for the Holmeses and their origins, no one knows where they're buried. They clearly invented themselves and then, when all their illusions came tumbling down, they vanished into obscurity, leaving no trace of their end. Perhaps they were the apparitions all along.

The last known entry in Eliza White's history is a theater bill, notices of which were mentioned in newspapers nationwide. Eliza utilized her infamy to make a career transition to the stage in a play called *Katie King; or, Spiritualism Exposed*.

WILLING THE GHOSTS TO LIFE

Molly and Matilda of the Sorrel Weed House

ANDREA

SAVANNAH, GEORGIA

The Sorrel Weed House circa 1933 by the Historic American Buildings Survey. Library of Congress, Prints & Photographs Division, HABS [or HAER or HALS], Reproduction number [e.g., "HABS ILL, 16-CHIG, 33-2"]

When considering ghostly legends, it is often said it doesn't matter if they're true; what matters is what they tell us about ourselves and our society. In the case of the Sorrel Weed House, what they tell us is rather troubling.

According to legend, the Sorrel Weed House is said to be one of the most haunted houses in Savannah. The 1840s Greek Revival mansion was built for wealthy merchant Francis Sorrel, a Haitian immigrant who married his wealthy, well-connected business partner's daughter, Lucinda, when she was just seventeen years old.[1] When Lucinda died of yellow fever just five years into their marriage, Sorrel promptly replaced her with her younger sister, Matilda. Most ghost tours in Savannah will tell you that Matilda was apparently emotionally unstable and prone to bouts of depression; her melancholy was exacerbated by her husband's continued infidelity, including affairs with one of their slaves, a girl named Molly, whom he kept as a mistress.* When Matilda caught Francis and Molly in flagrante, she became crazed with grief and jealousy and threw herself from a second-floor balcony. Distraught by Matilda's suicide, Molly hanged herself in the carriage house a mere two weeks later. In some versions of the story, Molly was actually murdered by Francis Sorrel to keep her quiet about the affair.

To this day, Molly still haunts the carriage house. Her spirit alternately screams, "Help me!" or simply stands and smiles seductively. Matilda is presumed to be the menacing "lady in black" seen floating about the place. Together, the spectral women replay their story on an endless loop.

The tropes, both sexist and racist, that pervade this bodice-ripper of a ghost story simply drip off the page like Spanish moss . . . or maybe like humidity on a hot Southern summer night. Pick your cliché. It doesn't matter because—guess what?—this story is prob-

* We kept the standard language of most ghost tours and guidebooks in our retelling here.

ably 98 percent false! And yet it's presented like fact on ghost tours, paranormal websites, and alllll over the city of Savannah. What gives? Where does this extremely triggering story, filled with euphemisms like "mistress," "affair," and "trusted servant," as Molly is sometimes called on the house tour, come from? And why was it not part of Savannah ghostlore until *after* the house was opened as a tourist attraction?

The answer reveals an intriguing web of greed and lies, commerce and capitalism, tragedy and real-life horror that puts any made-up ghost story to shame. To even begin to untangle it, we have to start with a bit of background on ghost tourism in Savannah.

The supernatural tourism industry in Savannah is pretty intense, to say the least. The city does a brisk trade in its "spooky South" offerings and is heavily invested in the promotion of its paranormal tourism. It's an extremely lucrative and highly competitive business, one central to the city's brand. (As of this writing, there are approximately twenty ghost tour companies operating in this city of 145,000 people.) After the smash success of *Midnight in the Garden of Good and Evil* (both the novel and the film) in the 1990s, the city embraced its dark tourism aesthetic, "transforming nightly into a flourishing necropolis."[2] Which is why it's difficult to have a discussion about Savannah's ghosts without talking about the city's ghost tourism industry. The two have become entwined and inseparable, creating a strange feedback loop in which history, ghost stories, and folklore are remixed and reinterpreted in ways that strain and challenge reality. The most salient example of this phenomenon is the ghost story of Molly and Matilda at the Sorrel Weed House, where we find a troubling intersection of race, gender, and exploitation that demonstrates the ethical entanglements in profiting from the stories of marginalized people.

Though the stories of Molly and Matilda are presented as fact on the Sorrel Weed House ghost tour, a bit of sleuthing reveals cracks in the story fairly quickly—if you know where to look. Savannah tour guide and blogger James Caskey has a very informative post, "Haunted by Bad History," that lays bare a number of inconsistencies in the story, and writers Colin Dickey and Tiya Miles have thoroughly debunked several aspects of the story in their respective books *Ghostland* and *Tales from the Haunted South*. To recap their excellent research, the main problem with the Sorrel Weed ghost narrative is that real-life records of Molly and Matilda do not match the story.

Let's start with Molly. Although some researchers have stated that there is no record of her in the census records or anywhere else, others have found a slave manifest showing a twenty-eight-year-old Black woman named Molly who was "owned" by Sorrel. However, she didn't die in Savannah, as far as we know; the manifest for the ship *Augusta* states that she sailed to New York City in 1857, and we have found no record of her after that.[3] As for Matilda, she actually fell to her death and died not at the Sorrel Weed House, but at the townhouse next door, where the family moved nine months before her death. Though she may indeed have suffered from depression in real life, as some letters and other sources allude, the suicide isn't a definite fact. The official cause of her death was a concussion due to a fall.[4]

So how did the story get started? Deep in the mists of time, rumor, and local lore? It seems not. The provenance of the tale seems to sit with the current owners of the house. According to Tiya Miles, investment bankers Stephen and Philip Bader bought the historic house in the 1990s, did shoddy restorations, ran out of money, and decided to rebrand their half-finished, financially ruined investment as a ghostly attraction.[5] It was a rather clever idea, actually. If only they hadn't chosen a story that would set off so many alarm bells! Almost immediately, visitors to the house found the tale of Molly and Matilda problematic. Author Caitlin Doughty was dismissive of the ghost tour on her YouTube channel, *Ask a Mortician*. She noted that the enslaved Molly was referred to as a "trusted servant" and questioned the ethical value of having her haunt the carriage house: "So you're telling me that this girl has to hang around for 150 years providing thrills to paying tourists? That's a level of hell that Dante forgot."[6] Stephen Bader has stated in the past that his information regarding the affairs and suicides (or murder/suicide) was obtained from private family letters, but he has never made these letters public, claiming they have been lost. I made multiple calls and sent emails to the house's administrators asking for their side of the story, but they have gone unreturned.

In light of this lack of any corroborating evidence, and the counter-research done by respected scholars, many have concluded that the stories told about Molly and Matilda on the Sorrel Weed House ghost tour are false.[7] Such fabrications and exaggerations trivialize the lived experiences of women like Molly, who really were enslaved and coerced into unwilling sexual relations with men in positions of power over them. More disturbingly, calling Molly a "mistress" not only glosses over these uneven power dynamics but also suggests that someone thought eroticizing the story would sell tickets to a haunted attraction.[8] The exploitation of the violence perpetrated against Molly is also upsetting: EVPs of Molly's ghost screaming, "Help me!" are all over the internet and are used as promotional material for the ghost tour. (EVPs, an acronym for Electronic Voice Phenomena, are digital recordings of disembodied voices thought to be evidence of spectral activity.) It's extremely disturbing to see the sexual coercion and enslavement of women sensationalized for financial gain. A former tour guide for the house felt similarly about the exploitation of both Molly and Matilda's pain, saying:

> *I don't remember when exactly it hit me that this wasn't a Halloween haunted house. Maybe it was when I first heard [a spirit] in the basement speak to me. These were real people with real stories and real traumas. And what they're work-*

> *ing through is trauma. What right did I have to make this family's tragedy a spectacle? I gave dozens of tours before one of the museum curators pointed out that the bricks in the garden still bear the fingerprints of the slaves who made them.*[9]

It was also disturbing for me to notice, when researching this story, that the truth is buried fairly deeply beneath several layers of marketing and media sensationalism. The city of Savannah seems content to allow the mythmaking to continue, as it only serves to bolster its haunted brand and businesses. Colin Dickey quotes former Savannah tour guide Elena Gormley as saying, "'The city's very obsessed with its brand.'" Dickey accuses Savannah's tourism officials of allowing "licensed tour companies [to] do a brisk business on fabricated stories and distortions."[10] And, because the house was featured on *Ghost Hunters* and other paranormal TV shows, the internet is flooded with ghostly EVPs and recaps of the featured episodes, further solidifying the myth of this as a haunted house. Then there are the myriad blog posts associated with other Savannah ghost tour companies, all of which have a vested interest in maintaining the paranormal narrative. So there are at least three layers of mythmaking to wade through before you get to anything even resembling the truth. (If you're really masochistic, you can wade through the low-rated Tripadvisor reviews of the Sorrel Weed House, where discerning customers voice their suspicions.) In fact, if you didn't have the luxury of time, or if you didn't know what you were looking for, you might never have any idea that the story contains numerous unsubstantiated claims, because it all seems to have the imprimatur of the city of Savannah and the tacit approval of the paranormal tourism and entertainment industries.

Some may scoff at the idea that there can ever be "truth" on a ghost tour. Many argue that it isn't necessary to be historically accurate on such tours because ghosts aren't "real" and we are all willing participants in a charade—similar to professional wrestling or paranormal reality TV, we understand that storytelling contains a performative element and selective editing. We are allowed to enjoy a good story we know to be untrue simply because it's, well, a good story—much as wrestling audiences still enjoy the performance while knowing it's a performance. And yes, as ghost tour guides, we do understand the nature of oral tradition and folklore as occupying a space between fact and reality, but at the same time we have to acknowledge that this space exists. The issue with the Sorrel Weed House ghost tour is that it doesn't make these acknowledgments, and by failing to provide any context, and by uncritically presenting a falsified, eroticized version of Savannah's history, it ceases to be of any value and becomes merely exploitative instead.

This is especially sad because the Sorrel Weed House is missing a unique opportunity to engage people in a more thoughtful discussion of how the ghosts of the past bear on the present. Ghost tour operators have an opening to discuss more difficult subjects than traditional/daytime tours do, because their clients already have a demonstrated interest in the dark side of the human experience. Ghost tours also have the potential to reframe traditional narratives in thought-provoking ways. As geographer Glenn Gentry writes: "[Ghost] tours mix deep reflection with entertainment, fun, and education. Although ghost walks present tragedy in a light-hearted manner, this does not preclude the presentation of counterhegemonic stories or tales of injustice."[11] There's also an issue of responsibility at play here. Author Bilal G. Morris points out that profiting from a system of slavery and patriarchy by reselling the ghost stories of enslaved people is, to put it mildly, morally questionable, unless one offers some additional context or framework for discussion: "Ghost hunters and haunted tour guides make millions from Molly's story. But if that story is gonna make you rich, then why not give it the angle it deserves?"[12] The Sorrel Weed House is especially well positioned to potentially offer a corrective to past (mis)representations of the women and enslaved people discussed on their tours, and can move toward more honest (and honestly much more frightening) ghost tours.

In fairness, there do seem to have been some apparent attempts by the Sorrel Weed House to tone down the inaccurate and sensationalized ghost tours; they recently commissioned an archaeological study to determine whether a depression in the cellar floor was due to the burial of human remains (it turned out to be a combination trash pit and latrine).[13] If they keep going in this direction of genuine historic inquiry and take it one step further, they might move from a symbol of the industry's problematic side to a stellar example of how ghost tourism can usefully help us process troubling feelings that have been suppressed for too long. Placing ghost stories in a framework of real, shared history would actually make the experience of touring the Sorrel Weed House far more moving.

For example, look at the representation of Matilda, of her "madness." Her ghost story could be contextualized within a conversation about the way the institution of slavery was psychologically harmful to all people involved in it, in this case to the women who tacitly accepted their husbands' infidelity with bondspeople likely coerced into sexual relations. Imagine having to go to bed with *that* image in your mind every night. Anyone participating in a reprehensible system like slavery suffers devastating psychic consequences: "the unfettered beast of sexual slavery" destroyed "black lives as well as white families . . ."[14] If Francis Sorrel's infidelity really happened, it is highly probable it would have created psychological distress for his wife when she discovered it. If it didn't happen, these ghost stories could at least be acknowledged as standing in for larger social patterns that were fairly commonplace at the time.

That doesn't mean it's necessary to vilify Francis Sorrel to make a point. There are a number of ways to talk about him without resorting to unfounded accusations (no letters or other evidence exist that mention any sexual liaison with Molly or any other enslaved person). Francis is an interesting figure because of his status as a Haitian immigrant. White slaveholders in the antebellum South lived in a state of constant anxiety. The fear of rebellion and uprising pervaded daily life then, just as it still seeps into the mythology and history of the region now. The Haitian Revolution in particular struck fear in the hearts of slave-owning Americans; it was a successful slave uprising, the worst fear of any plantation owner or overseer. Sorrel's Haitian heritage is a trigger point for this anxiety, which may be another reason why stories about him exert such a powerful hold on the white imagination. It may also be why early versions of the ghost story emphasized his "voodoo" dabbling. There was speculation he was partly Black and passing for white; some scholars still believe this, while others debate it, but either way he was Haitian.* He had the traumatic childhood experience of living through the Haitian Revolution, witnessing brutal murders at an age when most children are learning the alphabet. His mother died when he was six weeks old; later, he was separated from his family. Private letters from his daughter elicit a profound pathos: They describe how upset her father would get when describing the violent, horrifying things he witnessed as a young child during the Revolution, how even as an old man he would tremble when he spoke of it.[15] Considering Francis Sorrel in the context of his Haitian heritage opens up a far more interesting conversation than merely having him stand in as a kind of cipher for a generic Southern man.

By making room for thoughtful commentary within the framework of the Sorrel Weed narrative, we could all have a much more

---

* Sorrel lived to an unusually old age, well into his nineties. Some say he lived so long because he secretly practiced voodoo. This exoticized and othered him, creating a bit of subconscious tension by painting him as a citizen of a country populated by dark-skinned rebels with magical powers. (Again, to be fair, the house has recently toned down this voodoo angle.)

profound and unsettling conversation about the ghosts of the past. And while this particular ghost story would certainly benefit from some skeptical inquiry and critical analysis, there is no need to strip it entirely of its spiritual power. We don't have to discount the many profound experiences people have had when visiting the Sorrel Weed House. Whether members of the family are still present in some residual form, or the ghostly energy is a by-product of the house's proximity to the Siege of Savannah in 1779, which resulted in great loss of life, we cannot say. It is not up to us to decide whether someone else's subjective ghostly experience is true or false. And even if we did, the house is just metaphorically inhabited by the ghosts of unfinished business from the past; we don't judge any tourist for wanting to learn more about the troubling side of our history, or our hauntings. The life stories of Francis, Matilda, and Molly, *and* their afterlives as ghost stories, still deserve to be told. But we owe it to Molly—whoever she really may or may not have been—and to every woman like her whose story has been forgotten, to tell these stories in as honest and truthful a way as we can.

On a personal note, the more I tried to untangle the web of lies surrounding this story, the more deeply I began to wonder if it's possible that, by virtue of this story's repetition, Molly has in some ironic way become a "real" ghost. Like the *tulpa* (a sentient thought form traditional in Tibetan Buddhism), her ghost has almost been willed into existence. As I wrote this chapter, I found myself becoming increasingly drawn into her story. James Caskey and Tiya Miles have also written about similar experiences, referring to their feelings as "an obsession" and "a call" respectively.[16] During the daytime, when I researched and wrote about Molly, my stomach twisted itself into knots and my right eye twitched constantly as I became increasingly perturbed by what I read and tried to process the information. At night, I would find myself waking at three in the morning, thinking about Molly and Matilda, sometimes with tears streaming down my face. If I walked down the hall to go to the bathroom, I imagined I could see their figures reflected back at me in every mirror. I'm not the most diligent Catholic, but I had a strong urge to light a white candle for each of them. They floated through my dreams at night and I wished fervently for their souls to be at peace. The more time I spent with them, the more I became—and no other word will do here—haunted.

THE MYTHMAKING OF MARIE ROGÊT

LEANNA

HOBOKEN, NEW JERSEY

MARY CECILIA ROGERS HAD ALREADY MADE THE PAPERS BY being the "Beautiful Cigar Girl" who brought a robust traffic of admirers to Anderson's Tobacco Emporium, the downtown Manhattan tobacco shop where she worked and captivated high-profile clientele.

Her decomposing body in a ruined white dress was found floating in shallow waters by men who had been relaxing at the popular Sybil's Cave in Hoboken, New Jersey, on July 28, 1841.

Rumors immediately flew about the young woman's violent death. A brief coroner's examination at the site where her body had been taken ashore concluded that she had been strangled and violated. Mary's murder at approximately twenty years old remains an unsolved mystery to this day.

Sybil's Cave was a man-made excavation that led to a natural spring. Opened in 1832, the cave remained a popular tourist attraction throughout the mid-nineteenth century, made all the more mordantly popular by the subsequent deaths discovered beside it.

Rogers's fiancé, Daniel Payne, tormented by grief and accusations that he'd had something to do with her death, committed suicide by overdosing on laudanum while intoxicated. A remorseful note was tucked in with papers on his body, which was also found near Sybil's Cave on October 7, 1841. His sorrowful note read: "To the World—here I am on the very spot. May God forgive me for my misspent life."

Sybil's Cave was shut down in 1880 by the Board of Health, which deemed its spring not safe enough to drink from, and was destroyed in the 1930s when industry took over the area. The entrance was rediscovered in 2007, and its once grand—and admittedly eerie—Gothic-arched entryway has been rebuilt. Revived interest in the cave, naturally, prompted a fresh interest in its infamy.

Mysterious, luminous figures have been seen along the dramatic rocks near the entrance, searching for solace and, perhaps, for the truth.

Mary Rogers's unsolved death and the mythmaking that followed marks a turn into the creation and increasing popularity of "true crime" stories. She was, after all, beautiful. And now dead . . . the stuff of poetry.

Edgar Allan Poe used Rogers's death as inspiration for "The Mystery of Marie Rogêt," a story that features a rare treat: a continuing character in Poe's work. The detective C. Auguste Dupin made his first appearance in Poe's short story "The Murders in the Rue Morgue," published in 1841. He called these works his tales of "ratiocination," referring to the methodical process of logic and reason, and the stories have been widely considered to be the first detective fiction.

"The Mystery of Marie Rogêt," published in 1842, marks Dupin's second appearance. "The Purloined Letter," published in 1844, was the third and final appearance of the detective. Poe named

Dupin after the heroine of a story that had been printed in *Burton's Gentleman's Magazine* about the life of Vidocq, the French minister of police.

Poe set the story in Paris but used the details of Mary Rogers's death, a crime that remains one of the most puzzling unsolved murders of New York City. "The Mystery of Marie Rogêt" was presented by Poe to possible publishers with a savvy lure—that he had quite nearly solved the Mary Rogers murder by his own rigorous analysis. This, at a time when most readers would certainly have been aware of the details of that event and the wild flurry of reporting around it, would be a sound investment in a known intrigue. In *The Beautiful Cigar Girl: Mary Rogers, Edgar Allan Poe and the Invention of Murder,* Daniel Stashower discusses the absolute flash point that the Rogers case became in New York and New Jersey.

> *To some, she was an innocent lamb led to slaughter, illustrating the failures of law enforcement. "Nothing tending to elucidate the mystery hanging over the murder of poor Mary has yet transpired at the Police Office," wrote the* Herald. *Instead, the public appetite for news by "stories made to suit the gullibility of the gaping crowd . . . but, on enquiry, they are all found to be like the baseless fabric of a vision."*[1]

A distinct vision Edgar Allan Poe wanted to play a part in.

The first part of his serialized story was published in *Snowden's Ladies' Companion* in November 1842, the second part in December. An article published in an issue of the *New-York Tribune* that year caused Poe to delay the third installment's publication. New evidence arose suggesting that Rogers could possibly have died from complications of an abortion attempt—"premature delivery" being the verbiage of the time.

Poe edited his story to posit a similar possibility. By 1845, in a full reprint edition of the story, Poe included fifteen minor changes to suggest this angle as possible from the start. The tale explores multiple possibilities in its pursuit of clues, and the resolution itself is the exaltation of ratiocination as the requisite process for solving a mystery (even if Poe didn't actually end up solving anything concretely, in the end).

Poe names the *parallel* of Marie Rogêt to Mary Cecilia Rogers directly in the beginning and end of the story, careful to say that his meticulously crafted mirror shouldn't necessarily be taken as the *same* story nor treated as such; he tells the reader there's a danger in doing so:

> *It should be considered that the most trifling variation in the facts of the two cases might give rise to the most important miscalculations, by diverting thoroughly the two courses of events; very much as, in arithmetic, an error which, in its own individuality, may be inappreciable, produces, at length, by dint of multiplication at all points of the process, a result enormously at variance with truth.*[2]

In that paragraph, Poe explains so much about how we, as a society and as storytellers, may inadvertently stray "enormously at variance" from truths. Our ghost stories might be part of that "multiplication at all points of the process" he warns us about, folding in innumerable variables as we go.

Poe was nothing if not a master of the slippery nature of reality; he loved a good hoax, and derived immense pleasure from blurring the boundary between fiction and truth. In 1844 he published an article known as "The Balloon Hoax" in the New York *Sun*, a great jest in which he fooled New Yorkers into thinking a man had crossed the Atlantic in a hot-air balloon. Poe often adopted a pseudoscientific tone in his short stories, prompting one, "The Facts in the Case of M. Valdemar," to be reprinted as fact in British scientific journals.

American genre fiction, of which Poe is considered the great godfather, derives much of its terror and pleasure from the slippage between logic and the fantastic. It's appropriate, then, that Poe's own legacy is entangled with innumerable myths and half-truths, from whose shadows the "real" Poe may never emerge. We can only ever know the truth up to a certain point, as even primary sources can be biased both at their source and in their interpretation, and beyond that point lies the world of the imagination.

Every paranormally focused book, blog and article concerning Hoboken lists Sybil's Cave as a haunted location and discusses Mary's unsolved murder as a prompt for Poe. The actual accounts of ghosts there are entirely amorphous. But the site remains an unquestionably haunted location because of her violent, unresolved death. Everyone is focused on Mary's case and the story it birthed rather than the details of her spirit. Perhaps Rogers remains a phantom of our human need for answers and justice. She remains a liminal figure floating outside a poisoned spring welling up at her own cavernous entrance to the underworld, haunting the shores where she died because no one, not even one of the greatest American storytellers, could get her story quite right.

"AFTERWARD"

Sticks and Stones

LINDA D. ADDISON*

WORDS HAVE NO WEIGHT, OTHER THAN THAT GIVEN BY their use. Unlike the "Sticks and Stones" saying, words can hurt. A word can lift/enlighten or suppress/destroy depending on how it's used; context makes all the difference. When I was very young, another child in a playground called me a word that I interpreted to mean *dirty.* That was the first time I realized others might see me as less because my skin is brown. I was confused and deeply hurt. It took years to process that day and all the days after when others' behavior supported that interpretation of one word.

This memory came to mind when I thought about this book, because I've read so many tales of women ghosts. I've always been deeply curious about human psychology, especially in the area of the need to label people as a means to put them down. There's something about controlling others (or the fear of others) that comes into play.

---

* Linda D. Addison is an award-winning author, HWA Lifetime Achievement Award recipient, and SFPA Grand Master.

When I read classic tales of women ghosts I wonder about the reality that spawned those stories. The voices of women who suffered loss in the past are rarely part of the history written (until now).

It's fitting that this book gathers thoughts around the subject of women's tropes and ghost stories. The Gothic vision of a female ghost floating silently through rooms reminds me of a concept of women being beautiful, silent figures, floating from room to room, without a voice. Their human power reduced to two-dimensional versions of themselves. Seen, not heard.

I grew up watching scary movies at night with my mother. In these early movies, *ghosts* were cutout human forms levitating through walls, intending to scare the living. They usually had a backstory of some kind of wrongful death. Besides the chill the movie was creating, I also marveled at the idea that this being couldn't easily be hurt. I didn't question how real this concept of ghosts was—my active imagination loved the revenge stories.

If you ask someone about ghosts, few will admit to believing in them, but then they can recall a story from a relative (or themselves) of an encounter with supernatural entities. Ghost tours are on the list of vacation things-to-do for many when visiting other areas (definitely on my list).

Even though I became fascinated with math and science in school, it didn't interfere with my enjoyment of reading supernatural stories. I was comfortable with the fact that science has so much more to discover about how the universe unfolds. If you look up the words *spirit* versus *ghost* you'll get the impression that all living beings have a spirit, but only the dead are ghosts. The unknown can look like magic, until defined, so time will tell.

Two of the women who set the pattern for the version of my best life are my mother and my aunt Henrietta (my mother's oldest sister). They both passed over and are my favorite spirits to talk to every day, sometimes more than once a day. I thank them for the amazing life I have, ask for help for others, etc. I wouldn't call them ghosts, although they both have made themselves known with sounds in my home.

My aunt Henrietta makes small clicks in a different room than I'm sitting in, usually the dining room, when I'm in the living room. My mother (who had an incredible soprano voice) sings through my humidifier, but only if you stand in a certain place in the hallway. I smile and feel comforted when I hear these manifestations.

Words. I've learned to take care with what I say out loud. Some years ago a dearly loved pet cat, Tony, lay on our couch dying. I caressed him and said something like, "You can stay." A couple of weeks after he died I woke to him licking my hair (as usual). With my eyes closed, I waved him away and felt his weight as he bounced to the end of the bed. Then I realized it was his ghost. It kept happening. Along with his favorite plant being chewed up in the yard. I got used to Tony waking me up, seeing signs of him knocking things over, until I figured out he was there because of what I said as he was passing. I went room to room (including the yard) to speak words out loud releasing him. He didn't return after that day.

As described in the chapter "Mama Tried," a novel with an unforgettable story of a Black ghost tied to the concept of slavery is Toni Morrison's *Beloved*. I've read all of Morrison's books, but this one still makes my soul ache, because it was based on a real incident of a family escaping slavery and the mother who killed her child rather than have the daughter returned to the nightmare of enslavement. How to wrap the mind around making such an impossible decision as a way to protect your child, and have the ghost of that child return to haunt you, is the story line of a ghost novel and a horrible reality.

Morrison's book garnered huge acclaim, including the Pulitzer Prize. It's an emotional journey to read, not just because of the child ghost, but because slavery, the real horror that still haunts us, created that ghost.

What real-life terror lies behind the spectral tales that entertain us today? If we knew the story behind the story, how would that change our feelings about the ghost? Can we be haunted by a past version of ourselves? Would we call that version a *ghost*, a *memory*, a *spirit*? The speculative writer in me doesn't need a factual answer to these questions. I'm perfectly content spinning weird poetry and tales while listening to my mother sing in the sounds of the humidifier and smiling at the dings in another room from my aunt Henrietta, letting me know she still watches over me.

I'm excited about the birth of this book. To read women's thoughts on the hidden story behind the story of women *ghosts*. Seen, but no longer silent, the thought-provoking words written here will shatter some preconceptions, while entertaining and enlightening.

ACKNOWLEDGMENTS

LEANNA

FIRST AND FOREMOST, I WANT TO THANK MY INCREDIBLE CO-author, Andrea: you've simply amazed me with your work, heart, vision, and spirit throughout this process. I am blessed and in awe.

Endless thanks to our editor, Elizabeth May, for taking a chance on this book and for doing so much work to bring it all together, helping us shape separate pieces into a powerful whole; you're a champion. Thank you to the entire Kensington team for working so hard with us on this book; it means the world. Thank you, Paul Stevens of the Donald Maass Agency, for being an agent and caretaker for this book; thank you for all your help!

Janan Boehme of the Winchester Mystery House: that glorious place is so lucky to have you and I'm so blessed to have met you. You couldn't have been a better or bigger help on such an important chapter.

To my parents, Mike and Kathy Hieber, who have unconditionally supported every work of art I've ever undertaken and humored my every paranormal whimsy, I couldn't be more grateful. To my inimitable sister, Kelissa, and her partner, Kara, this book better (finally) get me to Denver. It's time for a book-based beer at Goldspot Brewery!

Thank you, Thom Truelove and Shveta Thakrar, for being such wonderful sounding boards along the way. Thank you, Sebastian Crane, for expert Salem advice!

As always, thanks to Ashley Lauren Rogers for sensitivity reading; my work always benefits from your input.

An enormous thanks to editor Lauren Knowles for coming to me with the idea for this book in the first place; you remain a part of this project, too.

And thank you, spirit world; may we continue to be a force for good.

ANDREA

I WOULD LIKE TO ACKNOWLEDGE THE AMAZING WORK OF MY INcredibly talented and passionate co-author, Leanna Renee Hieber, and our editor Elizabeth May, for skillfully managing a million moving parts.

This book would be incomplete without the advice and insight of Pi Gardiner, Anthony Bellov, Marguerite Durret, and everyone at the Merchant's House Museum, corporeal and incorporeal. (Thank you, Gertrude!)

Throughout this project I have been deeply indebted to Chris Woodyard, who has provided invaluable research tips and graciously and generously shared her insight, advice, and knowledge.

To a good friend of the fam, George Schmalz: thank you for reading over the West Virginia chapter and helping me do right by your home state!

Thank you to fellow tour guide and history geek Tim Krepp for your thoughts on Mary Surratt and her story, and to Hannah Kates for her insights on the Sorrel Weed House.

There's a special place in my heart for the entire Boroughs of the Dead staff: Marie Carter, SJ Costello, Liz Cousins, Carrie Napolitano, and Adrian Sexton; thank you for all these years of being part of my spooky, nerdy extended family! And thanks to our many loyal customers for all their support and enthusiasm—you're part of the family, too.

Enormous thanks, as always, to my parents and my sister for endless, lifelong encouragement and support, and much love to my in-laws in Buffalo for introducing me to Lily Dale.

To my husband, Robert: while the world lost its head, you kept your cool, and I will forever be in awe of your patience and calm. Thank you for holding it all together while I wrote this book.

And finally, to our wondrous Alice, thank you for respecting the sign on my office door that said "Mama Working: Do Not Enter." I love you. (See? I saved the best for last!)

SELECTED BIBLIOGRAPHY

INDUSTRIAL MONSTERS: GHOSTS OF THE TRIANGLE SHIRTWAIST FACTORY

Miles, Tiya. *Tales from the Haunted South: Dark Tourism and Memories of Slavery from the Civil War Era*. Chapel Hill: University of North Carolina Press, 2015.

Puglionesi, Alicia. "The Ethical Dilemmas of Fells Point Ghost Tours." *Baltimore City Paper*, October 31, 2015.

Von Drehle, David. *Triangle: The Fire That Changed America*. New York: Grove, 2004.

THE BEAUTIFUL STRANGER: KATE MORGAN AND THE HOTEL DEL CORONADO

Hotel del Coronado Heritage Department. *Beautiful Stranger: The Ghost of Kate Morgan and the Hotel del Coronado*. San Diego, CA: Hotel del Coronado, 2002.

DARK ACADEMIA: GHOSTS OF COLLEGE CAMPUSES

Barefoot, Daniel W. *Haunted Halls of Ivy: Ghosts of Southern Colleges and Universities*. Durham, NC: John F. Blair, 2004.

Hauck, Dennis William. *Haunted Places: The National Directory: Ghostly Abodes, Sacred Sites, UFO Landings, and Other Supernatural Locations*. New York: Penguin Books, 1996.

Tucker, Elizabeth. *Haunted Halls: Ghostlore of American College Campuses*. Jackson: University Press of Mississippi, 2007.

Windham, Kathryn Tucker, and Figh, Margaret Gillis. *13 Alabama Ghosts and Jeffrey*. Tuscaloosa: University of Alabama Press, 1969, 2014.

FOREVER MARITANA: GHOSTS OF THE DON CESAR HOTEL

Frethem, Deborah. *Ghost Stories of St. Petersburg, Clearwater and Pinellas County*, Tales from a Haunted Peninsula. Mount Pleasant, SC: Arcadia Publishing, 2007.

"The Haunted Ghosts of The Don CeSar Hotel." St. Petersburg, FL. *The Don CeSar* (blog). February 18, 2021. https://www.doncesar.com/blog/the hauntedghostsofthedoncesarhotel.

A RED PARAGON BODICE: BRIDGET BISHOP

Carlson, Carol F. *The Devil in the Shape of a Woman*. 2nd ed. New York: W. W. Norton, 1998.

Dickey, Colin. *Ghostland: An American History in Haunted Places*. New York: Viking, 2016.

Upham, Charles Wentworth. *Salem Witchcraft*. Vols. I & II. New York: Frederick Ungar, 1867.

TUGGING AT YOUR HEM: DOROTHY GOOD

Upham, Charles Wentworth. *Salem Witchcraft*. Vols. I & II. New York: Frederick Ungar, 1867.

OUR FAMILY TROUBLE: THE BELL WITCH

Arsenault, Emily. "Our Haunted Childhoods, 80s Poltergeists, and the Rage of Female Adolescence." *Crimereads*. July 13, 2021.

Blum, Deborah. *Ghost Hunters*. New York: Penguin Press, 2006.

Brown, Alan. *Haunted Tennessee: Ghosts and Strange Phenomena of the Volunteer State*. Mechanicsburg, PA: Stackpole Books, 2009.

Carrington, Hereward, and Fodor, Nandor. *Haunted People*. New York: Dutton, 1951.

Clarke, Roger. *A Natural History of Ghosts: 500 Years of Hunting or Proof*. London: Particular Books, 2012.

Goodspeed, Westin A. *The History of Tennessee from the Earliest Times to the Present*. Nashville: Goodspeed Publishing, 1886.

Hendrix, Grady. "Little Ghost on the Prairie." *Slate*, May 4, 2006.

Ingram, Martin Van Buren. *Authenticated History of the Bell Witch and Other Stories of the World's Greatest Unexplained Phenomenon*. 1894. Reprint, Adams, TN: Historic Bell Witch Cave, 2005.

Morton, Lisa. *Ghosts: A Haunted History*. London: Reaktion Books, 2015.

Nickell, Joe. "The 'Bell Witch' Poltergeist." *Skeptical Inquirer* 38, no. 1 (February 2014). https://skepticalinquirer.org/2014/01/the-bell-witch-poltergeist/.

Puchko, Kristy. "Why the Movies Love Telekinetic Women, and Why We Fear Them." *Vanity Fair*, March 2, 2015.

Roll, William, and Storey, Valerie. *Unleashed: Of Poltergeists and Murder: The Curious Story of Tina Resch*. New York: Gallery Books, 2004.

Rose, Lloyd. "Night of the Haunter." *Washington Post*, August 1, 1999.

Windham, Kathryn Tucker. *Jeffrey's Favorite 13 Ghost Stories from Alabama, Georgia, Tennessee, and Mississippi*. Montgomery: NewSouth Books, 2020.

Young, Nicole. "Psychic: I Know the Real Bell Witch Story." *The Tennessean*, October 27, 2015.

GRAVEYARD DANCE: THE WITCH'S CURSE

Jones, Merlin. *Haunted Places*. Globe Mini Mag 327. Boca Raton, FL: Globe Communications, 1945, 1999.

Ocker, J. W. *The New England Grimpendium*. New York: Countryman Press, 2010.

Van Winkle, Valerie. "Legends of Jonathan Buck." Bucksport, Maine, June 2021. https://www.bucksportmaine.gov/vertical/sites/%7B1700581E-144E-4C5D-B026-79CCA6D1E656%7D/uploads/Legends_of_Jonathan_Buck.pdf.

Verde, Thomas A. *Maine Ghosts and Legends: 26 Encounters with the Supernatural.* Camden, ME: Down East Books, 1995.

STILL CAPTAINING HER SHIP: THE GHOST OF MA GREENE

Abbott, Taylor. "Mary B. Greene: The Ohio River's Leading Lady." Part 1. *Wheeling Heritage.* https://weelunk.com/mary-b-greene-ohio-rivers-leading-lady-part-1/.

Casper, Teri and Smith, Dan. *Ghosts of Cincinnati.* Charleston, SC: History Press, 2009.

MAMA TRIED

Beatty, Judith Shaw, ed. *La Llorona: Encounters with the Weeping Woman.* Santa Fe, NM: Sunstone Press, 2004.

Boyd, Colleen E., and Thrush, Coll, eds. *Phantom Past, Indigenous Presence: Native Ghosts in North American Culture and History.* Lincoln: University of Nebraska Press, 2011.

Gordon, Avery. *Ghostly Matters: Haunting and the Sociological Imagination.* Minneapolis: University of Minnesota Press, 1997.

Hauck, Dennis William. *Haunted Places: The National Directory: Ghostly Abodes, Sacred Sites, UFO Landings, and Other Supernatural Locations.* New York: Penguin Books, 1994, 1996, 2002.

Taylor, L. B., Jr. *Haunted Virginia: Ghosts and Strange Phenomena of the Old Dominion.* Mechanicsburg, PA: Stackpole Books, 2009.

THE EVERLASTING FAINT: THE GHOSTLY WIVES OF WEST VIRGINIA

Appalachian Magazine's Mountain Superstitions, Ghost Stories & Haint Tales: A Collection of Mountain Memories & Tall Tales from the Mountains of Appalachia. Stately Ties Media, 2018.

Dougherty, Shirley. *A Ghostly Tour of Harper's Ferry.* Harper's Ferry, VA: Eigmid, 1993.

Elizabeth, Norma. *Lighthouse Ghosts.* Birmingham, AL: Crane Hill Publishers, 1999.

Guiley, Rosemary Ellen. *The Big Book of West Virginia Ghost Stories.* Guildford, CT: Globe Pequot, 2014.

Letcher Lyle, Katie. *The Man Who Wanted Seven Wives: The Greenbrier Ghost and the Famous Murder Mystery of 1897.* Charleston, WV: Quarrier Press, 1999.

Musick, Ruth Ann. *The Telltale Lilac Bush and Other West Virginia Ghost Tales.* Lexington: University Press of Kentucky, 1965.

Stoll, Steven. *Ramp Hollow: The Ordeal of Appalachia.* New York: Hill and Wang, 2017.

Stick, David. *Graveyard of the Atlantic: Shipwrecks of the North Carolina Coast.* Chapel Hill, NC: University of North Carolina Press, 1952.

Wilson, Patty A. *Haunted North Carolina: Ghosts and Strange Phenomena of the Tar Heel State*. Guildford, CT: Globe Pequot, 2019.

THE LADY OF THE HOUSE: ELIZA JUMEL

Blackhall, Susan. *Ghosts of New York*. San Diego: Thunder Bay Press, 2005.

Janes, Andrea. "How Eliza Became a Ghost" in *The Morris-Jumel Mansion Anthology of Fantasy and Paranormal Fiction*. Edited by Camilla Saly-Monzingo. New York: Riverdale Avenue Books, 2016.

AMERICAN SUCCUBI: SOILED DOVES OF THE FRONTIER

Enss, Chris. "Wild Woman Wednesday: Kitty LeRoy, Doomed Darling of Deadwood." *Cowgirl Magazine*, December 30, 2015.

Thrush, Coll. "Hauntings as Histories: Indigenous." *In Phantom Past, Indigenous Presence: Native Ghosts in North American Culture and History*. Edited by Colleen E. Boyd and Coll Thrush. Lincoln: University of Nebraska Press, 2011.

CONSPIRATOR TO AN ASSASSINATION: THE GHOST OF MARY SURRATT

Blakemore, Erin. "The Enduring Enigma of the First Woman Executed by the U.S. Federal Government." *Time*, June 30, 2015. https://time.com/3935911/mary-surratt/.

Farquhar, Michael. "That Haunting Tale of Mary Surratt." *Washington Post*, October 31, 1991. https://www.washingtonpost.com/archive/lifestyle/1991/10/31/the-haunting-tale-of-mary-surratt/8c1b67d6-7deb-401d-9274-cc540ff22482/.

Felde, Kitty. "'The Conspirator' Mary Surratt Still Haunts Washington." 89.3KPCC, April 25, 2011. https://archive.kpcc.org/news/2011/04/25/26050/the conspirator-mary-serratt-still-haunts-washingt/.

"Ghosts to Leave Surratt Home When Rebuilt." Seward *Daily Gateway*. March 20, 1925.

Hoover, Marc. "The Ghost of Mary Surratt Still Roams." *Clermont Sun*, October 11, 2018. https://www.clermontsun.com/2018/10/11/marc-hoover-ghost-of-mary-surratt-still-roams.

Krepp, Tim. Interview with Andrea Janes, April 4, 2022.

Larson, Kate Clifford. *The Assassin's Accomplice: Mary Surratt and the Plot to Kill Abraham Lincoln*. New York: Basic Books, 2011.

Larson, Kate Clifford. "The Lincoln Lectures—Assassin's Accomplice: Mary Surratt and the Plot to Kill Abraham Lincoln." US National Archives, December 29, 2009. YouTube. https://www.youtube.com/watch?v=4jqaJDBgQTw.

"Mrs. Surratt's House Haunted." Cleveland *Plain Dealer*, December 5, 1866. Reprinted in Chris Woodyard, "The Spirit of Mary Surratt," *Haunted Ohio*, 2016, http://hauntedohiobooks.com/news/ghosts-news/the-spirit-of-mary-surratt/.

"The Murderer of Mr. Lincoln: Extraordinary Letter of John Wilkes Booth." *New York Times*, April 21, 1865.

Ogden, Tom. *Haunted Washington*, DC: Federal Phantoms, Government Ghosts, and Beltway Banshees. Guildford, CT: Globe Pequot, 2016.

Paschall, Valerie, Goldchain, Michelle, and Acitelli, Tom. "DC's 15 Most Haunted Locations, Mapped." Curbed.com, September 27, 2019. https://dc.curbed.com/maps/haunted-house-scary-dc-washington.

Petito, Jackie. "Ghosts of Penn Quarter: Civil War Era Hauntings." *Face to Face* (blog). Smithsonian/National Portrait Gallery, https://npg.si.edu/blog/ghosts-penn-quarter-civil-war-era-hauntings.

Proctor, John Claggett. "Capital's Ghosts Walk Anew on Halloween Eve." *Washington Evening* Star, October 27, 1935.

Shogan, Colleen. "Things That Go Bump in the Blue Room: Why Is the White House Haunted?" White House Historical Association, https://www.whitehousehistory.org/things-that-go-bump-in-the-blue-room.

Vargas, Theresa. "Is the White House Haunted? A History of Spooked Presidents, Prime Ministers and Pets." *Washington Post*, October 30, 2017. https://www.washingtonpost.com/news/retropolis/wp/2017/10/30/is-the-white-house-haunted-a-history-of-spooked-presidents-prime-ministers-and-pets/.

Vowell, Sarah. *Assassination Vacation*. New York: Simon & Schuster, 2005.

Woodyard, Chris. *The Ghost Wore Black: Ghostly Tales from the Past*. Dayton, OH: Kestrel, 2014.

THE HAUNTING OF LIZZIE BORDEN

D'Agostino, Thomas. *Haunted Massachusetts*. Atglen, PA: Schiffer, 2007.

Pittman, Rebecca F. *The History and Haunting of Lizzie Borden*. Loveland, CO: Wonderland Productions, 2016.

Robertson, Cara. *The Trial of Lizzie Borden: A True Story*. New York: Simon & Schuster, 2019.

Wood, Maureen, and Kolek, Ron. *The Ghost Chronicles: A Medium and A Paranormal Scientist Investigate 17 True Hauntings*. Naperville, IL: Sourcebooks, 2009.

"MADWOMEN": INTRODUCTION

King, Moses. *King's Handbook of New York City 1892: An Outline History and Description of the American Metropolis*. Facsimile of first edition. Barnes & Noble, 2001

AN UNRELIABLE NARRATOR: JAN BRYANT BARTELL

Bartell, Jan Bryant. *Spindrift: Tales from a Psychic Sea*. New York: Hawthorn Books, 1974.

UNFINISHED BUSINESS: THE WINCHESTER MYSTERY HOUSE

Ignoffo, Mary Jo. *Captive of the Labyrinth: Sarah L. Winchester, Heiress to the Rifle Fortune*. Columbia: University of Missouri Press, 2010.

Dickey, Colin. *Ghostland: An American History in Haunted Places*. New York: Viking, 2016.

A CORRECT HISTORY OF THE LIFE AND ADVENTURES OF THE WANDERING WOMAN

Greenwood, Grace. "A Night of Years—The Maniac." *The Ladies' Garland and Dollar Magazine*, Philadelphia: Samuel D. Patterson, March 1848.

Hammond, Luna. *History of Madison County*. Syracuse, NY: Truair, Smith, 1872.

Haunted Places. "Cazenovia Lake." https://www.hauntedplaces.org/item/cazenovia-lake/.

Tranquille, Dante O. "The Press Scrapbook," *Utica Daily Press*, January 6, 1951.

MISS TREDWELL IS AT HOME

Bellov, Anthony, ed. *Some Say They Never Left: Tales of the Strange and Inexplicable at the Merchant's House Museum*. New York: Merchant's House Museum, 2007.

Blackhall, Susan. *Ghosts of New York*. San Diego: Thunder Bay Press, 2005.

Chokshi, Niraj. "The Ghosts of New York's Past." *New York Times*, October 28, 2018.

Dickey, Colin. *Ghostland: An American History in Haunted Places*. New York: Viking, 2016.

Erskine, Helen Worden. *Out of This World: A Collection of Hermits and Recluses*. New York: Putnam, 1953.

Knapp, Mary. *An Old Merchant's House: Life at Home in New York City*. New York: Girandole Books, 2012.

FROM MOTHER ANN TO SYBIL PHELPS: THE SPIRITS OF THE GREAT BURNED-OVER

Horowitz, Mitch. *Occult America: The Secret History of How Mysticism Shaped Our Nation*. New York: Bantam Books, 2009.

Guiley, Rosemary Ellen. *Harper's Encyclopedia of Mystical and Paranormal Experience*. New York: HarperCollins, 1991.

Smith, Hilary. "N.Y. Town Celebrates Birthday of Famed Spiritualist Sybil." *MetroWest Daily News* (Framingham, MA), October 17, 2007.

Tucker, Elizabeth. *Haunted Southern Tier*. Charleston, SC: Haunted America, 2011.

Unvericht, Patti. *Ghosts and Hauntings of the Finger Lakes*. Charleston, SC: History Press, 2012.

Whitacre, Tammy. "Spirit of Sybil: A Birthday Celebration of a Different Kind." Daily Messenger (Canandaigua, NY). October 17, 2013. https://www.mpnnow.com/story/news/local/2013/10/17/spirit-sybil-birthday-celebration-different/42381681007/.

THE WIDOW AND MRS. SPENCER

Briones, Isis. "Joan Rivers' 'Haunted' Upper East Side Penthouse Is Listed for $38 Million." *Architectural Digest*, May 12, 2021. https://www.architecturaldigest.com/story/joan-riverss-upper-east-side-penthouse-listed.

Finn, Kathy. "Joan Rivers Works Magic for Voodoo Priestess in New Orleans."

Today.com, August 24, 2012. https://www.today.com/news/joan-rivers-works-magic-voodoo-priestess-new-orleans-962960.

Gould, Jennifer. "Saudi Prince Guts Joan Rivers' 'Haunted' Home." *New York Post*, August 26, 2015. https://nypost.com/2015/08/26/saudi-prince-guts-joan-rivers-haunted-home/.

Grace, Lauren. "Joan Rivers Left Flowers Out for the Ghost in Her $28 Million Manhattan Penthouse." *Showbiz Cheat Sheet*, March 20, 2021. https://www.cheatsheet.com/entertainment/joan-rivers-left-flowers-ghost-28-million-manhattan-penthouse.html/.

Harris, Elizabeth A. "For Comedian, Leading Her Condo Board Is a Serious Matter." *New York Times*, June 12, 2012. https://www.nytimes.com/2012/06/12/nyregion/for-joan-rivers-role-on-condo-board-a-serious-matter.html.

Krepp, Tim. *Capitol Hill Haunts*. Charleston, SC: History Press, 2012.

MacCash, Doug. "Joan Rivers' Voodoo Priestess Friend Describes Haunting of Joan's House." *Times-Picayune*, August 14, 2012. https://www.nola.com/entertainment_life/arts/article_4bc19c41-e9b9-582c-85c3-3a14a35a5f65.html.

Miller, Mason. "Joan Rivers' Spiritual Guide Is Fighting Crime with Voodoo in New Orleans." *Vice*, September 22, 2014. https://www.vice.com/en/article/exmqwe/joan-rivers-spiritual-guide-is-fighting-crime-with-voodoo-in-new-orleans-945.

Miller, Tom. "The 1903 John Drexel House—No. 1 E. 62nd Street." *Daytonian in Manhattan* (blog), November 1, 2012. http://daytoninmanhattan.blogspot.com/2012/11/the-1903-john-r-drexel-house-no-1-e.html.

Jarrett, Seth, dir. *Celebrity Ghost Stories*. Season 1, episode 1, "Scott Baio/Joan Rivers/Teri Polo/David Carradine." Aired October 3, 2009 on Biography Channel. https://www.imdb.com/title/tt1532605/.

THE PRESTIGE OF KATIE KING

Hoover, Stephanie. *Philadelphia Spiritualism and the Curious Case of Katie King*. Charleston, SC: History Press, 2013.

"Doctor Robert Hare." *Scientific American* 13, no. 38, May 1858.

WILLING THE GHOSTS TO LIFE: MOLLY AND MATILDA OF THE SORREL WEED HOUSE

Caskey, James. "The Sorrel-Weed House: Haunted by Bad History?" Savannah Walking Tours, September 5, 2013. https://www.ghostsavannah.com/2013/09/the-sorrel-weed-house-haunted/.

Caskey, James. *Haunted Savannah: America's Most Spectral City*. Savannah: Manta Ray Books, 2013.

Cohen, Abraham J. "A. J. Cohen Collection on the Sorrel-Weed House." Georgia Historical Society. http://ghs.galileo.usg.edu/ghs/view?docId=ead/MS%201197-ead.xml.

Dickey, Colin. *Ghostland: An American History in Haunted Places*. New York: Viking, 2016.

Doughty, Caitlin. "Ask a Mortician—Deathstination: Savannah Georgia and

Ghost Tours." *The Order of the Good Death*. April 18, 2013. https://www.youtube.com/watch?v=YcMB27PeO7w.

Gentry, Glenn. "Walking with the Dead: The Place of Ghost Walk Tourism in Savannah, Georgia." *Southeastern Geographer* 47, no. 2 (November 2007): 222–38.

Gormley, Elena. "Ghost Tours Turn Women's Abuse into Family Friendly Entertainment." *Vice*, October 10, 2015. https://www.vice.com/en/article/3dxmy5/ghost-tours-turn-womens-abuse-into-family-friendly-entertainment.

Harris, Michael, and Sickler, Linda. *Historic Haunts of Savannah*. Charleston, SC: History Press, 2014. Page 43.

Hungate, Caitlyn. "Haunts and Jaunts: Examining the Effects of Dark Tourism on Savannah's Traditional Branded Image." Masters thesis. University of Georgia, 2017. https://getd.libs.uga.edu/pdfs/hungate_caitlyn_j_201712_mhp.pdf.

Miles, Tiya. *Tales from the Haunted South: Dark Tourism and Memories of Slavery from the Civil War Era*. Chapel Hill: University of North Carolina Press, 2015.

Morris, Bilal G. "The Antebellum Tale of Black Slave Girl Molly and the Haunting of Sorrel-Weed House." *NewsOne*, October 18, 2021. https://newsone.com/4234785/sorrel-weed-house-black-slave-girl-molly/.

Westfield, Kelly. "Excavations in the Carriage House Basement of the Sorrel-Weed House." *Digging Savannah Reports*, Spring 2017. https://digitalcommons.georgiasouthern.edu/cgi/viewcontent.cgi?article=1000&context=armstrong-dig-savannah.

THE MYTHMAKING OF MARIE ROGÊT

Poe, Edgar Allan. "The Mystery of Marie Roget," *The Complete Tales and Poems of Edgar Allan Poe*. New York: Barnes & Noble Books, 1992.

Stashower, Daniel. *The Beautiful Cigar Girl: Mary Rogers, Edgar Allan Poe and the Invention of Murder*. New York: Berkley Books, 2006.

NOTES

PART 1: DEATH AND THE MAIDEN

Industrial Monsters: Ghosts of the Triangle Shirtwaist Factory

1 Alicia Puglionesi, "The Ethical Dilemmas of Fells Point Ghost Tours," *Baltimore City Paper*, October 31, 2015.

2 *Tiya Miles, Tales from the Haunted South: Dark Tourism and Memories of Slavery from the Civil War Era* (Chapel Hill: University of North Carolina Press, 2015), 132.

The Beautiful Stranger: Kate Morgan and the Hotel del Coronado

1 Hotel Del Coronado Heritage Department, *Beautiful Stranger: The Ghost of Kate Morgan and the Hotel del Coronado* (San Diego: Hotel del Coronado, 2002).

Dark Academia: Ghosts of College Campuses

1 "Ghost Story: The Ghost of Clara Mills," October 30, 2013, https://www.nebrwesleyan.edu/about-nwu/news-center/ghost-story-ghost-clara-mills.

2 Elizabeth Tucker, *Haunted Halls: Ghostlore of American College Campuses* (Jackson: University Press of Mississippi, 2007), 140.

3 Dennis William Hauck, *Haunted Places: The National Directory* (New York: Penguin Books, 1994), 129.

4 Stassa Edwards, "Have You Heard the One About the Murdered Sorority Girls?" *Jezebel*, October 29, 2015.

5 Tucker, *Haunted Halls*, 136.

Forever, Maritana: The Ghosts of the Don CeSar Hotel

1 Deborah Frethem, *Ghost Stories of St. Petersburg, Clearwater and Pinellas County: Tales from a Haunted Peninsula* (Charleston, SC: Arcadia Publishing, 2007).

2 Ibid., 38.

3 "The Haunted Ghosts of The Don CeSar Hotel," *The Don CeSar* (blog), https://www.doncesar.com/blog/thehauntedghostsofthedoncesarhotel.

PART 2: "WITCHES"

A Red Paragon Bodice: Bridget Bishop

1 Carol F. Carlson, *The Devil in the Shape of a Woman*, 2nd ed. (New York: W. W. Norton, 1998), 75.
2 Charles Wentworth Upham, *Salem Witchcraft*, vols. I and II (New York: Frederick Ungar, 1867), 183.
3 Ibid., vol. 2, supplement.
4 Colin Dickey, *Ghostland: An American History in Haunted Place* (New York: Viking, 2016), 35.

Tugging at Your Hem: Dorothy Good

1 Charles Wentworth Upham, *Salem Witchcraft*, vols. I and II (New York: Frederick Ungar, 1867), 270.

Our Family Trouble: The Bell Witch

1 Hereward Carrington and Nandor Fodor, *Haunted People* (New York: Dutton, 1951).
2 For a full family tree, see https://www.genealogy.com/forum/surnames/topics/batts/322/.
3 Kristy Puchko, "Why the Movies Love Telekinetic Women, and Why We Fear Them," *Vanity Fair*, March 2, 2015, https://www.vanityfair.com/hollywood/2015/03/telekinetic-women-horror.
4 Deborah Blum, *Ghost Hunters* (New York: Penguin Press, 2006).
5 Guy Lyon Playfair, *This House Is Haunted: The True Story of a Poltergeist* (New York: Stein and Day, 1980).
6 Carol Gilligan, *Joining the Resistance* (Cambridge, UK; Malden, MA: Polity, 2011), 21.
7 Emily Arsenault, "Our Haunted Childhoods, 80s Poltergeists, and the Rage of Female Adolescence," *Crimereads*, July 13, 2021, https://crimereads.com/on-haunted-childhoods-80s-poltergeists-and-the-rage-of-female-adolescence/.
8 Kathryn Tucker Windham, *Jeffrey's Favorite 13 Ghost Stories from Alabama, Georgia, Tennessee, and Mississippi* (Montgomery, AL: NewSouth Books, 2020), 166.
9 Martin Van Buren Ingram, *Authenticated History of the Bell Witch and Other Stories of the World's Greatest Unexplained Phenomenon* (1894; repr., Adams, TN: Historic Bell Witch Cave, 2005), 66.
10 Windham, *Jeffrey's Favorite 13 Ghost Stories*, 167. Betsy would later go on to marry her childhood schoolteacher, William Powell.
11 Ingram, *Authenticated History of the Bell Witch*, 67.
12 Serafina Kent Bathrick, "*Carrie* Ragtime: The Horror of Growing up Female," *Jumpcut*, no. 14, (March 1977).
13 Barbara Creed, *The Monstrous Feminine: Film, Feminism, Psychoanalysis* (Abingdon, UK: Routledge, 1993), 78.
14 Heather Greene, *Lights, Camera, Witchcraft: A Critical History of Witches in American Film and Television* (Woodbury, MN: Llewellyn Press, 2021), 234.

Graveyard Dance: The Witch's Curse

1 J. W. Ocker, *The New England Grimpendium* (New York: Countryman Press, 2010), 225.

2 Merlin Jones, *Haunted Places,* Globe Mini Mag 327 (Boca Raton: Globe Communications, 1945, 1999), 44.

3 Thomas A. Verde, "One Foot on the Grave," in *Maine Ghosts and Legends: 26 Encounters with the Supernatural* (Camden, ME: Down East Books), 30.

4 Valerie Van Winkle, "Legends of Jonathan Buck," June 2021, https://www.bucksportmaine.gov/vertical/sites/%7B1700581E-144E-4C5D-B026-79CCA6D1E656%7D/uploads/Legends_of_Jonathan_Buck.pdf.

PART 3: MOTHERS AND WIVES

Introduction

1 See Adrienne Rich's *Of Woman Born* for more on the invisible violence of the institution of motherhood (New York: W. W. Norton, 1976).

2 American maternal mortality rates for BIPOC women are four to five times higher than for white women. See "Racial and Ethnic Disparities Continue in Pregnancy-Related Deaths: Black, American Indian/Alaska Native Women Most Affected," September 5, 2019, https://www.cdc.gov/media/releases/2019/p0905-racial-ethnic-disparities-pregnancy-deaths.html.

3 Adrienne Rich writes, "out of my weariness I would rage at [my] children for no reason they could understand. I remember thinking I would never dream again (the unconscious of the young mother—where does it entrust its messages when dream sleep is denied her for years?)" See *Of Woman Born: Motherhood as Experience and Institution,* 32.

4 Alexandra Sacks, "'The Birth of a Mother,'" *New York Times,* May 8, 2017, https://www.nytimes.com/2017/05/08/well/family/the-birth-of-a-mother.html.

5 For more on this topic, see Darcy Lockman's *All the Rage: Mothers, Fathers, and the Myth of Equal Partnership* (New York: HarperCollins, 2019).

Still Captaining Her Ship: The Ghost of Ma Greene

1 Taylor Abbott, "Mary B. Greene: The Ohio River's Leading Lady," Part 1, *Wheeling Heritage,* March 3, 2021, https://weelunk.com/mary-b-greene-ohio-rivers-leading-lady-part-1/.

2 Teri Casper and Dan Smith, *Ghosts of Cincinnati* (Charleston, SC: History Press, 2009), 34–35.

Mama Tried

1 L. B. Taylor Jr., *Haunted Virginia: Ghosts and Strange Phenomena of the Old Dominion* (Mechanicsburg, PA: Stackpole Books, 2009), 107.

2 Dolly's story lives on, online. See "Drivers Beware! 9 of the Most Haunted Roads in America," October 18, 2019, https://www.commercialtrucktrader.com/blog/2019/10/18/drivers-beware-9-of-the-most-haunted-roads-in-america/.

3 "Local Haunts," *Daily Press* (Newport News, VA), October 27, 2002; and Molly Feser, "Oddities & Curiosities: Haunting of Dorothy 'Dolly Mammy'

Pauls Messick," *WY Daily* (Williamsburg, VA), September 3, 2021, https://wydaily.com/our-community/series/oddities-curiosities/2021/09/03/oddities-curiosities-haunting-of-dorothy-dolly-mammy-pauls-messick/.

4 "Something Is Afoot in Marshes of Messick," *Daily Press* (Newport News, VA), October 30, 1983.

5 L. B. Taylor Jr., *Ghosts of Virginia's Tidewater* (Charleston, S.C.: Arcadia Publishing, 2011), 110.

6 Ibid., 109

7 Norman Tippens, "Poquoson Community Leader Jessie Fay Forrest Dies," *Daily Press* (Newport News, VA), July 15, 2000.

8 Obituary for Dolly Elizabeth Messick, *Daily Press* (Newport News, VA), January 19, 1937.

9 Dennis William Hauck, *Haunted Places: The National Directory* (New York: Penguin Books, 1994).

10 Mary Washington House Museum, http://hauntedhouses.com/virginia/mary-washington-house-museum/.

11 Betty J. Cotter, "Into the Mist: Tour of O'Neill Cottage Conjures Ghosts of the Past," *Grace Getting Out* (blog), August 17, 2011, https://www.theday.com/article/20110817/GRACE02/110819594.

12 In her lifetime, Shirley Jackson was as much noted for her writings on motherhood as she was for her dark fiction. Rather than see a conflict between these two worlds, astute readers of Jackson will see how motherhood informed her macabre aesthetic; in other words, Jackson definitely acknowledged the inherent weirdness of motherhood and of children, as her short story "Charles" demonstrates. For more, see Emma Nichols, "Shirley Jackson and the Mundane Horrors of Motherhood," *Book Riot*, December 21, 2017, https://bookriot.com/shirley-jackson/.

13 "Stow Lake Ghost," Golden Gate Park, https://goldengatepark.com/stow-lake-ghost.html.

14 Katie Dowd, "The True Tale Behind the Death That Sparked San Francisco's Most Famous Ghost Story: An Investigation of San Francisco's Famed White Lady of Stow Lake," *SFGate*, October 5, 2017, https://www.sfgate.com/sfhistory/article/san-francisco-ghost-stories-white-lady-stow-lake-12247189.php.

15 The idea that motherhood should involve "24-hour lifelong shifts of unconditional love" is a false construct designed to bolster conservative opinion that a mother's place is with her children in the domestic sphere. Despite Victorian-era ideals of upper- and middle-class "cults of true womanhood," history shows that mothers have been participating in the labor force since time immemorial, and research demonstrates that mothers have no more innate inclination to stay home with children than fathers do. For more, see Michaeleen Doucleef, "Working Moms Have Been a 'Thing' Since Ancient History," *Goats and Soda* (blog), NPR, November 30, 2017, https://www.npr.org/sections/goatsandsoda/2017/11/30/567262912/working-moms-have-been-a-thing-since-ancient-history; and Darcy Lockman, *All the Rage: Mothers, Fathers, and the Myth of Equal Partnership* (New York: HarperCollins, 2019).

16 As Erich Neumann writes in *The Great Mother: An Analysis of the Archetype* (Princeton, NJ: Princeton University Press, 2015), "To her belong all waters, streams, fountains, ponds and springs, as well as the

rain." The quotation referencing the "amniotic salinity of the sea" is from Angela Carter, *The Bloody Chamber and Other Stories* (1979; repr., New York: Penguin Books, 1990).

17 Adrienne Rich, *Of Woman Born: Motherhood as Experience and Institution* (New York: W. W. Norton, 1976, 1986), 115.

18 Jacob and Wilhelm Grimm, *Complete Fairy Tales of the Brothers Grimm*, ed. Jack Zipes (London: Bantam Press, 2003).

19 Rich, *Of Woman Born*, 115.

20 Hauck, *Haunted Places*, 185.

21 The Indian Removal Act was signed into law by President Andrew Jackson on May 28, 1830, authorizing the president to grant lands west of the Mississippi in exchange for Indian lands. For more, see guides.loc.gov/indian-removal-act.

22 White women's stories continue to be privileged over those of Indigenous women. For more, see Katie Robertson, "News Media Can't Shake 'Missing White Woman Syndrome,' Critics Say," *New York Times*, September 22, 2021,https://www.nytimes.com/2021/09/22/business/media/gabby-petito-missing-white-woman-syndrome.html.

23 For more on Indian burial ground tropes, see Colin Dickey, *Ghostland: An American History in Haunted Places* (New York: Viking, 2016).

24 The Battle of Wyoming, incidentally, took place on July 4. For more on Queen Esther, see Warren Hunting Smith, "Queen Esther," *Virginia Quarterly Review* 29, no. 3 (Summer 1953), 397–407.

25 A good starting point is *Phantom Past, Indigenous Presence: Native Ghosts in North American Culture and History*, ed. Colleen E. Boyd and Coll Thrush (Lincoln: University of Nebraska Press, 2011).

26 Avery Gordon, Ghostly Matters: Haunting and the Sociological Imagination (Minneapolis: University of Minnesota Press, 1997), 139.

27 Ibid., 142.

The Everlasting Faint: The Ghostly Wives of West Virginia

1 *Appalachian Magazine's Mountain Superstitions, Ghost Stories & Haint Tales: A Collection of Mountain Memories & Tall Tales from the Mountains of Appalachia* (Stately Ties Media, 2018), 15.

The Lady of the House: Eliza Jumel

1 Susan Blackhall, *Ghosts of New York* (San Diego: Thunder Bay Press, 2005), 99–100.

2 Andrea Janes, "How Eliza Became a Ghost," in *The Morris-Jumel Mansion Anthology of Fantasy and Paranormal Fiction*, ed. Camilla Saly-Monzingo (New York: Riverdale Avenue Books, 2016), 6.

PART 4: BAD GIRLS, JEZEBELS, AND KILLER WOMEN

Introduction

1 Erika Owen, *Lawbreaking Ladies: 50 Tales of Daring, Defiant, and Dangerous Women from History*. New York: Tiller Press, 2021, 85.

2 Clare McBride, "Lavinia Fisher, America's 'First Female Serial Killer' That Wasn't," *SYFY Wire*, October 2, 2020, https://www.syfy.com/syfy-wire/lavinia-fisher-americas-first-female-serial-killer-that-wasnt.
3 Erica Jackson Curran, "Bruce Orr Lets John and Lavinia Fisher's Skeletons Out of the Closet," *Charleston City Paper*, December 21, 2010, https://charlestoncitypaper.com/bruce-orr-lets-john-and-lavinia-fishers-skeletons-out-of-the-closet/.
4 See Thavolia Glymph, *Out of the House of Bondage: The Transformation of the Slaveholding Household* (New York: Cambridge University Press, 2008), 20–26, quoted in Tiya Miles, *Tales from the Haunted South: Dark_Tourism and Memories of Slavery from the Civil War Era* (Chapel Hill: University of North Carolina Press, 2015), 73.
5 Taylor Feingold, "Living Among the Dead: Julie, the Octoroon Mistress," *News with a Twist*, WGNO, October 19, 2016, https://wgno.com/news-with-a-twist/living-among-the-dead-julie-the-octoroon-mistress/.
6 David Pilgrim, "The Tragic Mulatto Myth," Jim Crow Museum, Ferris State University, November 2000, https://www.ferris.edu/HTMLS/news/jimcrow/mulatto/homepage.htm.
7 Feingold, "Living Among the Dead."

American Succubi: Soiled Doves of the Frontier

1 Chris Enss, "Wild Woman Wednesday: Kitty LeRoy, Doomed Darling of Deadwood," *Cowgirl Magazine*, December 30, 2015.
2 Caitlin Morton, "The 32 Most Haunted Places in America," Inspiration, *Condé Nast Traveler*, October 7, 2021, https://www.cntraveler.com/gallery/the-most-haunted-places-in-america.
3 Coll Thrush, "Hauntings as Histories: Indigenous," in *Phantom Past, Indigenous Presence: Native Ghosts in North American Culture and History*, ed. Colleen E. Boyd and Coll Thrush (Lincoln: University of Nebraska Press, 2011), 67.

Conspirator to an Assassination: The Ghost of Mary Surratt

1 Jeff Wallenfeldt, "AssassinationofAbrahamLincoln, "*Britannica*, zupdated April4, 2022, https://www.britannica.com/event/assassination-of-Abraham-Lincoln.
2 Kate Clifford Larson, *The Assassin's Accomplice: Mary Surratt and the Plot to Kill Abraham Lincoln* (New York: Basic Books, 2011), xiii.
3 "Johnson's Last Words on Mary Surratt," National Park Service, Andrew Johnson National Historic Site, Tennessee, last updated April 14 2015, https://www.nps.gov/anjo/learn/historyculture/mary-surratt.htm.
4 Larson, *The Assassin's Accomplice*, 229.
5 See the Susan Higginbotham's 2016 novel *Hanging Mary* and the 2010 film *The Conspirator* for proof of the continued fascination Mary Surratt's story holds on our imaginations.
6 Cleveland *Plain Dealer*, December 5, 1866, reprinted in Chris Woodyard, "The Spirit of Mary Surratt," Haunted Ohio, 2016, http://hauntedohiobooks.com/news/ghosts-news/the-spirit-of-mary-surratt/.
7 Seward *Daily Gateway*, March 20, 1915, 2.
8 Hauck, *Haunted Places: The National Directory*, 107.
9 History.com Editors, "Mary Surratt Is First Woman Executed by U.S.

Federal Government," *This Day in History*, July 7, 1865, History, November 13, 2009; updated July 6, 2020, https://www.history.com/this-day-in-history/mary-surratt-is-first-woman-executed-by-u-s-federal-government.

10 Marc Hoover, "Ghost of Mary Surratt Still Roams," *Clermont Sun* (Clermont, OH), October 22, 2018, https://www.clermontsun.com/2018/10/11/marc-hoover-ghost-of-mary-surratt-still-roams.

11 Michael Farquhar, "The Haunting Tale of Mary Surratt," *Washington Post*, October 31, 1991, https://www.washingtonpost.com/archive/lifestyle/1991/10/31/the-haunting-tale-of-mary-surratt/8c1b67d6-7deb-401d-9274-cc540ff22482/.

12 "The Surratt House," DC Ghosts, *Haunted Places* (blog), https://dcghosts.com/the-surrat-house/.

13 Kate Clifford Larson, "The Lincoln Lectures—Assassin's Accomplice: Mary Surratt and the Plot to Kill Abraham Lincoln," US National Archives, December 29, 2009, YouTube, https://www.youtube.com/watch?v=4jqaJDwgQTw.

14 Larson, *The Assassin's Accomplice*, 27.

15 Chris Woodyard, *The Ghost Wore Black: Ghostly Tales from the Past* (Dayton, OH: Kestrel, 2014), 230.

16 Larson, "The Lincoln Lectures—Assassin's Accomplice: Mary Surratt and the Plot to Kill Abraham Lincoln."

17 "The Murderer of Mr. Lincoln: Extraordinary Letter of John Wilkes Booth," *New York Times*, reprinted from the *Philadelphia Inquirer*, April 21, 1865, 3, https://www.nytimes.com/1865/04/21/archives/the-murderer-of-mr-lincoln-extraordinary-letter-of-john-wilkes.html.

18 Larson, *The Assassin's Accomplice*, xiv.

19 Sarah Vowell, *Assassination Vacation* (New York: Simon & Schuster, 2005), 25.

20 Theresa Vargas, "Is the White House Haunted? A History of Spooked Presidents, Prime Ministers and Pets," *Washington Post*, October 30, 2017, https://www.washingtonpost.com/news/retropolis/wp/2017/10/30/is-the-white-house-haunted-a-history-of-spooked-presidents-prime-ministers-and-pets/; and Tom Ogden, *Haunted Washington, DC: Federal Phantoms, Government Ghosts, and Beltway Banshees* (Guildford, CT: Globe Pequot, 2016), 7.

21 Timothy Walch and Maureen Harding, "American Mysteries, Riddles, and Controversies! New Exhibit at the Hoover Presidential Library Challenges Visitors to Ask Better Questions in the Search for Answers," *Prologue Magazine* 39, no. 2 (Summer 2007), https://www.archives.gov/publications/prologue/2007/summer/mysteries.html; and Vowell, *Assassination Vacation*, 21.

22 Vowell, *Assassination Vacation*, 54.

23 Valerie Paschall, Michelle Goldchain, and Tom Acitelli, "D.C.'s 15 Most Haunted Locations, Mapped," *Curbed* Washington, DC, updated September 27, 2019, https://dc.curbed.com/maps/haunted-house-scary-dc-washington.

24 Jackie Petito, "Ghosts of Penn Quarter: Civil War Era Hauntings," *Face to Face* (blog) Smithsonian/National Portrait Gallery, https://npg.si.edu/blog/ghosts-penn-quarter-civil-war-era-hauntings; and Colleen Shogan, "Things That Go Bump in the Blue Room: Why Is the White House Haunted?" White House Historical Association, October 9, 2020, https://www.whitehousehistory.org/things-that-go-bump-in-the-blue-room.

25 Kitty Felde, "'The Conspirator' Mary Surratt Still Haunts Washington," 89.3KPCC, April 25, 2011, https://archive.kpcc.org/news/2011/04/25/26050/the-conspirator-mary-serratt-still-haunts-washingt/.
26 Ibid.
27 Larson, "The Lincoln Lectures—Assassin's Accomplice: Mary Surratt and the Plot to Kill Abraham Lincoln."

The Haunting of Lizzie Borden

1 For a somewhat more detailed retelling of the case, see the excellent *The Trial of Lizzie Borden: A True Story* by Cara Robertson (New York: Simon & Schuster, 2019).
2 Michael Martins, "Lizzie Andrew Borden and the Paranormal," August 28, 2020, https://lizzieborden.org/CuratorsCorner/2020/08/28/lizzie-andrew-borden-and-the-paranormal/.
3 Robertson, *The Trial of Lizzie Borden*, 29.
4 *The Commonwealth of Massachusetts vs. Lizzie A. Borden, The Knowlton Papers 1892–1893*, Fall River Historical Society, Fall River, MA, 1994.
5 *The Curious Life and Death of Lizzie Borden*, Smithsonian Channel/Zinc Media, original air date September 6, 2020.
6 Robertson, *The Trial of Lizzie Borden*, 174.
7 Megan Abbott, "Why Do We—Women in Particular—Love True Crime Books?" *Los Angeles Times*, June 14, 2018, https://www.latimes.com/books/la-ca-jc-megan-abbott-true-crime-20180614-story.html.
8 Stefani Koori, "A Talk with Lee-ann Wilber: New Owner of 92 Second Street," *The Hatchet: The Journal of Lizzie Borden Studies* 2, no 2 (April/May 2005).
9 Robertson, *The Trial of Lizzie Borden*, 285.
10 Arianna MacNeill, "The Next Owner of the Lizzie Borden House Took an Ax—and Saw an Opportunity to Entertain Guests," Real Estate by Boston.com & Globe.com, *Boston Globe*, April 15, 2021, https://realestate.boston.com/buying/2021/04/15/lizzie-borden-home-sells/.
11 Erika Mailman, "With the Borden Murder House in New Hands, Will Real History Get the Hatchet?" *Smithsonian Magazine*, July 6, 2021.
12 Thomas D'Agostino, *Haunted Massachusetts* (Atglen, PA: Schiffer, 2007), 61.
13 Eleanor Thibault, quoted in "Lizzie Borden: Is the Home of Lizzie Borden a Haunted Vacation Spot?" *Unsolved Mysteries*, www.unsolved.com/gallery/lizzie-borden/; and Fall River Massachusetts, Lizzie Borden House, Haunted Houses, http://hauntedhouses.com/massachusetts/lizzieborden-house/.
14 Will Dowd, "Dead and Breakfast: He Spent the Night at Lizzie Borden's House and Lived to Write About It," *MetroWest Daily News* (Framingham, MA), October 28, 2018.
15 Rebecca F. Pittman, *The History and Haunting of Lizzie Borden* (Loveland, CO: Wonderland Productions, 2016), 793–801.
16 D'Agostino, *Haunted Massachusetts*, 61.
17 Pittman, *The History and Haunting of Lizzie Borden*, 787.
18 Kerri Roderick, quoted in "Lizzie Borden: Is the Home of Lizzie Borden a Haunted Vacation Spot?"

19 Martha McGinn, "Looking Back: My Life at 92 Second Street, 1960 Till Now," *Lizzie Borden Quarterly* 1 (January 1998), 6–7.
20 Ibid.
21 Ibid.
22 Andrea McDaniels, "When Martha McGinn would spend the night in her . . ." UPI Archives, July 31, 1996, https://www.upi.com/Archives/1996/07/31/When-Martha-McGinn-would-spend-the-night-in-her/6088838785600/.
23 McGinn, "Looking Back," 6–7.
24 Robertson, *The Trial of Lizzie Borden*, 9.
25 Ibid., 123.
26 Ibid., 253.
27 Ibid.
28 Pittman, *The History and Haunting of Lizzie Borden*, 799.
29 Recall that maid Bridget Sullivan's alibi was that she was washing windows. See Pittman, *The History and Haunting of Lizzie Borden*, 780.
30 Borden Trial Transcript, 1661–2, quoted in Robertson, *The Trial of Lizzie Borden*, 239.
31 Angela Carter, "The Fall River Axe Murders" in *Saints and Strangers* (New York: Penguin, 1985).
32 Robertson, *The Trial of Lizzie Borden*, 289.

PART 5: "MADWOMEN"

Introduction

1 Moses King, King's *Handbook of New York City* 1892 (Boston: Moses King; facsimile, Barnes & Noble, 2001), 424, 464.

An Unreliable Narrator: Jan Bryant Bartell

1 Jan Bryant Bartell, *Spindrift: Tales from a Psychic Sea* (New York: Hawthorn Books, 1974), 228–29, 233, 248.

Unfinished Business: The Winchester Mystery House

1 Mary Jo Ignoffo, *Captive of the Labyrinth*: Sarah L. Winchester, Heiress to the Rifle Fortune (Columbia: University of Missouri Press, 2010), 85.
2 Ibid., 176.
3 Colin Dickey, *Ghostland: An American History in Haunted Places* (New York: Viking, 2016), 67.
4 Ignoffo, *Captive of the Labyrinth*, 115.
5 Ibid., 137.

A Correct History of the Life and Adventures of the Wandering Woman

1 Grace Greenwood, "A Night of Years—The Maniac," *The Ladies' Garland and Dollar Magazine*, March 1848.
2 Luna Hammond, *History of Madison County* (Syracuse, NY: Truair, Smith, 1872).
3 Dante O. Tranquille, "The Press Scrapbook," *Utica Daily Press*, January 6, 1951.
4 "Cazenovia Lake," Haunted Places, https://www.hauntedplaces.org/item/cazenovia-lake/.

PART 6: SPINSTERS AND WIDOWS

Introduction

1 Corinne May Botz, *Haunted Houses* (New York: Monacelli, 2010), 21.
2 Ruth Franklin, *Shirley Jackson: A Rather Haunted Life* (New York: Liveright, 2016), 415.
3 Teri Casper and Dan Smith, *Ghosts of Cincinnati: The Dark Side of the Queen City* (Charleston, SC: History Press, 2009), 61.

Miss Tredwell Is at Home

1 Anthony Bellov, ed. *Some Say They Never Left: Tales of the Strange and Inexplicable at the Merchant's House Museum* (New York: Merchant's House Museum, 2007), 2.
2 "Vanderbilt's Relative Dies in Old Fourth Street," *New York Times*, October 13, 1906.
3 Letter to the Editor, *New York Times*, October 24, 1906.
4 Helen Worden Erskine, *Out of This World: A Collection of Hermits and Recluses* (New York: Putnam, 1953).
5 It begs the question: Why did so many of the Tredwell sisters never marry? They were wealthy, highly eligible young women from a good family. There may be a simple, even mundane explanation for the Tredwell sisters' decision not to marry. Historian Mary Knapp theorizes that seeing their older sisters' marriages and childbirths may have been a factor in their remaining single: "Such a time I never want to witness," Phebe wrote to her younger sisters about their sister Elizabeth's labor. (Phebe Tredwell to her sisters, November 1, 1854, Nichols Box, Manuscript Division [New York: New-York Historical Society], quoted in Mary Knapp, *An Old Merchant's House*, page 105.) Elizabeth delivered her daughter, Lillie, at home on East 4th Street, and lived in the family home with her daughter and husband for an unusually long time, fourteen years. Mary Adelaide, too, lived at home after marrying her husband, and bore and raised three children there. Perhaps, after seeing the birth and rearing of so many children, the younger girls simply didn't want to become mothers and wives.
6 Colin Dickey, Ghostland: *An American History in Haunted Places* (New York: Viking, 2016), 62.
7 Mary Knapp, *An Old Merchant's House* (New York: Girandole Books, 2012), 203.
8 Niraj Chokshi, "The Ghosts of New York's Past," *New York Times*, October 28, 2018, https://www.nytimes.com/2018/10/28/nyregion/halloweenghoststories.html?searchResultPosition=1.
9 Interview with Anthony Bellov, November 2021.
10 Interview with Marguerite Durret, November 2021.
11 Ibid.
12 Susan Blackhall, *Ghosts of New York* (San Diego: Thunder Bay, 2005), 30.
13 "Just Like Papa Would Have Wanted" is the title of Susan Blackhall's chapter on Gertrude and the Merchant's House Museum in *Ghosts of New York*, 26.

From Mother Ann to Sybil: The Spirits of the Great Burned-Over

1 Mitch Horowitz, *Occult America: The Secret History of How Mysticism Shaped Our Nation* (New York: Bantam Books, 2009), 13.

2 Rosemary Ellen Guiley, *Harper's Encyclopedia of Mystical and Paranormal Experience* (New York: HarperCollins, 1991), 538.

3 "Phelps General Store and Residence," Historic Palmyra, https://www.historicpalmyrany.com/phelps-general-store.

4 Patti Unvericht, *Ghosts and Hauntings of the Finger Lakes* (Charleston, SC: History Press, 2012), 86.

5 Hilary Smith, "N.Y. Town Celebrates Birthday of Famed Spiritualist Sybil," *MetroWest Daily News* (Framingham, MA), October 17, 2007.

6 Tammy Whitacre, "Spirit of Sybil: A Birthday Celebration of a Different Kind," *Daily Messenger* (Canadaigua, NY), October 17, 2013, https://www.mpnnow.com/story/news/local/2013/10/17/spirit-sybil-birthday-celebration-different/42381681007/.

7 Smith, "N.Y. Town Celebrates Birthday of Famed Spiritualist Sybil."

The Widow and Mrs. Spencer

1 Catherine Wessinger, "Sallie Ann Glassman," Island Salvation of Botanica, https://www.islandofsalvationbotanica.com/about.html#/.

2 Mason Miller, "Joan Rivers's Spiritual Guide Is Fighting Crime with Voodoo in New Orleans," *Vice*, September 22, 2014, https://www.vice.com/en/article/exmqwe/joan-rivers-spiritual-guide-is-fighting-crime-with-voodoo-in-new-orleans.

3 Tim Krepp, *Capitol Hill Haunts* (Charleston, SC: History Press, 2012), 63.

4 Ibid., 64–65.

PART 7: FRAUDS, FAKES AND MYTHMAKING

The Prestige of Katie King

1 Stephanie Hoover, *Philadelphia Spiritualism and the Curious Case of Katie King* (Charleston, SC: History Press, 2013), 26.

2 "Doctor Robert Hare," *Scientific American* 13, no. 38 (May 1858), 301.

Willing the Ghosts to Life: Molly and Matilda of the Sorrel Weed House

1 "A. J. Cohen collection on the Sorrel-Weed House," Georgia Historical Society, http://ghs.galileo.usg.edu/ghs/view?docId=ead/MS%201197-ead.xml.

2 Caitlyn Hungate, "Jaunts and Haunts: Examining the Effect of the Dark Tourism Industry on Savannah's Traditional Branded Image" (master's thesis, University of Georgia, 2017), 2, https://getd.libs.uga.edu/pdfs/hungate_caitlyn_j_201712_mhp.pdf.

3 Kelly Westfield, "Excavations in the Carriage House Basement of the Sorrel-Weed House," *Digging Savannah Reports* (Spring 2017), 41, https://digitalcommons.georgiasouthern.edu/armstrong-dig-savannah/1/.

4 Michael Harris and Linda Sickler, *Historic Haunts of Savannah* (Charleston, SC: History Press, 2014), 55.

5 Tiya Miles, *Tales from the Haunted South: Dark Tourism and Memories of Slavery from the Civil War Era* (Chapel Hill: University of North Carolina Press, 2015), 32.
6 Caitlin Doughty, "Ask a Mortician—Deathstination: Savannah Georgia and Ghost Tours," *The Order of the Good Death*, April 18, 2013, https://www.youtube.com/watch?v=YcMB27PeO7w.
7 Hungate, "Jaunts and Haunts," 28.
8 Miles, *Tales from the Haunted South*, 26. "Someone had concocted her story of racial and sexual exploitation as a titillating tourist attraction."
9 Hannah Kates, email interview with authors, April 12, 2022.
10 Colin Dickey, *Ghostland: An American History in Haunted Places* (New York: Viking, 2016), 232.
11 Glenn Gentry, "Walking with the Dead: The Place of Ghost Walk Tourism in Savannah, Georgia," *Southeastern Geographer* 47, no. 2 (2007), 223.
12 Bilial G. Morris, "The Antebellum Tale of Black Slave Girl Molly and the Haunting of Sorrel-Weed House," *NewsOne*, October 18, 2021, https://newsone.com/4234785/sorrel-weed-house-black-slave-girl-molly/.
13 Westfield, "Excavations in the Basement of the Carriage House of the Sorrel Weed House."
14 Miles, *Tales from the Haunted South*, 36.
15 Gilbert Moxley Sorrel, "In Memoriam, Francis Sorrel of Savannah Georgia, 1793–1870," Sorrel Papers, Southern Historical Collection, quoted in Miles, *Tales from the Haunted South*, 41; for more biographical information on Francis Sorrell, see https://www.wikitree.com/wiki/Sorrel-40.
16 See James Caskey, *Haunted Savannah: America's Most Spectral City*, Kindle edition location 3830; and Miles, *Tales from the Haunted South*, 24.

The Mythmaking of Marie Rogêt

1 Daniel Stashower, *The Beautiful Cigar Girl: Mary Rogers, Edgar Allan Poe and the Invention of Murder* (New York: Berkley, 2006), 99–100.
2 Edgar Allan Poe, "The Mystery of Marie Roget," *The Complete Tales and Poems of Edgar Allan Poe* (New York: Barnes & Noble Books, 1992), 433.

ABOUT THE AUTHORS

Leanna Renee Hieber is an award-winning author and paranormal history expert. A regular speaker at Sci-Fi / Fantasy and paranormal conventions, she's appeared on film and television on shows including *Mysteries at the Museum* and *Beyond the Unknown*. She's a three-time Prism Award winner for her debut novel, *The Strangely Beautiful Tale of Miss Percy Parker*, and a Daphne du Maurier Award finalist for *Darker Still*. After earning a BFA in theatre performance and a focus study on the Victorian Era, she spent many years in the professional regional theatre circuit, skills that serve her well as a speaker and a ghost tour guide for Boroughs of the Dead in New York. Leanna lives in New York City, and can be found online at LeannaReneeHieber.com.

Andrea Janes is the founder and owner of Boroughs of the Dead, New York City's premier ghost tour company, which has been featured in the *New York Times, Jezebel, Bustle, Cosmopolitan, Huffington Post, Gothamist*, and NPR.org, among others. Andrea is also the author of the YA novel *Glamour*, several short horror stories, and horror novel *Boroughs of the Dead*, the inspiration for her company. More at www.boroughsofthedead.com.

CPSIA information can be obtained
at www.ICGtesting.com
Printed in the USA
LVHW091246021022
729765LV00003B/461

9 780806 541587